PENGUIN BOOKS

THE RETIREMENT SAVINGS TIME BOMB . . . AND HOW TO DEFUSE IT

Ed Slott is a highly sought-after professional speaker, CPA, and tax advisor. His diverse client list includes major corporations such as Fidelity Investments, American Express, Merrill Lynch, Nationwide Insurance, and Oppenheimer Funds. Slott's writing frequently appears in national publications such as *The Wall Street Journal, The New York Times,* and *USA Today,* and he has appeared on broadcast television and radio stations nationwide. He is publisher of the popular monthly newsletter *Ed Slott's IRA Advisor.* For more information, visit his Web site: www.irahelp.com.

Praise for *The Retirement Savings Time Bomb . . . and How To Defuse It*

"Unless you consider cat food a viable dinner option, it's wise to take action now to bulletproof your retirement assets. Sooner or later, we pay taxes. But why allow your retirement savings to become a windfall for Uncle Sam when the money should go to you and your heirs? Slott's book will show you how to keep your cash all in the family."
—*USA Today*

"Ed Slott's advice could save your retirement plan from something worse than a Bear Market—the tax collector!"
—Terry Savage, author of *The Savage Truth on Money* and personal finance columnist for the *Chicago Sun-Times*

"Ed Slott's easy-to-understand tax strategies mean money in your bank account, not the IRS's."
—Jan M. Rosen, coauthor of *Wall Street Secrets for Tax-Efficient Investing* and financial columnist for *The New York Times*

"Ed Slott knows his stuff. If you want your retirement savings to stay in the family and not go to Uncle Sam, READ THIS BOOK!"
—Grace W. Weinstein, columnist for the *Financial Times* and author of *J.K.Lasser's Winning with Your 401(k)*

"Ed Slott guides you through the maze of retirement-plan rules with a sense of humor and a firm grasp of the costly pitfalls that await the unwary."
—Priscilla Brandon, editor, *Kiplinger's Retirement Report*

"If you have questions about IRAs or other retirement plans, you'll find every last answer in this easy-to-understand and hugely informative book. Ed Slott is truly Mr. IRA."
—Lynn O'Shaughnessy, author of *The Retirement Bible*

"Ed Slott's blueprint for protecting your retirement savings shouldn't be missed."
—Karin Price Mueller, writer of the "Money Manager" column for *The Boston Herald* and author of *Online Money Management*

"If you have assets in a retirement plan *The Retirement Savings Time Bomb* will save you money."
—Natalie B. Choate, author of *Life & Death Planning for Retirement Benefits: The Essential Handbook for Estate Planners*

"A book on retirement plan distributions that's easy to follow—and this is even more amazing—fun to read. . . . This is an eye-opening take-action book directed at those who have saved their money and now risk losing most of it. . . . Rich in context but written in an easy-to-follow, engaging style, the book tells readers how to keep the tax man at bay and take advantage of the most recent tax law and IRA rule changes. . . . We highly recommend Slott's book to those who are serious about protecting their retirement savings."
—Diane Lade and Humberto Cruz, *The Sun-Sentinel*

THE RETIREMENT SAVINGS TIME BOMB . . . AND HOW TO DEFUSE IT

A Five-Step Action Plan for Protecting
Your IRAs, 401(k)s, and Other Retirement Plans
from Near Annihilation by the Taxman

BY **ED SLOTT**

PENGUIN BOOKS

PENGUIN BOOKS
Published by the Penguin Group
Penguin Group (USA) Inc., 375 Hudson Street, New York, New York 10014, U.S.A.
Penguin Group (Canada), 90 Eglinton Avenue East, Suite 700, Toronto,
  Ontario, Canada M4P 2Y3 (a division of Pearson Penguin Canada Inc.)
Penguin Books Ltd, 80 Strand, London WC2R 0RL, England
Penguin Ireland, 25 St Stephen's Green, Dublin 2, Ireland (a division of Penguin Books Ltd)
Penguin Group (Australia), 250 Camberwell Road, Camberwell,
  Victoria 3124, Australia (a division of Pearson Australia Group Pty Ltd)
Penguin Books India Pvt Ltd, 11 Community Centre, Panchsheel Park, New Delhi – 110 017, India
Penguin Group (NZ), cnr Airborne and Rosedale Roads,
  Albany, Auckland 1310, New Zealand (a division of Pearson New Zealand Ltd)
Penguin Books (South Africa) (Pty) Ltd, 24 Sturdee Avenue,
  Rosebank, Johannesburg 2196, South Africa

Penguin Books Ltd, Registered Offices: 80 Strand, London WC2R 0RL, England

First published in the United States of America by Viking Penguin,
a member of Penguin Putnam Inc. 2003
Published in Penguin Books 2004

20 19 18 17 16 15 14 13 12 11

Grateful acknowledgment is made for permission to reprint "Tips for Achieving NUA Success"
and "Sample NUA Information Request Letter" by David A. Foster. Used by permission of David
A. Foster.

The Retirement Savings Time Bomb . . . and How to Defuse It seeks to provide the most accurate
and up-to-date information available about complicated tax topics. This information may be
changed, become outdated, or be rendered incorrect by new legislation or official rulings, however.
Therefore, neither the author nor the publisher assumes liability or responsibility for any losses that
may be sustained or alleged to be sustained, directly or indirectly, by the use of the information
contained in this book, and any such liability is hereby expressly disclaimed.

THE LIBRARY OF CONGRESS HAS CATALOGED THE HARDCOVER EDITION AS FOLLOWS:
Slott, Ed.
The retirement savings time bomb and how to defuse it : a five-step
action plan for protecting your IRAs, 401(k)s, and other retirement plans
from near annihilation by the taxman / by Ed Slott.
p.   cm.
Includes index.
ISBN 0-670-03236-0 (hc.)
ISBN 0 14 20.0377 8 (pbk.)
1. Pension trusts—United States.   2. Pension trusts—Taxation—United States.
3. Retirement income—United States—Planning.   4. Finance, Personal—United States.
I. Title.
HD7105.45.U6 S486 2003
332.024'01—dc21   2002032422

Printed in the United States of America
Designed by BTD Design

To my dad, who truly lived a wonderful life
To my wife, Linda,
and our children, Rachel, Ilana, and Jennifer

AUTHOR'S NOTE

This book is about the jeopardy you—and everyone you know—will face when the taxman shows up at distribution time, regardless of the type of tax-deferred retirement savings plan you have. Every type of plan is affected, be it an Individual Retirement Account (IRA), a 401(k), a 403(b), a 457, a Keogh plan, a SEP-IRA, a SIMPLE IRA, or a mixture of accounts. I'll be using the term *IRA* throughout the book as an umbrella term for all these retirement savings plans because the tax rules governing IRAs are generally the same as those for every type of retirement account. However, in those areas where the rules for a particular plan differ from those of IRAs, I will clearly point out the difference to you. Likewise, I'll be using the term *company plans* throughout this book as an umbrella for all types of employer plans, not just qualified plans (see "Talking the Talk" for the difference).

This edition takes into account the new reduced income and capital gains tax rates from the Jobs and Growth Tax Relief Reconciliation Act of 2003 (the 2003 Tax Act).

I want to give a special nod upfront to Beverly DeVeny and Mark LaVangie of Fleet Private Clients Group for the incredible job they did checking and double-checking the manuscript for technical accuracy. They went well beyond generously contributing their time and energy to make this book as reliable and error-free as possible. Thanks Beverly and Mark for helping me defuse the retirement savings time bomb. I can assure my readers that any inaccuracies that may still lurk herein are mine, and I take full responsibility for them.

Ed Slott

Contents

PLAYING THE "BACK 9"

*"Combined, income and death taxes could boost what your kids pay on
the remainder of your 401(k) [and IRA] to more than 80 percent."*
—*The Wall Street Journal*, editorial page, February 25, 2002

I n the not so distant past, the issue of protecting retirement savings rather than investing for retirement might have been considered putting the cart before the horse.

Not any longer.

Today, Americans have invested trillions of dollars in retirement
plans, turning them into the biggest, most valuable asset they
own—often worth more than even their homes. As a result, *savings protection* has become the name of the retirement plan game.

Most, if not all, retirement planning strategists, however, focus
on why you should save for retirement and how to grow your
money through a variety of investment vehicles.

That's valuable information, but it's not enough.

Look at it this way. What good is making even a 50 percent return on an investment if, at the time of withdrawal, taxes will step
in to claim 70, 80, or maybe even 90 percent of it?

Think of it like coming down the stretch of the U.S. Open Golf
Championship. The "Front 9" is where you position your lead by
building up your assets; holding onto your lead—i.e., protecting

your assets from excessive taxation—is the "Back 9" where, ultimately, you win or lose.

Crucial Component

This book addresses the critical issue that every other retirement-related and tax-related book on the market ignores: *protecting the assets you've spent a lifetime building from excessive taxation.* No single factor is more significant to your living the lifestyle you've been saving all of your life for, or to passing your hard-earned savings on to those you love.

Why is this component so crucial?

Due to a complex combination of distribution and estate taxes that kick in at retirement or death, millions of you are at risk of losing much—perhaps even most—of your retirement savings.

Already happening now, this dire turn of events will put a huge financial burden on you, your children, and on society as the ranks of the retiring and already retired swell to historic proportions in the coming years when the retirement savings time bomb explodes (see Chapter 1).

And so, the overriding purpose of this book is to give savers such as you the knowledge and the tools to defuse that bomb on your own—or with the help of your professional financial advisor—before detonation occurs.

Complex Web

I'll expose the complex web of dark secrets and traps in the tax code governing retirement savings in layman's terms, and I'll present, for the first time, an easy-to-use plan for helping the millions of you who are at risk to save a fortune in retirement income—income that might otherwise be lost to you and your families forever.

I'll deal with all aspects of IRA distribution planning, which encompasses virtually any type of retirement account you might have—401(k), 403(b), 457 Plan, SEP-IRA, SIMPLE IRA, Keogh, corporate pension plan—since virtually all retirement money is distributed according to what is commonly referred to as the "IRA distribution rules." These are among the most complicated rules in the entire U.S. tax code.

I'll go beyond the tax rules to provide easily understood explanations of the planning opportunities available and clear answers to some of the most perplexing and frequently asked questions ("I know the rule says X, but how can I accomplish Y without problem Z?").

I'll cut through the complexities of these rules and make them easy to grasp so that you'll be able to secure your retirement nest egg from being decimated by taxes, and you can keep your savings in the hands of your family, not the IRS.

In addition, if you're already a knowledgeable professional financial advisor, I will give you the tools to better guide and communicate with your clients, thereby attracting and retaining more assets under management, the key to growing your business.

A Total Solution

This book will help you devise and implement a simple, workable strategy to protect your retirement assets and keep your hard-earned money in the family—and growing—for generations.

My strategy grew out of my more than 20 years of experience "in the trenches" as a CPA preparing tax returns, and has evolved over my years on the circuit as a keynote speaker, teacher, and coach to consumers and professional financial advisors. I have conducted more than 500 seminars and workshops during the past five years, honing my action plan into one that works for *anybody* with an IRA, 401(k), or other retirement account—from hard-working folks such as teachers, doctors, and CPAs who have accumulated modest but still substantial retirement assets, to high–net-worth corporate executives and entertainers.

The result of my efforts is a **total solution**, one that you don't have to be a tax expert to achieve or to benefit from, regardless of what the stock market and economy are doing. It is a solution that will show how to

- Protect company stock owned in a 401(k).
- Make the most of retirement savings.
- Save a fortune in excessive, often needless taxation.
- Pass more assets on to loved ones and other beneficiaries.
- Keep retirement assets in the family for decades, even generations, with minimal or no taxes.
- Get more bang for your buck from your financial advisor.
- Expand knowledge of retirement distribution planning.
- Tap retirement funds for emergency cash—without paying a big tax penalty.
- Take advantage of the latest tax law and IRA rule changes.
- Integrate a retirement account with an overall estate plan to create the *perfect* estate plan.
- Avoid falling into tax traps with inherited IRAs or other retirement accounts.
- Protect retirement accounts from creditors, divorce, bankruptcy, lawsuits, or other problems that could expose them to confiscation.

As you read each chapter, keep in mind what I wrote at the outset of this introduction: Retirement planning is like a golf tournament. Building assets is just part of the game—and only the "Front 9," to boot.

There are nine more holes left to go in the equally, and perhaps even more, tortuous "Back 9"—the final holes where holding onto the assets you've built up becomes the biggest challenge of all.

Remember, where taxes are concerned, it's what you keep that counts!

Talking the Talk

A Foolproof Primer to Essential
But Often Confusing Tax Terms and Definitions

> *"If I seem unduly clear to you, you*
> *must have misunderstood what I said."*
> —Alan Greenspan, Federal Reserve chairman

You don't have to become a CPA to understand tax lingo (I'm a recovering CPA myself). But you will need to grasp a few key technical terms in order to get the most out of this book as well as any other information you may come across on the topic of retirement distribution planning and savings protection.

Rather than do the standard type of boring glossary that is usually stuck at the rear of a book, requiring you to constantly flip back and forth between pages, accumulating a lot of paper cuts along the way, I've created a primer right here at the beginning, where it'll be more useful and convenient for you (and require no Band-Aids).

Also, instead of going the typically sleepy A-to-Z route, I've livened up the format with a fresher presentation called "What's the Difference between . . . ?"

My rationale (apart from wanting to educate in an entertaining manner) is this: As you read through this book, there will be times when you will need to know not only what a specific tax term means but also how it differs from another tax term that may appear on the surface to have a similar meaning.

2 ■ THE RETIREMENT SAVINGS TIME BOMB

How could such conflicts occur?

The writers of our tax rules—Congress and the IRS—have at times conspired to create a broad panoply of easily recognizable words, which, in tax talk, have completely different meanings than in their common usages.

At other times, these writers just make up words out of convenience, words that cannot possibly be defined with any known form of logic—in our lexicon, anyway. (I know they're made up because they don't appear in any spell check software I've ever seen.)

Likewise, there are terms that some of you may *think* you know because they seem familiar—but if you guess wrong, the mistake could cost you a bundle at tax time.

Reading through this section to familiarize yourself with these terms before moving on not only will help you to avoid such potentially expensive misinterpretations, but will take much of the mystery out of all that follows in the coming chapters.

WHAT'S THE DIFFERENCE BETWEEN . . . ?

Adjusted Gross Income (AGI) vs. Taxable Income

AGI is your gross income before any exemptions, deductions, or tax credits. It's an important term to know because many provisions in the tax code are based on AGI, not the income on which you are actually taxed.

After-Tax vs. Pre-Tax Money

Either of these can be a good option, depending on your preference. For example, if you scarf up your vegetables fast to get them out of the way so you can get on with dessert, you're a "pay-me-later" (after-tax money) person. But if you like to put the veggies off to last and start with dessert, you're the "pay-me-now" (pre-tax money) type. For example, money that goes into a Roth IRA is after-tax money because you had to earn it as ordinary income first and pay tax on it before you could contribute it to the Roth. By contrast, 401(k) contributions are pre-tax money because you received a tax deduction on the portion of your salary you contributed, and will pay tax later when the funds are withdrawn. Most money accumulating in tax-deferred retirement accounts is pre-tax funds.

It comes down to this: After-tax money is taxable now; pre-tax money is taxable later. It's important to know the distinction so that you don't get into a situation where you're inadvertently shelling out tax money you've already paid. Also, the IRS requires you and your plan to keep track of after-tax and pre-tax funds so that it knows how much is taxable when you begin withdrawals.

Basis vs. Cost

Cost is what you paid for a property, whether a stock, a bond, a mutual fund, or a home. Basis is the amount used for figuring any gain or loss when property is sold. To calculate basis, certain adjustments are added to or subtracted from your cost. Here are some examples:

- For a home, the amount you pay for improvements will be added to the home's original purchase price to arrive at an *increased* basis.
- For a stock, any reinvested dividends on which you paid tax in the year they were earned will be added to the purchase price of the stock to arrive at an *increased* basis.
- For, say, equipment used in business, such as a tractor on a farm, any depreciation taken will be subtracted from the purchase price of the tractor to arrive at a *decreased* basis.

Increasing basis results in a decrease in capital (or ordinary) gains and the tax you'll pay, while decreasing basis results in an increase in capital (or ordinary) gains and the tax you'll pay. You must earn basis. It is earned by spending after-tax dollars. When you invest money that you have already paid tax on, you create basis. Basis is reduced by any tax deductions you receive. For example, if you contribute $3,000 to a tax-deductible IRA, you do not have basis, because the tax deduction reduced your basis to zero. If on the other hand you contribute to a nondeductible IRA or Roth IRA (which is nondeductible by definition), you have created basis. When the dust settles, and you completely distribute your IRAs, if you do not recover your basis you may have a deductible loss (see Chapter 9).

The basis concept is needed to figure out how much of your IRA distribution will be taxable under the pro rata rule (see Chapter 3) when you withdraw from an IRA and you have made nondeductible contributions to your IRA or your IRA includes after-tax funds rolled over to your IRA from your company plan. After-tax funds and nondeductible IRA contributions are basis in an IRA because they represent funds that have already been taxed. They will not be taxed again upon withdrawal, but to make sure that happens you must keep track of your IRA basis.

Beneficiary vs. Designated Beneficiary

In everyday English these two terms are interchangeable, but in tax language *designated beneficiary* has special meaning under the retirement distribution rules. It's the named beneficiary on an IRA or company plan beneficiary form, and must be a person—in other words, someone with a pulse and a birthday. If you cannot prove that you have both, you fall into the nonhuman or "other" column suitable only for "beneficiary" status—for example, a trust (although beneficiaries of trusts can also be designated beneficiaries if the trust meets certain requirements; see Chapter 8), an estate, a charity, or any other nonperson in your life, including pets, imaginary friends such as Peter Pan, Spiderman, Darth Vader, and all the characters on the TV show *Friends* (my daughter thinks they are real people).

Deceased relatives also fall into the nonperson category because, even though they have birthdays, they lack the second requirement, a pulse. Good, that's out of the way; now, here's something else you must know. A beneficiary can be a person who is *not* a designated beneficiary. Shall I repeat that? Yes, a beneficiary can be a person who is *not* a designated beneficiary. For example, say you do not name a beneficiary for your IRA on the IRA beneficiary designation form before you die. But after your will is probated, and the loving, but greedy family is finally through slugging it out, your son (whom you would have named as beneficiary if you'd gotten around to filling out the form) winds up inheriting your IRA anyway.

So, what's the difference? Even though your son is a person, he is *not* a designated beneficiary because he inherited through your estate (the nonperson beneficiary of your account, according to the IRS); he is instead a "beneficiary." On the surface, this may seem like a lot of tortuous nuancing since the outcome in our example is the same either way. But the distribution rules for a "beneficiary" and a "designated beneficiary" can be different (see Chapter 4), and there may be significant tax consequences, depending upon which you have.

Capital Gain vs. Ordinary Income

Capital gains are what everybody wants and *ordinary income* is what most people get. A capital gain results from the sale of what is called a "capital asset," which is generally defined as anything you own: stocks, bonds, mutual fund shares, your home. Income from your trade or business, or IRA distributions on the other hand, is defined as "ordinary," which means it gets taxed at a higher rate for many taxpayers. For example, if you are in a 35 percent tax bracket, you would pay 35 percent on ordinary income, whereas a capital gain would be taxed at a maximum of 15 percent if the property was held more than one year before it was sold.

Conversion vs. Recharacterization

What language are we speaking here? This is an example of the IRS using two words to describe the same thing—the transfer of assets to and/or from a traditional IRA and a Roth IRA—and stumping spell check once again. In IRS jive, a *conversion* is not when you undergo a spiritual change but when you transfer funds from a traditional IRA to a Roth IRA. A *recharacterization* (find that one in any dictionary!) is when you transfer funds back to where they originally came from, thereby annulling the conversion (and thus any liability if it was a taxable conversion). Conversions can be accomplished through a rollover or a trustee-to-trustee transfer (see "direct transfer" later in this chapter); a recharacterization can only be accomplished via a trustee-to-trustee transfer.

Deductible IRA vs. Nondeductible IRA

A contribution to a *deductible IRA* can be taken as a current tax deduction, and becomes taxable only when withdrawn. A contribution to a *nondeductible IRA* receives no current tax deduction, but also is not taxable when withdrawn. The traditional IRA is an example of an IRA that can be deductible (as long as you don't make too much money while you're active in your company's plan), whereas a Roth IRA is an example of a nondeductible IRA. You never receive a tax deduction for money contributed to a Roth IRA.

Direct Transfer vs. Rollover

A *direct transfer* is the process of actually moving funds from one retirement account to another. It is also referred to as a *trustee-to-*

trustee transfer, which means that the funds go directly from one bank or brokerage firm to another without your touching the money en route. This is my preferred method of moving money because it's not only safe, but also tax-free. The IRS prefers you to use it too, but for a different reason—they tremble at the thought of your taking the money, failing to redeposit it, and not telling them. With a trustee-to-trustee transfer, the IRS is assured (as are you) that your funds arrive safely at their new destination.

A *rollover* is when you actually withdraw money from your IRA or qualified plan, such as a company 401(k), and redeposit it in an IRA or into your new company's qualified plan. If you choose the rollover rather than the direct transfer method, the IRS allows you 60 days to redeposit the money into an IRA or your new company's plan. If you miss the deadline, the withdrawal becomes taxable—*the end of your retirement account!* If you still prefer the rollover method as opposed to the trustee-to-trustee transfer after reading that, be advised that you can do a 60-day IRA rollover only once a year. On the other hand, you can do as many direct transfers as you like in a year, as long as the funds go from trustee to trustee.

EGTRRA 2001 vs. Job Creation and Worker Assistance Act of 2002

EGTRRA 2001 (the *Economic Growth and Tax Relief Reconciliation Act of 2001)* was signed into law on June 7 of that year as part of the Internal Revenue Code, which all tax laws fall under. EGTRRA 2001 includes numerous tax provisions that impact retirement plan contributions and distributions, rollovers, plan portability, education and retirement tax incentives, as well as estate tax relief. Whenever I refer to an EGTRRA 2001 provision in the book, I will also give its effective date because most of the provisions of EGTRRA 2001 will not be effective until sometime in the future.

The *Job Creation and Worker Assistance Act of 2002* was signed into law on March 9 of that year. Most of the provisions involving retirement accounts were aimed at correcting mistakes due to lack of proofreading in EGTRRA 2001 or earlier legislation, and make the corrections retroactive. For example, EGTRRA 2001 specified the maximum allowable SEP-IRA deduction as 15 percent. This was a typo. The amount is 25 percent, and the Job Act corrected the error.

Estate Tax vs. Income Tax

Income tax is the one you're still alive to complain about.

Final Tax Return vs. Estate Tax Return

The *final tax return* refers to your last income tax return (Form 1040) for the year of death. The *estate tax return* (Form 706) is used to calculate how much estate tax the estate owes now that you're no longer here to say different.

Gift vs. Bequest and Gift Tax vs. Estate Tax

A *gift* is something that you present while you are alive, whereas a *bequest* is presented after your death through a will or trust. *Gift tax* is assessed on taxable gifts such as property, made by the giver during his or her lifetime. The giver is responsible for paying the tax, if there is one. *Estate tax* is levied on assets in an inherited estate after death, and is paid out of the estate. The tax system in place for gift and estate taxes is supposed to establish that whether you give something away while you are alive or it gets taxed in your estate after you're gone, the tax will be the same. But this doesn't always happen; paying a gift tax will cost less than paying an estate tax on the same amount of property.

IRC vs. TRA86

The *Internal Revenue Code (IRC)* is the tax law as written by Congress. For example, if you see a reference to "IRC Code Section 408," this means Section 408 of the Internal Revenue Code, and it's the law. *TRA86 (The Tax Reform Act of 1986)* is part of the tax code and is the notorious legislation that gave birth to most of the arcane rules on retirement plan distributions that are putting our savings in jeopardy of IRS confiscation today.

Life Expectancy (for Taxes) vs. Life Expectancy (Actual)

Making the most out of your IRA means keeping it growing tax-deferred over your life expectancy and that of your beneficiary. For tax purposes, life expectancy is based on the IRS life expectancy tables (see Chapter 4). These tables are based on actuarial assumptions of how long people of a given age will live. They have nothing to do with predicting *actual* life expectancy (that's left to crystal balls). If you work out, eat right, and have genes suggesting a longer potential lifespan than the IRS estimate, that's all well and good, but from the point of view of extending your retirement plan's growth, it's the IRS estimate that counts—and that estimate will be the same for you as for someone else your age who has given up that gym membership and eats hamburgers and french fries for breakfast every morning (with a side order of bacon, of course). In fact, it will be the same for a 50-year-old who is healthy and one who is terminally ill.

Probate Estate vs. Taxable Estate

The *probate estate* is the amount of your estate that is wholly in your name and passes to your heirs through your will. It may be estate taxable or nontaxable. The *taxable estate* is the amount of your estate subject to tax, and may include both probate and non-probate property. For example, a house bequeathed by a decedent is considered probate property and thus taxable, unless it—together with other items in the estate—is valued at less than the federal estate exemption. On the other hand, an IRA with a designated beneficiary is an example of nonprobate property, and is included in the taxable estate.

Qualified Plan vs. Nonqualified Plan

In order for an employee retirement plan to be *qualified,* the benefits generally have to be offered to all eligible employees, not just a chosen few. Qualified plans provide tax advantages generally unavailable to nonqualified plans. The major advantages are these: Employers receive current tax deductions for contributions to the plan made for the employees, and employees pay no tax on these contributions (or their own, for which they also get a deduction), which grow tax-deferred until distributed, usually in retirement. Examples of qualified plans are a company 401(k) and other profit-sharing plans; defined benefit plans; defined contribution plans; and Keogh plans. Section 403(b) tax-deferred annuity plans and 457 deferred compensation plans are technically not qualified plans but as a result of the Economic Growth and Tax Relief Reconciliation Act of 2001 (better known as EGTRRA 2001), they generally follow the same distribution rules. Similarly, individual retirement accounts (IRAs), simplified employee pension plans (SEP-IRAs), and savings incentive match plans for employees (SIMPLE IRAs) are not company plans or qualified plans. They are personal retirement savings accounts, but they too follow similar distribution rules.

Nonqualified plans do not have to meet the same stiff IRS requirements as qualified plans, such as being offered to all employees. Nor are they subject to spousal consent and discrimination rules. But they also do not enjoy the same tax benefits as qualified plans. So, why would anyone want a nonqualified plan? Employers use them to provide special benefits to certain employees and executives, such as special tax-deferred compensation packages, pension arrangements, insurance, or annuities. In other words, they're a vehicle for attracting and taking care of the "really important people" in a company—the brilliant, high-paid executives who often run it into the ground, as Enron, WorldCom, and many others have demonstrated so magnificently.

Regs vs. PLRs vs. Revenue Rulings

Regs is short for *regulations*. It is interchangeable with *rules*. I'll be using both words throughout the book not only for variety but to be very clear that something isn't "optional." Once a tax bill is passed by Congress and signed by the president, it becomes law. As Congress and the president typically have no idea what they passed and signed, the IRS is charged with interpreting the bill as "Proposed Regulations," which are then released for public comment. At some point thereafter, the IRS makes any changes deemed appropriate and necessary from the public's inspection, and issues "Final Regulations"; these represent the IRS's official interpretation of the bill's measures and thus, as Regis might say, the "final answer," which must be accepted by all. Until Final Regs are issued (which can take years and years), however, we're stuck with following the Proposed Regs, even though they're under review.

I can hear you now: "But how can they be 'rules' if they're only 'proposed'?" Good question, to which I have no good answer, except to say, "That's how the system works." For 15 years, the TRA86 provisions on retirement accounts were Proposed Regs. They were reproposed with a major overhaul in January 2001, but it wasn't until April 2002 that they became final. And so, except where noted, all references to Regs or "rules" in this book are to the Final Regs that the IRS took just shy of two decades to figure out.

A *PLR (private letter ruling)* is the IRS's official written response to a request from a taxpayer like you or me to clarify a regulation impacting our situation specifically, which falls into a particular gray area (I know, the whole tax code seems like a gray area). Used here, the word *private* is a bit misleading though because the IRS makes its pronouncements on these cases available to the public also; many professional financial advisors then use them as a tool for gauging how the IRS might rule on their clients in a similar regulatory predicament. For example, some taxpayers who converted from traditional IRAs to Roth IRAs in 1998–99, unaware that they didn't qualify for the conversion, found themselves faced with the fact that the deadline to "recharacterize" had elapsed (see Chapter 7). The Regs had never considered this possibility, and so the taxpayers, feeling screwed, requested PLRs. In most cases, the IRS has ruled to allow the late recharacterization, offering a hint, but no guarantee, of how it might come down in your case.

Requesting a PLR from the IRS is both time-consuming and expensive. You can't simply dial up the IRS and ask, "Hey, can I do this?" The process involves filling out pages and pages of application forms and questionnaires, and being familiar enough with the tax code to form a sound legal argument favoring your side of the regulatory issue you want resolved. Professional fees (lawyers, CPAs, etc.) for researching, preparing, writing, and submitting a PLR request can cost from $5,000 to $10,000 depending on the complexity of the issue, and then you're hit with the IRS's own fees, which can run from $600 to $2,000-plus for a PLR. It's not unusual for the IRS to take upward of nine months to get back to you. And you may wind up not getting a favorable ruling! So, unless there are big bucks at stake, it's not often worth it to request a PLR. I've described what it is because I'll be referring to some PLRs along the way to show which way the IRS ruled on a specific provision that was unclear in the law or the Regs.

When the IRS feels a clarification has broad application to all taxpayers and not just an individual case, it issues a *revenue ruling*. This is an authoritative position taken by the IRS that every taxpayer or financial advisor can rely on with respect to how the IRS will rule in their own or a respective client's case. The IRS also uses revenue rulings as vehicles for closing any perceived loopholes in the tax code.

Rollover IRA vs. Conduit IRA

Here's another example of two terms for the same thing: money that goes from a company plan to an IRA. In the past, it was important to keep this money separate from other IRA money so that it could be rolled over to a new company plan if you change jobs. The so-called "conduit IRA" account would contain just the funds that were rolled over from the company plan plus the earnings on those funds. If you mixed any other IRA contributions with those funds, you would "taint" the conduit IRA, and it would no longer be considered, or enjoy the benefits of, "pure rollover" money. Now, all taxable IRA funds can be rolled over to company plans, not just conduit (AKA rollover) IRA funds, and so it is no longer important to worry about "tainting." The only situation where you would need to keep the funds in a conduit IRA "pure" is if you qualify for 10-year averaging tax treatment (see Chapter 3), where this is required.

Rollover vs. Distribution vs. Lump-Sum Distribution

All cats are animals, but not all animals are cats. Similarly, all rollovers are distributions, but not all distributions are rollovers. Funds withdrawn from a retirement account at any time are considered a *distribution*. But if these funds then get transferred into another retirement account, you've got a rollover situation. If funds are withdrawn but never transferred, you have a distribution, but no rollover. Rollover money is tax-free because it goes into another tax-sheltered account. Throughout this book, when I refer to a rollover as "tax-free," I mean that there is no current income tax on the transfer of funds from one retirement account to another. But that money is not free of tax forever. It will be taxed later when it is withdrawn (and not rolled over to another tax-deferred account). Distribution money is taxable (unless after-tax funds are being distributed) and, therefore, not sheltered any more.

The term *lump-sum distribution* refers to money received from a company plan, not an IRA. It may sound like it applies only to folks with big bucks. After all, why would it be called a "lump" if it were just peanuts? But a lump-sum distribution doesn't always equal a boatload of cash. It's to empty that plan by withdrawing the entire balance, regardless of its size.

For example, if you left your old job, which you hadn't had very long, to take a new job with another company, you might have only accumulated, say, $612 in your old company's 401(k). If you withdraw the whole $612, it's a lump-sum distribution, even though it's not a very sizable lump. Taking a lump-sum distribution doesn't always mean that you must take the money and run. It can be, and often is, rolled over to an IRA tax-free. Taking a lump-sum distribution may also qualify you for favorable tax breaks, under special circumstances (see Chapter 3).

Simplify vs. Complicate

These words are used frequently in connection with taxes—in fact, I use them often throughout this book. So, I think I should explain what they mean. In English, they are opposites—like *fat* vs. *thin* or *rich* vs. *poor*. But when it comes to tax law they mean the same thing—"to render incomprehensible." Therefore, whenever you read or hear of Congress or your state and local legislators "simplifying" the tax laws, you've got a heads-up that "something complicated this way comes."

Tax Audit vs. Tax Examination

There is no difference. They both stink.

Tax Avoidance vs. Tax Evasion

Tax avoidance is legal; *tax evasion* isn't. For example, this book will help you to *avoid* taxes, not evade them.

Tax Bill vs. Tax Law

A *tax bill* spells out what prognosticators tell you coming tax law changes will be. A *tax law* spells out what they actually turn out to be.

Tax-Free vs. Tax-Deferred Money

Tax-free means you never have to pay the piper. *Tax-deferred* means you don't have to pay the piper now but you will in the future. For example, retirement accounts are tax-deferred because you pay no tax on the income earned until the funds are withdrawn.

Traditional IRAs vs. Roth IRAs vs. Coverdell Savings Accounts (Formerly Known as Education IRAs)

Legend has it that the *traditional IRA* is named after an IRS pension specialist named *Ira* Cohen (no, I'm not making this up). In addition, it is an acronym—for "Individual Retirement Account," right? Wrong! It stands for "Individual Retirement *Arrangement*." I'm tossing this in so that when your friends want to go double or nothing in a game of Trivial Pursuit after falling victim to the Ira Cohen answer, you can stump them again and clean up. The traditional IRA is what might be called the "plain vanilla" IRA, which has been around since 1975, when it supposedly got its name from Mr. Cohen. The contributions you make to an IRA can be tax-deductible or not, depending upon your level of income and whether you are active in a company plan. You cannot contribute to a traditional IRA after you reach age 70½; you cannot withdraw from a traditional IRA before you reach age 59½ (but there are exceptions); and you must begin taking the money out of your traditional IRA when you reach age 70½ (see Chapter 4).

Named after former Senate Finance Committee Chairman William Roth from Delaware, who championed their creation, the *Roth IRA* arrived in this world in 1998. Contributions to a Roth IRA are not tax-deductible but, unlike a traditional IRA, distributions are tax-free—as long as you play by the rules (see Chapter 7). Contributions to a Roth IRA can be made annually or by converting a traditional IRA to a Roth IRA. When you convert, you pay tax on the funds that are converted. Unlike with a traditional IRA, you never have to withdraw from a Roth; if you qualify, you can keep contributing after you reach age 70½ or beyond.

Coverdell (after the late Georgia Senator Paul Coverdell) *education savings accounts* are not retirement accounts; they are education-funding vehicles. Because they are not retirement accounts (even though they were lumped in with IRAs when they first came out), this is the only reference to them you will find in this book.

So, who'll be the next lawmaker to have an IRA named after him (or her)? How about a restriction-free "Traficant IRA"—after former Ohio Congressman James Traficant—for people who don't like being bound by rules?

PART ONE

WHAT TO DO WITH THE BIGGEST CHECK YOU'LL EVER GET

ONE

The Crime of the Century

*"There was a time when a fool and his money
were soon parted, but now it happens to everybody."*
—Adlai E. Stevenson (1900–65), presidential candidate and U.S.
representative to the United Nations

L et me tell you about Ann, a woman with a nest egg consisting mainly of her 403(b), a tax-deferred retirement account for employees of nonprofit entities such as schools and hospitals. A widow, she was retired from her job of 30 years as a New York City schoolteacher. Ann's sole wish at the end of her life was to leave her entire savings to her two children: Jessica and Tom.

When Ann died suddenly in 2000, just two years into her retirement, Jessica and Tom came to me for advice. They explained how they'd been brought up in a modest, middle-class home where the emphasis was on living within one's means and always saving for a rainy day. They were amazed that although their mom, being a teacher after all, was clearly not a rich woman, she had, during 30 years of disciplined saving, accumulated more than $800,000 in her retirement account!

As Jessica and Tom both had good jobs with decent incomes, I suggested that they try to delay receiving that money since any distributions taken now would be subject to income tax, and they were both in high brackets. I explained that by "stretching" the distributions from their mom's 403(b) over their own lifetimes (Jessica was 40, and Tom was 36), the $800,000 could compound tax-free into an even bigger fortune as I'm sure Mom would have liked.

That was the good news.

However, as I learned more about the arrangements their mother had made—or, rather, had *not* made—I then had to give them the bad news: They wouldn't be able to take advantage of this option.

From Bad to Worse

Although Ann had never lived like a wealthy woman, according to our tax system, her combined estate of $1.2 million (her house, some minor savings, and other personal property, plus the $800,000 retirement plan) was large enough to be subject to estate tax.

Furthermore, as in all high-tax states (she was a New Yorker), her retirement plan distributions were subject to estate and income taxes on both the federal and state levels, as well as a city income tax!

Once I revived Jessica and Tom, I had to give them even more bad news.

As the estate tax exemption was only $675,000 (today it's $1.5 million) and their mother's estate was worth $1.2 million, they would have to pay a combined federal and New York State estate tax of $207,000, or almost 40 percent, on the $525,000 balance ($1.2 million − $675,000 = $525,000) of the inheritance. Neither Jessica nor Tom was in a position to shell out such a hefty amount, so Ann's retirement account itself would have to be tapped since there were few other liquid assets in the estate besides the account.

But it got worse.

Once the money was withdrawn from their mom's retirement

account to pay the estate taxes, the withdrawal itself would be hit with federal, state, and city income taxes of another $80,000!

Then came the worst news of all.

Under the best payout option offered by their mom's 403(b) plan, they would have to empty the account within five years, even if they didn't need the cash.

Thus, there would be no lifetime stretch option, no 40-plus years of additional tax-free compounding—which, even at a modest rate of interest, might conceivably have grown the account as high as $10 million.

Instead, their mom's retirement account, which represented a lifetime of sacrifice and saving, would be reduced by a snowball effect of taxation on taxation to less than $150,000 for each child.

Moral: Ignorance is not always bliss.

If Ann had known enough to roll her 403(b) over into an IRA when she retired, and had protected her account with sufficient life insurance, this terrible tax trap could easily have been avoided— and Jessica and Tom could have parlayed Mom's retirement account into $10 million for both of them—maybe even more.

Imagine that.

Worst Rollover Attempt Ever

Horror stories occurring to average people just like you abound. Here's another:

In a notorious 1993–98 tax case, a Mr. Albert Lemishow decided to take advantage of the IRS rule that allows you to withdraw funds from one retirement account and roll them over into another within 60 days without incurring taxes and penalties. His purpose was to use the cash to buy some shares of stock, and roll over the stock in what he thought would be a tax-free transaction.

Unfortunately, Mr. Lemishow missed the fine print.

He took the following distributions from his Keogh self-employment plan and IRA accounts to buy the stock:

Type of Account	Amount
Keogh	$250,651
Keogh	50,130
IRA	13,939
Keogh	153,828
IRA	6,377
IRA	5,489
Total Distributions	$480,414

Federal tax was withheld on the $50,130 and $153,828 Keogh withdrawals, but for some reason was ignored on the $250,651 Keogh. The combined tax withholding was $43,297. Therefore the net amount of the Keogh and IRA distributions was $437,117.

Since Mr. Lemishow withdrew the funds on December 14, 1993, he had until February 12, 1994, to complete the rollover within the required 60 days.

In the meantime, Mr. Lemishow completed a subscription to buy $450,000 worth of the stock he had his eye on. However, he was only able to buy $377,895 worth of that stock, which, on February 11, 1994, he deposited into a new IRA. He did not roll any of the other cash into the IRA.

When he filed his 1993 federal tax return, Mr. Lemishow reported no taxable Keogh or IRA distributions and claimed credit for the $43,297 tax withheld. However, the IRS assessed, and the tax court held, that all of the Keogh and IRA distributions were taxable, and disallowed any tax-free treatment on the stock that was rolled over to the IRA.

As a result, Mr. Lemishow got hit with a staggering tax bill of $170,968 plus penalties and interest that effectively wiped out his pension!

Why? Here's what was in the fine print.

When withdrawing cash from an IRA or other plan for the purpose of rolling it over to another IRA, only the same property (i.e., cash) can be rolled over tax-free. If a different property (in this case, stock) is rolled over, the distribution is taxable, as well as subject to early withdrawal and other applicable penalties (see Chapter 3).

Time Bomb

There are almost as many variations to these two horror stories as there are run-on sentences in the tax code. But the common denominator among them is this: The number of such stories is growing because of two unprecedented events in our nation's history that are converging: the passing away of the World War II generation and the retirement of that generation's offspring, the so-called baby boomers.

The convergence of these two events is fostering the greatest transfer of wealth our planet has ever seen as all the people of the WWII generation, who've spent their lives saving, bequeath their savings to their children, the baby boomers, who are just now beginning to retire in record numbers and starting to take distributions from their own retirement accounts.

This is resulting in two scenarios:

Many pre-retirees of the baby boom generation who are inheriting money from their parents are suddenly finding themselves well fixed (perhaps even wealthy) and are running up against some hard, costly estate taxes not taken into account by their parents, and they're going into shock ("How did this happen? My folks saved 40 years, and you say it's all gone? How is that possible? How is that fair?").

Simultaneously, retiring baby boomers are leaving their jobs with the biggest check they've ever had (and biggest asset they own)—their retirement savings—and thus potentially opening themselves up to a big financial problem.

Having been so busy chasing investment returns all their working lives, they've probably neglected the distribution part of the equation, and thus risk losing a whopping amount of what they've saved to the taxman.

As this greatest transfer of wealth in human history reaches its apex in the coming years, there will be an explosion of excessive taxation that will reach epidemic proportions (especially given the population affected), an explosion that will give millions of ill-prepared and underprotected American savers like yourself the financial shock of their lives.

The fallout from this "retirement savings time bomb" will continue to affect you, your children, the economy, and society for years and years to come.

How much at risk are YOU personally?

Turn the page and see.

TWO

What's Your Risk IQ?

"A good scare is worth more to a [person] than good advice."
—Ed Howe (1853-1937), American editor and novelist

Genius or Idiot—The IRS Doesn't Discriminate

I have a client who's a genius. It's true. He's one of the most brilliant research scientists in the world. His IQ is somewhere up there in the high triple digits. Unfortunately, none of his remarkable gray matter renders him immune from making the same boneheaded mistakes the rest of us make where our retirement savings are concerned. In fact, his smarts may even make things worse for him.

After soliciting my advice on his retirement account, he proceeded not to listen to me as I tried to persuade him that a decision he was considering would put his entire savings at risk. He's apparently such a genius that he only needs to listen to himself. I have no idea why he even asked me for advice since it's clear that all he wanted was an accomplice.

The Wiz, I'll call him, had a substantial IRA; it was created when he left a former job where he had a 401(k) and rolled the money over. Now he was working for a new company and was participating in its 401(k) plan. When he read in the newspapers about a new tax law that would allow him to roll his IRA back into his new 401(k), he called to ask if this was true. I said it was but asked why on earth he would consider such a move since its long-term consequences could spell disaster for him and his family.

"Simple," he said. "My 401(k) investments are doing better than my IRA investments."

"Then change your IRA investments," I said, sounding like Henny Youngman.

I explained that, first of all, an IRA offered literally thousands of investment choices whereas his 401(k) offered only eleven. Second, I knew from past meetings with him that he wanted to leave his retirement savings to his children since his wife had sufficient assets of her own and didn't want his retirement money. For most people, especially this family, the IRA is the best vehicle for this because you can leave an IRA to anyone you wish—while creating the opportunity to build a powerful pile of cash in the bargain.

Under federal law, however, the Wiz had to leave his 401(k) to his spouse, unless she signed a waiver in favor of the children, which she had yet to do because he, being a research scientist, felt compelled to do more research on the subject before she took pen to paper. This meant that if he dropped dead suddenly, the children would be out of luck.

But let's say Mrs. Wiz has signed a waiver. That just opens up another can of worms. You see, a typical 401(k) does not allow taking distributions over an extended period of time, as is permitted with an IRA. On the contrary, the beneficiary—in this case the Wiz's children—would have to take the entire payout from the 401(k) within one year after their father's death and pay all the deferred tax on the account in one fell swoop. As a result, they would suddenly find themselves owing a fortune in taxes that they likely wouldn't be able to pay, which means that the IRS would reach into their father's retirement savings to collect. Presto, there goes their bequest (or most of it anyway) and Dad's legacy in the blink of an eye.

On the other hand, if the Wiz spends his time doing scientific research instead of analyzing tax law and leaves his IRA alone rather than rolling it over into his new company's 401(k), his children will inherit everything immediately upon his death—and be able to keep the inheritance growing tax-deferred for another 40 years into their own dotage if they so desire.

You tell me which strategy is better.

My recommendations fell on deaf ears, however. Focusing on the Small Picture rather than the Big Picture—i.e., current returns rather than savings protection—the Wiz bulldogged ahead and rolled his IRA money over into his new 401(k), setting up a scenario for disaster.

Shortly afterward an event occurred that neither of us would have predicted, whose repercussions added even more fuel to the fire of his bad decision. The nightly news broke the scandalous story of the financial failure of Enron, America's seventh largest corporation. Although the Wiz did not work for Enron, his company, like so many others, was scorched by the Enron effect as stock prices plummeted. So, on top of what he'd done to put his retirement savings at risk on his own, fate had stepped in to take away a substantial amount of the value of his new 401(k) as well.

I'll bet that the return on his old IRA looks pretty good to him about now.

Unfortunately, his is not an isolated case. When it comes to cashing in on our errors, the IRS doesn't discriminate. Genius or idiot, we're all in the same boat.

Most people don't—or, worse, won't—see the forest for the trees when it comes to things financial. For example, I've found that they'll devote more time going over their supermarket receipts to make sure they haven't been overcharged than they'll spend keeping their life savings from becoming a windfall for Uncle Sam. As a matter of fact, I've actually had clients cancel their estate planning appointments with me to hit a sale at their local Price Club wholesaler. Believe me, they'll have to score some mighty big bargains there, plus rob several banks, to make up the percentage of their life savings they'll lose to taxes if they don't get smart.

That's what seeing the Big Picture is all about, and I've spent the better part of the past 15 years pointing it out.

"Everybody Should Know About This!"

When the distribution rules for IRAs and all other retirement plans were first issued by the IRS in July 1987, they received virtually no attention. The country was still reeling from the savings-and-loan debacle, better known as the greatest bank robbery in American history, and that story was a whole lot sexier (and easier to untangle) than a bunch of complicated tax rules on retirement accounts. And yet these rules were setting in motion a plan that effectively would rob America's savers of their nest eggs down the road—a road that is now a minefield of tax traps.

Another reason that attention wasn't paid back then is that IRAs were not the sizable portion of an individual's retirement savings that they are today. Most of the big retirement money was in company pension plans, so the fate of an IRA at the hands of the taxman was dismissed as a minor issue.

Today, most company pension money ultimately ends up in an IRA, through either rollovers or inheritances. This means that more money is now going into IRAs than into any other type of retirement plan. Rollovers from 401(k)s and other plans into IRAs are now in the trillions of dollars. As the baby boomers retire and inherit from their parents, IRAs are fast becoming the largest single asset people own! This constitutes a major economic change in the distribution of wealth. So, the big deal about those complex IRA distribution rules issued back in 1987 is their impact today on the tax-deferred savings of us all, regardless of what type of retirement plan we're in.

For example, an executive from a major television network came to me for help in evaluating the tax ramifications of his 401(k) plan. As we focused on tax planning for his retirement account, I went through the same five steps with him for keeping the taxman at bay that I'll present to you in this book. They're applicable to anyone, rich or poor, with any type of retirement plan. (In fact, the less you have, the more important it is to protect it.)

At the conclusion of our session, the network exec expressed amazement at how little of his retirement money would now be going to the government and how much of it would be going to his family due to following my five simple steps. He could not believe how much of a difference they had made in the financial legacy he would now be able to leave to his family, and was absolutely thrilled. On his way out, feeling as if he'd just slain the tax dragon, he said, "Ed, this is unbelievable. It's bigger than Enron. *Everybody* should know about this!"

I agreed. "People think Enron's bad," I said. "Think how they'd feel if it was *their* retirement account that vanished. How they would feel if it vanished legally, confiscated by their own government—and, if unlike the employees at Enron, they had only themselves to blame!"

Within three days I was on his network's nightly news, at his urging, talking about this very subject. And yet tens of millions of Americans are still largely in the dark that their retirement savings are at risk.

What this means is that if you don't know that there is a problem, it doesn't bother you. Or, to put it another way, "Out of sight, out of mind."

Until it bites.

The Roach That Came to Dinner

I'm reminded of another story, a parable really, about a man and his wife who eat regularly at a favorite local restaurant because the food there is absolutely scrumptious.

They are unaware that the restaurant has a roach problem in the kitchen. Yet even if they did know, while obviously not cottoning to the idea, they'd probably still keep coming back for the food just as long as the roaches stayed unseen.

Once the creatures started crawling onto their plates, however, the man and his wife would probably get so upset that they'd call the board of health. By then, of course, it would be too late. The place would have to be shut down because the problem had become an epidemic.

It's the same with your IRAs and other plan savings.

Most of you haven't yet experienced the shock of losing the bulk of a retirement account to taxes. But when this happens, you'll wish something could be done to reverse the damage. But by then it'll be too late. Unfortunately, it's human nature to not call in the exterminator until the roaches are on our plates.

Where our retirement savings are concerned, the roaches aren't out of the kitchen yet, but they're on the way.

If you don't address the issue of protecting your 401(k), IRA, or other retirement plan distributions from excess taxation now, while you're still breathing, your family will pay the price. Worse, they'll spend the rest of their lives wondering how you could have worked so hard and been so smart and so disciplined as to have accumulated such an impressive nest egg only to have been careless or ignorant enough to have left it to the IRS.

How Safe Is *Your* Retirement Account?

Now that I've put a good scare into you with my prognostication of things to come, here's where seeing is believing.

Take this simple self-evaluation of your personal retirement plan risk. It is designed to flush out the biggest mistakes people make with retirement distribution planning. Each question highlights a situation that could lead to the demise of your 401(k), IRA, or other retirement savings if you're not careful.

As you read these questions, the point of some may elude you at this stage. That's OK. What's important now is this: Going through them will get you started thinking seriously about protecting your retirement money now because each situation could by itself, or in combination with others, be the death knell for your life savings and be a pot of gold for Uncle Sam depending upon your response.

Here's the deal. Answer "yes" or "no" to each of these 20 questions. Give yourself five points for each "yes" answer, and five points for each "no" answer. When you're finished, tally the total number of "yes" points and "no" points in the blanks provided, then check the scoring box to find out your risk IQ—i.e., how much or how little your retirement savings are at risk.

TEST YOUR RISK IQ

■ ■ ■ ■ ■ ■ ■ ■ ■

1. Do you have most of your retirement savings in a company 401(k), 403(b), or 457 retirement plan? _____YES_____NO

2. Do you have company stock in your 401(k)?
_____YES _____NO

3. Is your retirement plan one of the largest assets you own?
_____YES _____NO

4. Have you recently left your company or retired, or will you be retiring soon? _____YES _____NO

5. After you retire, will you be leaving your retirement account with your former employer? _____YES _____NO

6. Will you be taking a lump-sum distribution from your company plan at any time? _____YES _____NO

7. Will your retirement account savings pass according to the terms in your will? _____YES _____NO

8. Have you named a trust to be the beneficiary of your retirement plan? _____YES _____NO

9. Is your estate the beneficiary of your retirement plan?
_____YES _____NO

10. Will you be leaving your retirement assets to your spouse?
_____YES _____NO

11. Have you put off instructing your beneficiaries what to do—and what not to do—with your retirement plan when they inherit? ____YES ____NO

12. Do you want to be able to control the payouts on your retirement account(s) after your death to prevent your beneficiaries from squandering the money? ____YES ____NO

13. Will you be inheriting a retirement account from anyone? ____YES ____NO

14. Are you confident that your bank, broker, or mutual fund company will have all the necessary documentation on your retirement account that your beneficiaries will need? ____YES ____NO

15. Are you unsure of the exact amount that the IRS requires you to withdraw from your retirement account, and when? ____YES ____NO

16. Do you own a life insurance policy? ____YES ____NO

17. Will you be rolling cash, stock, or other property over from one retirement account to another? ____YES ____NO

18. Has it been more than a year since you last updated the beneficiary forms for every retirement account you own? ____YES ____NO

19. Will you need to tap into your retirement savings before you reach age 59½? ____YES ____NO

20. Have you heard of the Roth IRA but taken no steps to find out more or set one up yet? ____YES ____NO

TOTAL POINTS: _____ YES _____ NO

■ ■ ■ ■ ■ ■ ■ ■ ■ ■ ■ ■ ■ ■ ■ ■ ■ ■ ■

SCORING YOUR RISK IQ

The total number of "yes" points represents the approximate percentage of your retirement savings that will probably go to the U.S. Treasury, and the total number of "no" points represents an approximation of how much you and your family will likely keep.

Most probably you're now reeling from shock—unless your risk IQ beat the taxman soundly, which, while possible, of course, is not probable. I've given this evaluation to tens of thousands of consumers, tax professionals, and financial advisors over the years in my seminars and workshops, and most find their retirement accounts to be woefully exposed to extreme taxation.

But I'll give you the benefit of the doubt and say that you did come through relatively unscathed, holding onto more of your retirement savings than the government will take. If so, here's a promise. My next book will be about YOU! I'll call it *The Retirement Savings Time Bomb Survivor* and we'll sell it to Hollywood. I smell Oscar!

As for the rest of you who are just now coming out of shock at the prospect of spending a lifetime building your savings only to wind up leaving it to the government, take heart.

As you dive into this book and sail through its five easy steps for leaving your loved ones with more and the taxman with less, dream instead about what to do with all that extra cash—and shuck off the nightmare about having your confiscated nest egg come back to you some day in the form of a meager monthly Social Security check (assuming the Social Security fund is still solvent when that time comes).

Your retirement savings is *your* money. Protect it! If you truly want you and your family to be able to enjoy the fruits of your lifetime of labor and success, turn the page *now* and start getting even with—and getting over on—the taxman!

■ THREE ■

Roll Over, Stay Put, or Withdraw?

"In all things, success depends upon previous preparation,
and without such preparation, there is to be such failure."
—Confucius (551–479 BC), philosopher

I t's the first day of the rest of your life.

You're about to retire, just retired, left a company to take another job, or have been downsized (AKA rightsized or whatever they're calling it these days), having built up a sizable retirement account.

Now what?

You're going to get the biggest check of your life—your lump-sum distribution. Surely this calls for some thought or pre-planning about what to do with it. And I don't mean leafing through Disneyworld brochures or inquiring about car rentals at Brinks.

Fortunately there aren't a ton of options to make your head spin. You've got three choices for what to do with your money:

- Option #1: Roll over to an IRA.
- Option #2: Stay put in the company plan (if or for as long as allowed) or roll to a new employer's plan.
- Option #3: Take a lump-sum distribution and pay the tax now.

The choice you make here is probably the most important financial decision of your lifetime. In a way, it's like deciding where to park your car for easy access, convenience, and safety when it's off the road. In tandem with the five simple steps for protecting your retirement savings I'll present in Part 2, your decision here can make or break your retirement.

To gauge the tax ramifications of each option, take the following factors into consideration:

1. **When will you need the money?** Will you need it to retire on? Or sooner rather than later? Your answer will determine whether you're better off rolling your money over into an IRA (option #1) or taking a lump sum and paying tax on the distributed amount at ordinary income tax rates or special tax-favored rates (option #3).

2. **What will your tax bracket be in retirement?** It is not uncommon to be in a higher tax bracket in retirement than during your working years. If your postretirement bracket will be significantly higher, the required annual distributions from option #1, which are tax-deferred until withdrawn, will be taxed at that higher rate, leaving less for you to live on. Therefore, taking a lump-sum distribution and paying the tax on it now, but at a lower rate under special tax treatment (option #3) if you qualify, might be a better long-term retirement strategy for avoiding excessive taxation.

3. **How is your health?** If you're seriously ill or old enough to have one foot in the grave already, you'll want to be able to extend the tax deferral on your retirement account distribution over the longer life expectancy of your beneficiary. Option #1 will allow you to do this.

4. **How much money will you need for retirement?** Maybe you have a sufficient amount of non–tax-deferred savings to support your retirement to be able to choose option #1 or #2. But

if you feel that you will have to tap into your pension money to make ends meet, option #3 may be a must.

5. **How much is the lump-sum distribution?** If it is large, taking the tax hit up-front probably won't pay because of the unlikelihood of your being able to make up the shortfall in your remaining years. Therefore, options #1 and #2 are more viable. If the lump-sum distribution is a small amount, you'll pay proportionately less in current tax under option #3.

6. **How old are you?** The minimum age you can begin taking distributions without getting socked with a 10 percent early-withdrawal penalty is 59½ (for more on this rule and its exceptions, see Chapter 4). More to the point, however: The younger you are, the more years you will have to keep building tax-deferred money, which you will need more of, because retirement is such a long way off. So, if you're younger than 59½, consider option #1. But if you're older, you have a lot more flexibility for avoiding taxes and penalties in all three options than those young whipper-snappers.

7. **What is your estate plan?** With an IRA rollover (option #1), the money can continue building up tax-deferred for your heirs after your death. Or it might pay to take a lump-sum distribution (option #3) if you need to correct a faulty estate plan—i.e., one with insufficient funds to pay the estate tax after you're gone without draining key assets. You can also withdraw to equalize assets between you and your spouse to maximize each of your estate tax exemptions. This may be necessary when one spouse has most of the couple's assets in his or her IRA and the other spouse has few assets.

8. **Who will pay the income tax?** Can it be shifted to your beneficiaries at lower rates, or will it be cheaper for you to pay the income tax now with the special tax treatment offered by option #3? If not, option #1 might be better. It will allow you to convert the rolled-over funds to a Roth IRA (if you qualify; see Chapter 7), whereby you pay the income tax on those

funds upon conversion, relieving your beneficiaries from ever having to sell off key assets to pay that tax. Furthermore, you will have reduced the size of your estate that will be subject to estate tax by the amount of tax you paid on the conversion.

9. **Will you be working again?** If there's a chance that you will be rehired or want to go back to work again after you've retired, option #1's portability feature—the ability to park your money temporarily in an IRA rollover account and then roll it back into your new employer's plan—may be most attractive to you. However, in most cases it is best to roll the funds to an IRA and leave them there (do not roll them back to your new employer's plan). If you already have a new job lined up, you may want the flexibility of rolling your money right from your prior employer's plan into your new employer's plan to take advantage of loan provisions or creditor protection (if your state does not already protect IRAs from creditors) (option #2). Then again, if there's a chance that you'll be working again, but you need the money now, option #3 may be your best choice because you may qualify for special tax treatment. If not, you may as well select option # 1 and withdraw what you need from the IRA as you need it. If you need tax-free cash now for bills or other pressing expenses, you might consider withdrawing any after-tax funds from your company retirement plan and rolling the rest of the company plan money to an IRA. The after-tax money withdrawn will be tax-free to you to spend as you wish, because you already paid tax on that money before it was contributed to the plan.

10. **Is creditor protection a big issue for you?** Most states afford IRAs protection from creditors; if your state does not protect IRAs from creditors, however, and this is an important issue for you, you might want to consider leaving the funds in your company plan or rolling them over to a new employer's plan (option #2). Option #3 (taking a lump-sum distribution) exposes your pension money to creditor claims, such as lawsuits, malpractice, divorce, bankruptcy, or other creditor problems.

But you should not let the issue of creditor protection tip the scales and sway you because most people do not have judgments on their retirement accounts. You must really give some thought here as to which is more important to you—creditor protection or having all the advantages of the IRA rollover—by asking yourself, for example, "Would I want to give up the opportunity to stretch my IRA (see Chapter 6) for my beneficiaries in exchange for creditor protection I may never need?"

CAUTION!

Don't base your decision on any one factor alone, unless that factor is a major issue for you.

As I delve in detail into your three options for what to do with that Biggest Check You'll Ever Get, keep reviewing your responses to the 10 factors you should consider—and remember that more than one road leads to Rome. Each option is not always all-or-nothing. You may, for example, want to roll part of your company plan money over (option #1) while withdrawing some for expenses (option #3). That's perfectly legal and doable! Remember, it's your money—and it's my job to ensure that you hold on to as much as possible, so you and your family can enjoy it for years to come.

Option #1: Roll Over to an IRA

The IRA rollover is the best option for most people. It's the most liberal and flexible. Once your funds are rolled to an IRA, you can take advantage of everything the tax law allows. That is not necessarily true of company plans. Believe it or not, some 401(k)s, for example, impose far more restrictive rules than even the IRS!

With this option, you roll your lump-sum distribution into an

IRA account and park it there until you're ready to take withdrawals. (You could also roll the distribution to your new employer's plan, but if your old plan had a lot of restrictive rules, you'll probably be subject to the same ones in your new plan—so you'll be no better off.)

Because it's a rollover, the distribution is tax-free, provided the rollover is completed within 60 days of the day you receive the distribution; otherwise you'll have to pay income tax on the whole withdrawal (plus that pesky extra 10 percent penalty if it's also an *early* withdrawal, which is a withdrawal made before you are 59½ years old, or before age 55, if the age 55 exception (see page 56) applies). This so-called *60-day rule* is strictly enforced, although the IRS has the authority to waive it under special circumstances where delay is beyond your control due to "casualty, disaster, disability, hospitalization, death, or incarceration" (though it seems to me that these last two especially would make violating the 60-day rollover rule the least of one's worries).

The 60-day rule can also be waived due to restrictions imposed by a foreign country (such as being trapped behind enemy lines if war breaks out), postal errors (inconceivable as this may seem), an error committed by your financial institution (impossible!), or any other situation where denying a waiver would be unfair or against good conscience.

Whose good conscience?

Good question.

That's why even though a 60-day waiver is available, I advise that the best way to do a tax-deferred lump-sum rollover is *directly* from one company plan to another, or to an IRA, via trustee-to-trustee transfer. In this way, the distribution never comes in contact with your hot little hands, so you never have to worry about the unexpected coming along to gum up your ability to comply with the 60-day rule. For example, you may have every intention of withdrawing the money from one bank and walking it directly across the street for deposit into another bank, completing the rollover in less than 60 minutes, let alone 60 days. But in your haste to set a new world record for a completed rollover, you don't look both ways crossing the street and get smacked by a bus. Do the trustee-to-trustee transfer instead. It's safer. Plus you can do as many trustee-to-trustee transfers a year as you like, whereas IRA rollovers are limited to one per year. That's not a calendar year, mind you, but *one rollover every 12 months.*

If you have more than one IRA, however, the 12-month rollover rule applies to each one separately, which means that although you have to wait another 12 months to roll over the *same funds,* you can roll over *different funds* in another of your IRAs (and, of course, wait another 12 months to roll those funds over again).

EXAMPLE

If you roll over $200,000 from one IRA to another IRA in November 2003, you cannot roll the $200,000 over again to another IRA two months later in January 2004, even though it's a new calendar year. You have to wait a *full 12 months* (until November 2004) to do another rollover with the same funds. But if you have, say, another IRA worth $40,000, you could roll those funds over in January 2004 (even earlier), since it's not the same money. But you couldn't roll the $40,000 over again until January 2005.

The 20 Percent Tax Trap on Rollovers

This is another reason why I recommend using the trustee-to-trustee (direct) transfer method instead of the rollover method when withdrawing money from a company plan and putting it in an IRA.

If you go the rollover route, the plan is required to withhold 20 percent federal income tax from the rollover amount. This means that instead of rolling over 100 percent of your account balance,

20 percent of it is withheld by your plan for taxes, leaving you 80 percent to roll over.

Yes, I know. Rollovers are supposed to be tax-free, so why does the tax law require 20 percent—or any amount—of your distribution withheld?

Here's why: If you do a rollover rather than a direct transfer, the government is not assured that you will indeed redeposit 100 percent of that big fat check in the IRA or other retirement account. It simply does not trust you with your own money. Therefore, the government covers itself by forcing company plans to withhold 20 percent from your distribution before giving you a dime.

"But if I do the rollover and have the 20 percent withheld, I won't owe anything, so I'll get the 20 percent back as a tax refund, right?"

Right. But the problem is this: If you don't roll over the entire amount (100 percent), the amount not rolled over is taxable—even subject to the 10 percent early-withdrawal penalty if you're under 59½ (or under age 55 if the age 55 exception applies). "Gotcha!" says the IRS.

The 20 percent withholding tax requirement applies to rollovers from company plans to IRAs, but not to rollovers from IRAs. Nevertheless, I still advise going the direct trustee-to-trustee transfer route because you avoid the 60-day rule and the one-rollover-per-year limitation.

The 20 percent withholding requirement also does not apply to rollover distributions of company stock in a qualified plan—when that is the only asset in the plan. (For more on this exception, see option #3.)

EXAMPLE

You have $500,000 in your 401(k) and roll it over to an IRA. The 401(k) plan will cut you a check for $400,000, (80 percent, of your account balance). The plan is required to send other 20 percent ($100,000) to the IRS, and you'll get credit for it when you file your tax return. Unless you have an extra $100,000 under a mattress you can use to replace the 20 percent shortfall, you can't do a complete rollover (all $500,000), so you'll wind up owing tax on that 20 percent that wasn't rolled over—plus a 10 percent penalty if you're younger than 59½ (or under 55 if the age 55 exception applies). This is a killer tax trap that could cost you and your family decades of tax-deferred compounding on that 20 percent of your retirement savings. What a nightmare! That's why you should always do a trustee-to-trustee transfer when moving retirement money from a company plan to another retirement account.

Allowable Rollovers

In the past, rollovers were limited. For example, 403(b) tax-sheltered annuities could be rolled over to an IRA but not to another qualified plan, such as a 401(k); Section 457 plan balances could not be rolled over at all; and only taxable funds (the pre-tax funds) could be rolled over. After-tax funds (contributions made to a plan that are not deductible from an employee's income because they represent basis) were simply withdrawn tax-free since the tax on that money was already paid. Now after-tax funds from a qualified plan can be rolled over to another qualified plan or to an IRA.

Taxable retirement account distributions from company plans such as 401(k)s, 403(b)s, and governmental Section 457 plans are permitted to be rolled over to another 401(k), 403(b), or 457 or to an IRA. Only taxable amounts can be rolled from an IRA to a company plan. Amounts rolled over are called eligible rollover distribution (ERDs), and it is the rollover that makes the distribution tax-free.

Certain plan distributions are not eligible to be rolled over. These include

- Required minimum distributions (see Chapter 4).
- Any distributions that are part of a series of substantially equal periodic payments or distributions over another specified period of 10 years or more (called Section 72[t] payments; see Chapter 9).
- Hardship distributions. Some company plans may allow participants to withdraw to pay for a medical emergency, funeral, or other pressing need. The reason that the IRS will not let you roll over hardship distributions to an IRA is because it feels that if you had such a pressing need for the cash, then the cash must be used for that pressing need. In other words, the IRS saw this as a potential loophole and closed it.
- Distributions to plan beneficiaries—except for spouse beneficiaries (see Chapters 4 and 6).

Rollover Rules

After-tax funds (the nontaxable amounts) from a 401(k) plan still cannot be rolled over to 403(b) plans. Section 457 plans do not accept after-tax contributions, so no after-tax money can be rolled into or out of a 457. If after-tax funds are shifted from one 401(k) plan to another 401(k), the rollover must be a direct trustee-to-trustee transfer, and the receiving plan must agree to keep a separate accounting of both the taxable and the after-tax funds, as well as of the income earned on those funds.

A separate accounting of after-tax funds rolled into them is not required for IRAs, since that is done by the IRA's owner and reported to the IRS on Form 8606 ("Nondeductible IRAs and Coverdell ESAs"), which is filed with the IRA owner's personal tax return.

The problem with rolling after-tax money to an IRA is that you cannot simply withdraw that money tax-free from the IRA. This is because once it's in the IRA, it gets treated the same as nondeductible contributions under what is known as the *pro rata rule*.

The pro rata rule applies to withdrawals of *basis* in an IRA, which, as you'll remember from "Talking the Talk," is the amount of nondeductible IRA contributions and after-tax contributions rolled into an IRA from another plan. Basis is actually a good thing because it's already-taxed money and, thus, can be withdrawn tax-free. The hitch is accounting for the basis in an IRA when you actually withdraw from the account—since the pro rata rule will not allow you to withdraw only the basis and pay no tax on that money.

The rule states that all distributions from your IRA represent a "proportionate share" of both basis and taxable money. The percentage of each IRA distribution that is nontaxable is calculated by dividing the amount of nondeductible contributions (including rollovers of after-tax money from another plan) by the balance of all your IRAs, including SEP- and SIMPLE IRAs.

For example, assume you have $100,000 in your IRA plus a $300,000 401(k) that includes $40,000 of after-tax contributions (basis) and $260,000 of taxable funds (no basis), which you roll over. Your IRA balance is now $400,000. Then some unexpected bills arrive and you need money to pay them. So, you withdraw the $40,000 of basis from your IRA. The $40,000 cannot be withdrawn completely tax-free because of the pro rata rule. Only 10 percent ($4,000) of the withdrawal would be tax-free; you're taxed on the other $36,000. The total of your after-tax funds is $40,000 and the total IRA balance (after the rollover) is $400,000. $40,000 divided by $400,000 = 10 percent. So, 10 percent of the $40,000 IRA withdrawal equals $4,000, the amount that is tax-free; and 90 percent ($36,000) of the $40,000 IRA withdrawal will be taxable (see Figure 1).

The best analogy I can think of for the pro rata rule is a cup of coffee and cream. The coffee is your IRA and the cream is the after-tax money rolled into the IRA (or the nondeductible IRA contributions). Once the cream is poured into the coffee, you can't separate the two. In other words, you cannot just withdraw the after-tax funds and pay no tax. Every drop has a set percentage of both cof-

Figure 1. The Pro Rata Rule

After-tax money rolled over from plan + Nondeductible IRA contributions (the IRA basis) / Balance in all traditional IRAs, including SEP- and SIMPLE IRAs × Amount of IRA withdrawal = Tax-free Portion

$$\frac{\$40,000}{\$400,000} = 10\% \times \$40,000 = \$4,000 \text{ tax-free}$$

fee and cream. The only way to change the percentage is to add more coffee or more cream.

So, if you need some or all of that after-tax money in your company plan, don't roll it to an IRA—because, according to the pro rata rule, you won't be able to withdraw it tax-free unless you withdraw the entire IRA balance.

But if you have no current need for the money and your plan for the IRA is to leave it intact for your beneficiaries (except for the annual required distributions you must take after you turn 70½ years old; see Chapter 4), then it pays to roll the after-tax money to your IRA where it can continue to grow tax-deferred.

SO, YOU THINK YOU SPOTTED A LOOPHOLE?

Q. Ed, what if I withdraw the after-tax money from my 401(k) and roll it over to a separate, secret new IRA account, in a different bank, in a different state? You know, like the big corporations do when they hide their cash in the Cayman

Islands? Then I can withdraw the after-tax money I kept
segregated from my other IRA funds tax-free, right?
A. Wrong! The IRS is way ahead of you on that one, bub.
The regs say that whether you have one IRA in the bank
across the street, a second in a bank in a different state,
and a third in an offshore bank, you must aggregate all
your IRA accounts when computing the pro rata rule.
Don't compare yourself to the big corporations. They
know how to beat the system; they just shred everything. It's up to us small fry to pay the country's bills.

IRA Rollovers to Company Plans

Only the taxable amount (the pre-tax money) distributed from an
IRA can be rolled over to a company plan. The after-tax funds (basis) in an IRA cannot be rolled over. They can be rolled into an
IRA from a company plan, but not out to a company plan. They're
like the guests at the Roach Motel—they check in, but never check
out. After-tax funds must remain in the IRA. Also, any nondeductible contributions (which are also basis) cannot be rolled to a
company plan. But both after-tax funds and nondeductible contributions can still be rolled over into other IRAs. As with rollovers
from a company plan to an IRA, the transfer is subject to the 60-
day rule if it is not made directly via trustee-to-trustee.

"Why would I want to roll over from an IRA to a company
plan?" you ask.

"Because when IRA funds are rolled to a company plan, the pro
rata rule is negated!" I answer.

Here's the picture.

Let's say you have three IRAs with a total balance of $200,000.
IRA #1 has a taxable (no basis) balance of $100,000. IRA #2 has
a balance of $70,000 made up of $40,000 in after-tax funds (basis) rolled over from another plan, while the remaining $30,000 is
taxable. IRA #3 has a balance of $30,000 including $20,000 in

nondeductible IRA contributions (basis); the remaining $10,000 is taxable.

IRA #	Total IRA Amount	Basis (Not Taxable)	No Basis (Taxable)
1	$100,000	–0–	$100,000
2	70,000	$40,000	30,000
3	30,000	20,000	10,000
Totals	$200,000	$60,000	$140,000

Of the combined $200,000 balance between the three IRAs, a total of $140,000 is taxable, and a total of $60,000 is basis (non-taxable). Because the combined $100,000 balance ($70,000 + $30,000) of IRAs #2 and #3 is less than the total taxable amount of $140,000, you can roll IRAs #2 and #3 into a company plan— at which time the combined basis figure of $60,000 will be transferred to IRA #1. The money itself is not actually moved to IRA #1 as there is no money to move, since IRAs #2 and #3 were emptied when they were rolled over into the company plan.

As a result, IRA #1 has the same $100,000 balance it had before, but now only $40,000 will be taxable, and the remaining $60,000 will be basis, or nontaxable— which means that only the taxable $40,000 in IRA #1 can be rolled into a company plan.

Let's take this example a step further and say you roll the remaining $40,000 of taxable IRA money into a company plan. Now left with $60,000 in IRA #1 (your only remaining IRA), you can withdraw the entire $60,000 tax-free because it is all basis. To even greater advantage, you could then convert the withdrawal tax-free to a Roth IRA if you qualified (see Chapter 7).

As you see, you have to do a bit of a rollover jig to negate the pro rata rule, and in the end it may not be worth the effort because there's this obstacle to consider: Even though the IRS allows IRA money to be rolled over to a company plan, the plan—a 401(k), for example—doesn't have to accept that money, and many company plans don't. Why? Because they don't want the additional administrative headache of having to keep track of your IRA and your 401(k), too.

CAUTION!

Think twice before rolling IRA money to a company plan. Even though this is allowable and could enable you to bypass the pro rata rule, the best retirement distribution, investment, and withdrawal options are in the IRA. Once IRA funds are rolled to a company plan, they become plan assets, and are thus subject to plan restrictions and federal laws.

Stock Rollovers

With all that stock building up in your retirement plan, it's likely that you may want to roll some or all of that over too.

Tax-free rollovers of company stock (defined as stock in the company that employed you)—as well as other noncash property—from a qualified plan or IRA to another IRA (and vice-versa) are permitted by the IRS. Distributions are taxed at ordinary income tax rates based on the fair market value of the stock at the time of distribution. This fair market value then becomes your foundation for computing gain or loss on the future sale of the stock.

However, if the company stock in your retirement plan is highly appreciated, you may not want to roll it over to an IRA (even though the conventional wisdom tells you to do so) but take a lump-sum distribution instead (see option #3).

Figure 2. Allowable Rollovers at a Glance

PERMITTED ROLLOVERS UNDER THE TAX LAW

The 2001 tax law (EGTRRA 2001) greatly expanded rollovers between company plans and IRAs. The new liberalized rollover rules also apply to surviving spouses who are beneficiaries of their deceased spouse's company plans or IRAs.

Rollovers of taxable funds are permitted between all the plans listed in the chart below. The chart shows which plans can also roll over after-tax funds to other plans. Even though the tax law permits these rollovers, company plans are not required to accept rollovers.

Rollovers from:	Rollovers to:			
	IRA	401(k) Plan	403(b) Plan	457 Plan
IRA	All taxable (eligible) funds can be rolled over to other IRAs.	All taxable (eligible) funds can be rolled over to a 401(k) plan.	All taxable (eligible) funds can be rolled over to a 403(b) plan.	All taxable (eligible) funds can be rolled over to a 457 plan.
	After-tax funds rolled into IRAs from plans and nondeductible IRA contributions can be rolled over to other IRAs, but not to company plans.	After-tax funds rolled into IRAs from plans and nondeductible IRA contributions cannot be rolled to a 401(k) plan.	After-tax funds rolled into IRAs from plans and nondeductible IRA contributions cannot be rolled to a 403(b) plan.	After-tax funds rolled into IRAs from plans and nondeductible IRA contributions cannot be rolled to a 457 plan.

Figure 2. Allowable Rollovers at a Glance (*continued*)

Rollovers from:	Rollovers to:			
	IRA	401(k) Plan	403(b) Plan	457 Plan
401(k) plan	All taxable (eligible) funds can be rolled over to an IRA. After-tax 401(k) contributions can be rolled into an IRA.	All taxable (eligible) funds can be rolled over to other 401(k) plans. After-tax 401(k) contributions can be rolled to other 401(k) plans.	All taxable (eligible) funds can be rolled over to a 403(b) plan. After-tax 401(k) contributions cannot be rolled to a 403(b) plan.	All taxable (eligible) funds can be rolled over to a 457 plan. After-tax 401(k) contributions cannot be rolled to a 457 plan.
403(b) plan	All taxable (eligible) funds can be rolled over to an IRA. After-tax 403(b) contributions can be rolled to an IRA.	All taxable (eligible) funds can be rolled over to a 401(k) plan. After-tax 403(b) contributions can be rolled to a 401(k) plan.	All taxable (eligible) funds can be rolled over to other 403(b) plans. After-tax 403(b) contributions can be rolled to other 403(b) plans.	All taxable (eligible) funds can be rolled over to a 457 plan. After-tax 403(b) contributions cannot be rolled to a 457 plan.
457 plan (governmental 457 plans only)	Section 457 plans do not accept after-tax funds, so no after-tax funds can be rolled into or out of a 457 plan. The taxable plan balance can be rolled to an IRA, 401(k), 403(b), or another 457 plan. The expanded rollover rules do not apply to Section 457 plans of nongovernmental tax-exempt organizations.			

The Same-Property Rule

Remember the woeful tale of Mr. Lemishow's rollover attempt in Chapter 1?

The IRS lets you roll over stock or other property from a qualified plan to an IRA, but the rollover must be of the same property that was distributed from your plan. This is called the *same-property rule*.

For example, you cannot hold onto the stock, substitute an equivalent amount of cash or other property, and roll that over to an IRA in lieu of the stock. What you can do is sell the stock and roll over the cash you received for it. But even that can only be done when rolling over from a plan to an IRA. It cannot be done when rolling over from one IRA to another. With IRA rollovers, the same property must be rolled over. You must roll over stock for stock, cash for cash, bonds for bonds, mutual funds for mutual funds, blueberries for blueberries, and so on.

ADVANTAGES OF ROLLING TO AN IRA

1. **Stretch distributions for beneficiaries.**
   - Heirs can keep the money growing over their life expectancies after your death (see Chapter 6).
   - Heirs must take required distributions (see Chapter 4), but with proper estate and beneficiary planning, the amount remaining can continue to build up, tax-deferred.
   - Although a nonspouse designated beneficiary of an IRA can stretch distributions on the inherited IRA over his or her life expectancy, many plans do not allow this stretch option even though the IRA rules permit it. This is the trap Ann fell into in our earlier story. Had she rolled over her 403(b) plan to an IRA, her children would have been able to stretch the

distributions on the inherited IRA over more than 40 years, but instead they were cashed out by the 403(b) in five years. Since her children were nonspouse beneficiaries, they could not roll over the inherited 403(b) plan to their own IRAs and, therefore, lost the ability to stretch their inherited account.

2. **Smoother estate planning.**
- Assets in an IRA can more easily be coordinated with your overall estate plan than assets in a company plan such as a 401(k).
- You can name anyone you wish as your beneficiary, and even split accounts, naming several primary and contingent beneficiaries.
- Funds in a company retirement plan are subject to federal law, which for the most part requires that you name your spouse as beneficiary—unless your spouse signs a waiver. An IRA rollover does not avoid the spousal waiver; it must be filed with the plan before you roll the funds, but once the funds are in your IRA, you're not required to name your spouse as beneficiary.

3. **More investment choices.**
- You have a universe of investment choices to pick from plus the ability to customize your investment choices to meet your personal needs; this is an important consideration in economically volatile times.
- You can instantly make changes that fit your risk tolerance and retirement needs rather than going through a bureaucracy where you are now an exemployee and thus receive little personal attention.

4. **Roth conversion ability.**
- You leave the door open to becoming eligible to convert from a traditional IRA to a Roth IRA (see Chapter 7), and allow income to pass tax-free to your beneficiaries.

5. Annuity investment.

- You can invest some of your IRA in an annuity, a feature that is generally not available with other types of retirement plans. I know that everything you've read elsewhere says not to do this because the annuity is already tax-deferred. But that thinking is wrong. I have annuities in my own IRA and if I died while the market was tanking, my beneficiaries would receive a guaranteed death benefit at the higher (stepped-up) predecline value.
- You've got a hedge against an unstable market.

6. Greater flexibility, availability, and control.

- You have no withdrawal restrictions with an IRA, whereas company plans may have some—for example, a 401(k) might not release money to you, even for a personal hardship, if you're under the minimum age requirement of 59½.
- You have immediate access to your funds, regardless of your age. Of course, you'll have to pay tax and, if no exception applies, a 10 percent penalty for the early withdrawal (see Chapter 4).
- You are in complete control and don't have to ask anyone's permission to take your money out, whereas even if a company plan did allow you immediate access, if you're no longer working there because of a layoff or taking a new job elsewhere, getting your hands on that cash may take you some time. And if you need the cash right away, this will just put pressure on you at a time when the last thing you need is more pressure.
- You exercise greater control over the amount of tax you pay by withdrawing more in low-income years—whereas with a lump-sum distribution (option #3), it's all or nothing; the entire account balance must be taken out, even if you don't need all that money, at the time of distribution.

7. Account consolidation.

- You can consolidate all your retirement plans under a single umbrella and not have to worry about keeping track of different distribution requirements and withdrawal options for each plan.

▪ You'll relieve yourself of so much paperwork. People are drowning with the monthly, quarterly, and annual statements they receive and tax reporting required for each retirement account.

▪ You'll save countless trees!

8. **Plan portability.**

▪ If you aim to keep to working, you're able to roll the taxable money in your IRA account back into your new company's plan with no sweat (but you cannot roll after-tax IRA money back into a company plan). After-tax IRA money would consist of nondeductible IRA contributions and any after-tax funds rolled into an IRA from a company plan.

9. **Access to professional advice.**

▪ IRAs are handled by retirement plan professionals whereas company plans such as 401(k)s are typically handled by know-nothing clerks in the Human Resources Department.

▪ No more "one-size-fits-all" plan management; you get an advisor who works for you, not the company you work for, to help customize your plan decisions.

▪ You'll be better able to formulate a long-term retirement and estate plan for you and your family.

Option # 2: Stay Put in the Company Plan (if or for as Long as Allowed) or Roll to a New Employer's Plan

This option lets you park your retirement savings with your old employer, depending upon whatever restrictions may apply. For example, some company plans don't allow this or allow it for only a set period of time.

Or, you can roll your money from your old company plan to

your new employer's plan. Even though this is called a rollover, it amounts generally to the same as staying put in your old employer's plan because your retirement money is still in a company plan and, therefore, subject to company plan rules.

ADVANTAGES OF STAYING PUT

1. **Federal creditor protection.**
- You're protected against personal bankruptcy, malpractice, divorce, lawsuits, and any other bids on your assets from current or potential creditors on the federal level (whereas IRAs receive creditor protection on the state level). Heck, how do you think O.J. makes ends meet?

2. **Borrowing ability.**
- If you find yourself suddenly strapped for cash, you can get a quick loan from a qualified plan, whereas you cannot borrow from an IRA. This privilege can be an important one, but for obvious reasons should be exercised only as a last resort. If you feel that you may need to borrow in the future, you might want to roll the funds into your new company's plan and keep that option open—that is, if the new company's plan allows borrowing. Not all company plans allow borrowing.

3. **Affordable life insurance.**
- Money in a qualified company plan can be used to buy life insurance, whereas IRA money cannot be used for that purpose. Why is this important? Life insurance offered through your company plan may be the only life insurance you qualify for or can afford. Leaving the plan and trying to continue the insurance on your own may prove too costly.

4. The "still-working exception."

- You can put off the age 70½ required minimum distribution (RMD) (see Chapter 4) until you're fully retired. This still-working exception to the RMD rules does not apply to distributions from IRAs.

5. The "age-55 exception."

- If you're at least 55 years old when you left your job and need to tap your retirement funds immediately, distributions from a company plan will be subject to income tax but no 10 percent early-withdrawal penalty (see Chapter 4). This exception does not apply to distributions from IRAs.

Option #3: Take a Lump-Sum Distribution and Pay the Tax Now

This option lets you withdraw all your pension monies in one fell swoop and get the tax bite over now. You might select this option if you need the balance in your retirement account right away for living expenses, medical costs, or other pressing bills, and if that balance is relatively small. But if the balance in your plan(s) is substantial, then you'd be better off with option #1—rolling to an IRA—and withdrawing only what you need rather than being taxed on the whole enchilada.

Option #3 actually comes with several choices. Each involves withdrawing the entire amount from your company plan, but two of the three offer special tax breaks if you qualify for them.

The choice with no tax breaks is withdrawing your entire account balance without the benefit of any special tax treatment on the distribution. This is the most expensive way to go and should, for obvious reasons, be avoided, unless you really, *really* need all your pension money, or most of it, at once. Then you'll have to do what you have to do, of course, but it will surely cost you a bundle in taxes (maybe even a penalty too if you withdraw early).

The other two choices offer special tax breaks that may at least soften the blow of withdrawing your funds.

Special Tax Break #1:
Net Unrealized Appreciation (NUA)
on Distributions of Company Stock

This allows you to take company stock from your qualified plan and pay ordinary income tax on the original cost of the stock rather than on its fair market value at the time of withdrawal. The difference in the value of the company stock from the time it was purchased to the time of distribution is called the *net unrealized appreciation (NUA)*. Provided you withdraw *all* the funds in your plan, you can then defer the tax on the NUA until you actually sell the stock—at which time (even if it's the day after the distribution), you pay the 15 percent maximum capital gain rate *on the appreciation only.*

Company stock means shares in the company you work for—e.g., if you're a Microsoft employee, only withdrawals from your plan of shares of Microsoft qualify for NUA.

To qualify, the distribution must be a lump sum, meaning the entire plan balance, not just the stock, must be withdrawn in one tax year. Other noncompany stock assets (cash, funds, etc.) in your plan, however, can be rolled over tax-free to an IRA or to another qualified company plan. (All or part of the company stock can be rolled over as well, but then there's no need to think about NUA because there is no current tax on rollovers to an IRA.)

Let's hang some numbers on the words and get a picture of how the NUA tax break works.

Say, for example, the original cost of the company stock in your plan was $200,000, and its current fair market value is $1 million. At the time of distribution, you pay regular income tax on the $200,000, but the stock continues to grow tax-deferred. You pay no current income tax on the $800,000 of NUA. The stock is now out of your company plan and in a regular taxable brokerage account. When you eventually sell it, you pay a maximum 15 percent on the NUA. So, assume you sell the stock immediately after distribution when it is worth $1 million. This gives you an $800,000 capital gain ($1 million current value less $200,000 original cost) taxed at 15 percent, and you pay $120,000 in taxes.

On the other hand, if you were to roll the stock over to an IRA, there would be no tax on the rollover, but when the stock is eventually withdrawn, it would be taxed as ordinary income (which could run as high as 35 percent) at its full market value.

CAUTION!

When you take advantage of the NUA tax break on company stock, there are no mandatory IRA withdrawal requirements (see Chapter 4) because the stock is no longer in an IRA. You can hold your stock well into your dotage if you like and keep it growing tax-deferred for your beneficiaries. But remember that any dividends on the stock are taxable!

The NUA tax break is most beneficial when the company stock in your plan has appreciated substantially from the time it was purchased. If the current value of the stock at distribution is roughly the same as the original cost, you would pay ordinary income tax on practically the whole amount of the distribution, thereby rendering the tax break virtually worthless. Taking company stock out and paying tax now rather than rolling it over doesn't pay off either if the stock has a high basis or is not highly appreciated.

Let's change the facts in the example and see why.

Say the basis is the same as before ($200,000) but the value of the shares at distribution is only $250,000. It just wouldn't be worth it to withdraw the stock and have to pay regular income tax now because the appreciation is not much higher than the basis.

You would owe tax on the $200,000 immediately, and all of it would be taxed at ordinary income rates. Better to roll the stock over to an IRA and keep it growing tax-deferred.

What happens though if you hold onto the stock rather than withdrawing it and taking distributions, and then it appreciates even more?

Let's use our example's initial figures. The stock's original cost (the basis) is $200,000 and the stock is worth $1 million at withdrawal. Now what? As before, you will pay ordinary income tax on the $200,000, but the NUA (the $800,000) isn't taxed until you sell the shares. Say you sell the stock three months after distribution, and by then it's appreciated another $100,000. You'll pay the 15 percent capital gains rate on the $800,000 (because that is the NUA), but the additional $100,000 of appreciation after the distribution will be taxed at ordinary income tax rates.

You pay 15 percent on the NUA regardless of when you sell the stock, but for any further appreciation to qualify for special tax treatment, the stock must be held more than one year from the date of distribution.

So, if you held the stock more than one year and then sold it for $1.1 million, the additional $100,000 of appreciation would now qualify for the 15 percent capital gain rate as well.

OK, now let's look at another scenario 10 years later.

You've held onto the stock all that time; it's now worth $2 million, and you die without selling it, so it's part of your estate. What tax will your beneficiaries pay if they sell the inherited stock? Do they get to use the fair market value of the stock at the time of your death as the basis in figuring any NUA (or loss) between that time and when the stock is actually sold?

This is called a *step-up in basis,* and the answer is NO.

Your beneficiaries will receive the same tax treatment you would have received had you lived and sold the stock; they'll pay the maximum 15 percent capital gains rate (assuming that's still the maximum rate when they inherit) on the $800,000 of NUA. They will receive, however, a step-up in basis on all appreciation since the date of the distribution (giving them a basis of $1.2 million).

So, if they sell all the stock for $2 million the day after your death (and it's even been known for some beneficiaries, unlike vultures, to wait even *two* days to swoop in and start feasting), they will pay capital gains tax on the $800,000 of NUA. They will receive a step-up (increase) in basis from the $1 million the stock was worth at distribution to the date of your death of another $1 million, on which they pay no income tax. Any further appreciation on the now $2 million worth of stock, however, will be subject to income tax. If the beneficiaries wait and the company stock appreciates from $2 million to, say, $2.3 million, they will pay a capital gains tax on the $800,000 of NUA plus the $300,000 of appreciation since your death. Or, to look at it another way, their basis for figuring gain is $1.2 million (the $200,000 of tax you paid when you originally withdrew the company stock from your plan, plus the $1 million step-up in basis for your beneficiaries).

TAX TIP!

If you have not yet reached age 55 in the year you leave the company, you would owe a 10 percent penalty on the cost of the company stock at distribution time, but would pay the penalty only on the amount that is taxable, which for NUA-qualifying stock would be the cost. You will escape the 10 percent penalty on the NUA due to the age-55 exception because it is not currently taxable. But if the appreciation is high enough, it actually might be advantageous to pay the 10 percent penalty in order to preserve the tax deferral on the NUA. If instead you choose to roll over the stock to an IRA, it's true that you will not be hit with the 10 percent early-withdrawal penalty below age 59½, but you will eventually pay ordinary income tax on the full market value of the stock as you withdraw it. The age-55 exception from the 10 percent penalty applies only to early distributions from qualified plans after separation from service and does not apply to IRAs.

Partial Distributions and NUA

If your plan consists of employer securities and other assets (cash, funds, etc.), you can roll the noncompany stock portion of your plan (the cash and funds) into an IRA rollover account and transfer the company stock portion to your taxable (non-IRA) brokerage account. The company stock still qualifies for the tax break on the NUA. On a partial rollover, however, you will still pay ordinary income tax on the cost of your shares. You could also roll part of your company stock into the IRA if you don't want to pay tax on the entire cost of the shares.

DOUBLE TAX BREAK (FOR SOME)

If your plan consists of assets in addition to company stock and you do not roll that portion of your plan over when you take the full distribution, not only can you defer the tax on the NUA, but the taxable portion (the cost of the shares plus the other assets) may qualify for special 10-year averaging (see "Special Tax Break #2" later in this chapter). In addition, if you contributed to your plan before 1974, you may also qualify for the maximum 20 percent capital gains break on the taxable portion. The downside here is that to gain the double tax break, you must also distribute and pay tax now on the noncompany stock assets that could have otherwise been rolled over to an IRA tax-free and kept growing tax-deferred.

Electing Not to Defer Tax on NUA

Deferring tax on NUA means you don't pay tax until you sell the company stock. But you can elect to take the distribution on the company stock and not defer the tax as well. Why would anyone in his or her right mind do this? Because if you qualify, you could then have the entire value of the stock (including the NUA) taxed using 10-year averaging (see "Special Tax Break #2"). If there has been little or if no appreciation, or if the distribution is small, the tax may be less using this strategy.

No 20 Percent Withholding on NUA, but . . .

As you'll remember from my discussion of option #1 (rolling to an IRA), generally employers are supposed to withhold 20 percent of distributions from a qualified plan (unless it's a trustee-to-trustee transfer) and send the money to the IRS.

There is, however, a little known exception to this rule when the only remaining asset in the plan is employer stock. Distributing $500,000 worth of NUA stock might cause $100,000 to be sent to the IRS, diminishing the amount rolled over, as long as the NUA stock is not the only asset in the plan at the time of the distribution. Not good! To avoid such an outcome, it pays to make certain that your employer will first send the plan's other assets (often cash) directly to the IRA custodian, which might be a bank or a brokerage firm, with nothing withheld because it's a trustee-to-trustee transfer. Then the NUA shares can be distributed "in-kind," with nothing left in the account to withhold for the IRS.

Timing Is Critical

The entire NUA transaction must take place within one calendar year in order to qualify as a lump-sum distribution and thereby merit the tax advantage. An NUA transaction may take several weeks, however, from the time the employer makes the in-kind distribution to the time the transfer agent issues new shares.

The IRS is merciless on such matters, when all reported dates must be within a given year. Therefore, you should never to ask for in-kind distributions of company stock after mid-December; it's better to wait a couple of weeks until the beginning of the next year.

No Mix and Match

You should not commingle NUA stock with other employer stock. For example, if you own other company stock that's not in your plan but in a separate brokerage account, you should not put distributed NUA shares in that account as well. Doing so may interfere with the record keeping necessary to ascertain the cost basis of the NUA stock, which would make it more difficult to claim the tax break.

To avoid such complications, simply set up a separate account (even with the same broker) under the same name in order to hold the NUA shares.

NEW NUA TAX BREAKS!

The Jobs and Growth Tax Relief Reconciliation Act of 2003 reduced capital gains tax rates to 15 percent for sales of stock made on or after May 6, 2003. This lower rate enhances the benefit of using the NUA tax break, since it also applies to sales of NUA shares.

In addition, there is now a special capital gains tax rate of 5 percent for low-bracket taxpayers. This means higher-bracket taxpayers who would otherwise have to pay up to 15 percent capital gains on sales of NUA shares can now give away those shares to someone in a lower tax-bracket—their fourteen-year-old child for example; then have the child turn around and sell the shares at his or her 5 percent rate on the untaxed appreciation.

But wait . . . there's more! This special 5 percent capital gains rate for low-bracket taxpayers drops to zero percent (that's right, zero percent!) in 2008. But—here's the catch—*only for that one year.*

Ordinary income tax rates have also been lowered slightly. For example, the top tax rate for ordinary income is now 35 percent, but that is still 20 points higher than the capital gains rate, increasing the appeal of the NUA tax break.

It doesn't get much better than this—unless, of course, you want Uncle Sam to pay *you* when you sell your stock. Hey, that's not a bad idea!

Actually Getting the NUA Tax Break May Take Work

I've given you the theory, but it's up to you to put theory into practice, and here's where you may hit some roadblocks—because many people working in human resources employee benefits departments who typically oversee company plans have never heard of the NUA tax break. So, it will probably fall in your court, or that of the financial advisor acting on your behalf (another good reason for having one), to avoid the bum's rush.

"On paper, the NUA tax break is tremendously appealing," says Peggy Cabaniss, a top financial planner and colleague of mine in Orinda, California. "But in the 'real world,' the tax benefits may be hard to come by. For example, I have two clients, each of whom works for a very large, presumably sophisticated, corporation, and they both ran into difficulties trying to use this strategy—not with the IRS, but with their own employee benefits people."

In each case, no one in human resources knew anything about the NUA tax provision or how to handle the necessary paperwork, she says. "But we persisted. For one client, we wound up talking with the firm that acts as custodian for the company's 401(k) plan. Finally, we reached a senior person in the retirement planning department who knew what to do." And how's her other client faring? "We're still working on it," Peggy tells me. "We're still hoping to find *someone* who can help."

Does going after the NUA stock break always have to be such a hassle? Not necessarily, says David Foster, a fellow CPA and ace financial planner in Cincinnati, and an expert on this issue. "Many of my clients work for Procter & Gamble, which is very knowledgeable about NUA stock and very helpful. P&G publishes the cost basis of employer stock on each employee's annual profit-sharing statement, a practice that all companies should adopt. But many companies outsource the administration of their employee retirement plans and won't get involved at all. Even the largest brokers and mutual fund companies seem to be unfamiliar with NUA stock."

So how does he help clients overcome such situations? Here are some of David's recommendations:

TIPS FOR ACHIEVING NUA SUCCESS

- *Start early.* At least six months before retiring, begin your search for someone who can help you.
- *Get it in writing.* Demand formal documentation of the cost basis of your employer stock as well as your employer's promise to make an in-kind distribution of the company shares.
- *Be a pit bull.* Chances are, the first person you speak with won't know NUA from the NFL, but someone in the organization will. Keep saying, "This transaction is permitted by the tax code so I'd like to speak with your supervisor."
- *Know the technicalities.* The greater your own familiarity with NUA issues, the more likely you'll get someone in authority to comply with your wishes.
- *Don't be sidetracked by IRS Publication 575.* Some employers will cite this publication as "proof" that the NUA strategy is not allowed if any part of the lump sum is rolled over. They are misinterpreting the information, which is presented in the context of discussing special averaging of lump-sum distributions.
- *Accept reality.* In some cases, the NUA tax benefits won't be available, perhaps because the plan does not permit in-kind distributions of company stock. If you're told that this is the case, don't give up easily. Insist upon seeing the plan provision forbidding the practice.

"In most circumstances, if you are persistent, you will be able to find someone who's knowledgeable," David says. "That person might work for your employer, the plan custodian, or the third-party administrator, but will be able to provide exactly what you need, including a properly executed Form 1099-R that reports the transaction to the IRS."

Because the issue of basis is so important, he adds, "You should consider whether it pays to limit the amount of company stock you are buying or stop buying company stock altogether inside your company plan as you near retirement."

Also, active trading of employer shares inside a plan is not advised, as retirement comes closer. Such activities will raise their average cost per share and devalue the tax benefit.

"If you want to buy more employer stock in the last few years preceding retirement, you should do so in a brokerage account, outside of your retirement plan. 'Overloading' in employer stock can be dangerous to your wealth, as the employees of Enron and some other less infamous boom-to-bust companies learned to their detriment," David says.

What if an employer says that it can't compute the basis of the company stock in the retirement plan? As David explains, "When you take a distribution from an employer-sponsored retirement plan, the employer must report your NUA in box 6 of your 1099-R, file that form with the IRS, and send you a copy, as well. The IRS will use that information to see how much tax an individual must pay on in-kind distributions of company stock.

"So, you see, given the reporting requirements, computing your basis isn't exactly an option even if an employer says it is. They have to do it. But it's hard to get them to, so you must press them on it."

Figure 3 illustrates a sample letter David has prepared for you to use to make sure that you get your NUA. Adapt it accordingly, and send it to your plan administrator at least six months before you retire. Once you connect with a person who can respond to the questions in it, send follow-up letters to keep track of your basis in the company shares. In this manner, you'll always know the

Figure 3. Sample NUA Information Request Letter

GreatStock.com Retirement Plan Administration Dept.
Oceanside, NY 11572
Re: John Doe SS# 123-45-6789

Dear (Name of Contact Person):

The purpose of this letter is to gather some information regarding my account balance with the GreatStock.com Retirement Plan. I have purchased GreatStock.com stock in my plan with both my tax-deferred contributions and company matching contributions. I have some very specific tax questions that are critical in my long-term retirement planning.

1. Does the plan allow for distributions at retirement of the common stock of GreatStock.com Corporation?

2. I would like to know the cost basis of the shares of stock that have accumulated in my retirement plan. Can you give me that information?

3. Under the Internal Revenue Code, Section 402(e), distributions of appreciated employer securities receive favorable tax treatment. In particular, if these shares are distributed to me in-kind as part of a lump-sum distribution, I will only be taxed on the cost basis of the shares. Do you agree with that? Will the company properly complete the 1099R for the year of distribution and complete Box 6 for net unrealized appreciation (NUA) in employer securities?

4. Please let me know the name and number of the person in your department who knows the most about distributions of employer stock and NUA issues.

This is very important to me and I would like to hear from someone knowledgeable in your department regarding these issues. You can respond either in writing or by phone to my financial advisor, Ed Slott, CPA, at

> E. Slott & Company, CPAs
> 100 Merrick Road – 200 East
> Rockville Centre, NY 11570
> 516-536-8282
> or e-mail: slottcpa@aol.com

Thank you for your prompt attention to this matter.

Sincerely:

_____

John Doe

amount of your NUA and will be well prepared to decide whether to proceed with the NUA strategy.

Special Tax Break #2: 10-Year Averaging

At one time, this special break tax break for easing the burden on lump-sum distributions from company plans was available two ways: using 5-year averaging or 10-year averaging. Now just 10-year averaging is used if you qualify for this tax break.

QUALIFYING FOR 10-YEAR AVERAGING

1. You must have been born before 1936.
2. The distribution must be from a qualified plan, such as a 401(k).
3. The distribution of your entire plan balance, excluding your voluntary employee contributions, must be made in one tax year. You cannot roll any part of the distribution over to an IRA or other company plan.
4. You must have been in the plan for at least five years before the year of the distribution.
5. You cannot have used 10-year averaging for any previous distribution after 1986.
6. If you are a beneficiary, the person you inherited from must have been born before 1936.

You would use 10-year averaging to lower your liability if you need to take all of your plan balance out now for living expenses, medical bills, or other pressing bills—or just because your balance is so small that you would have withdrawn it all anyway as the tax bite wouldn't be huge.

If you have a large plan balance, however, and don't need all your money now, you're better off rolling over to an IRA and withdrawing only what you require—because 10-year averaging demands that you withdraw your *entire* plan balance.

The 10-year averaging tax is figured separately from your regular tax (see Figure 4), and the income is not added to your adjusted gross income (AGI). Thus, the distribution won't cause you to lose tax deductions, credits, or other benefits keyed to AGI. Another goodie is that a lump-sum distribution that qualifies for 10-year averaging won't trigger the dreaded alternative minimum tax (AMT) as other retirement plan distributions might.

If you and your spouse are each receiving lump-sum distributions, 10-year averaging could reduce the marriage penalty as well, because each spouse is permitted to calculate his or her 10-year averaging tax separately. Although such a scenario might seem unlikely, it could easily happen, say, with a family business that may have closed due to poor economic conditions. If both spouses were participants in the business's retirement plan, they could each receive a lump-sum distribution in the same year.

If part of your lump-sum distribution is from pre-1974 plan participation, you can also elect to pay a flat 20 percent capital gains rate on that portion (not reduced to 15 percent under the 2003 tax act). You may choose as well not to elect capital gain treatment where 10-year averaging produces a lower tax.

For lump-sum distributions under $70,000, you're able to exclude a certain amount from your 10-year averaging calculation. This amount is called your *minimum distribution allowance* (see Figure 4), and it works as an exemption from the sum that is taxable under averaging.

Minimum distribution allowance is defined as the lower of $10,000 or one-half of the distribution. For example, on a $10,000 distribution, the minimum distribution allowance is $5,000 since $5,000 is the lower of $10,000 or one-half of the total distribution. (I know what you're thinking: What deranged mind comes up with this stuff? I can assure you, 'tain't mine.) If your distribution exceeds $20,000, the allowance is reduced by 20 percent of the amount over $20,000. For example, on a $50,000 distribution, the minimum distribution allowance is $4,000 ($10,000 less $6,000 = $4,000). The $6,000 is 20 percent of $30,000 (the amount by which the $50,000 distribution exceeds $20,000).

Figure 4. TAX RATE SCHEDULE FOR THE 10-YEAR TAX OPTION

Crunching the 10-year Averaging Numbers

(These are the 1986 tax rates for single taxpayers.)

If one-tenth of the
lump-sum distribution is:

Then one-tenth*
of the tax is:

Over	But not over		Of the amount over
$0	$1,190	11%	$0
1,190	2,270	$130.90 + 12%	1,190
2,270	4,530	260.50 + 14%	2,270
4,530	6,690	576.90 + 15%	4,530
6,690	9,170	900.90 + 16%	6,690
9,170	11,440	1,297.70 + 18%	9,170
11,440	13,710	1,706.30 + 20%	11,440
13,710	17,160	2,160.30 + 23%	13,710
17,160	22,880	2,953.80 + 26%	17,160
22,880	28,600	4,441.00 + 30%	22,880
28,600	34,320	6,157.00 + 34%	28,600
34,320	42,300	8,101.80 + 38%	34,320
42,300	57,190	11,134.20 + 42%	42,300
57,190	85,790	17,388.00 + 48%	57,190
85,790	———	31,116.00 + 50%	85,790

*The result is multiplied by 10 to arrive at the tax under 10-year averaging.
Note: Five-year averaging no longer exists. It was repealed for distributions after 1999.

Figure 4. TAX RATE SCHEDULE FOR THE 10-YEAR TAX OPTION *(continued)*

10-Year Averaging Tax on Various Lump-Sum Distributions (Only Available to Those Born Before 1936)

Amount of Lump-Sum Distribution	10-Year Averaging Tax (Using 1986 Tax Rates)	Effective Tax Rate
$25,000	$ 1,801*	7.2%
50,000	5,874*	11.7
75,000	10,305	13.7
100,000	14,471	14.5
125,000	19,183	15.3
150,000	24,570	16.4
175,000	30,422	17.4
200,000	36,922	18.5
225,000	43,422	19.3
250,000	50,770	20.3
275,000	58,270	21.2
300,000	66,330	22.1
350,000	83,602	23.9
400,000	102,602	25.7
450,000	122,682	27.3
500,000	143,682	28.7
550,000	164,682	29.9
600,000	187,368	31.2
650,000	211,368	32.5
700,000	235,368	33.6
750,000	259,368	34.6
800,000	283,368	35.4
850,000	307,368	36.2
900,000	332,210	36.9
950,000	357,210	37.6
1,000,000	382,210	38.2
1,500,000	632,210	42.1
2,000,000	882,210	44.1

*The tax on lump-sum distributions under $70,000 is reduced by the minimum distribution allowance calculated on Form 4972.

Figure 4. TAX RATE SCHEDULE FOR THE 10-YEAR TAX OPTION
(continued)

To qualify for 10-year averaging, the plan participant must meet the following tests:

1. The distribution must be from an IRS qualified plan.
2. The distribution of your entire plan balance (not including your voluntary employee contributions) must be made to you in one taxable year, and no part of the distribution can be rolled over.
3. You must have been born before 1936. (Beneficiaries can elect averaging, but only if the participant was born before 1936.)
4. You must have been in the plan for at least five years before the year of the distribution.
5. You cannot have used averaging for any previous distribution after 1986.

10-year special averaging is calculated on IRS Form 4972, "Tax on Lump-Sum Distributions." The 20% capital gain election for any pre-1974 plan participation and the tax on NUA are also figured on Form 4972.

CAUTION!

Walk, don't run, to use 10-year averaging! I can't tell you how many people born before 1936 tell me they want to use 10-year averaging, even though they don't know the first thing about it. They've just heard that it's a benefit people in their age group are entitled too, so they're determined to get it—much like early-bird specials for seniors. Just because they qualify, they'll move Heaven and Earth, even jeopardize their lives by driving like maniacs, to reach the restaurant by 6 P.M. for the cut rate—even if the food stinks and makes them sick. Well, qualifying for 10-year averaging doesn't automatically translate to saving a lot in tax—you just save some of what you would have forked over later by taking all your money out and paying tax on it now. To estimate the size of the check you'll be writing to get this special tax break, see Figure 4. You may find out that paying the IRS well before you have to is like that early-bird special. In other words, don't run to do 10-year averaging until you know what it will cost you.

Beneficiaries and 10-Year Averaging

Your beneficiaries will qualify to withdraw and pay tax on a lump-sum distribution from your estate using 10-year averaging too, regardless of their age, provided you qualified for averaging at the time of your death, and, of course, the distribution meets all the other requirements—such as the mandatory withdrawal of the entire balance in one tax year.

Other Property Distributions

Noncash property such as real estate or limited partnership interests can be distributed (as well as rolled over) from a company plan or IRA. Determining a value may be sticky, however.

Finding the value of listed stocks or mutual fund shares is generally easy. Look them up in *The Wall Street Journal* or your daily newspaper. But how do you put a value on nonconventional investments such as real estate property or interests in a limited partnership? Most likely they'll need to be appraised—and that appraisal had better be a good one because it will be the foundation for determining your taxable distribution. And if the distribution is required, there could be a 50 percent penalty imposed by the IRS if the taxman feels your valuation falls short of the required distribution amount. (Noncash property rollovers don't pose the same problem because the shift is tax-free regardless of the property's value. Only on the day when the other property must be withdrawn from the rollover account will an appraisal be needed.)

ADVANTAGES OF TAKING YOUR LUMPS

1. **Special tax breaks:**
- You may qualify for NUA stock or 10-year averaging tax relief.
- If your plan consists of assets (cash, funds, etc.) in addition to a company stock, and you withdraw everything in a lump sum, not only are you able to defer tax on the NUA, but the taxable portion may even qualify you for 10-year averaging, giving you a double tax break.
- If you participated in the plan before 1974, you may even qualify for 20 percent capital gains treatment on that portion.

2. **Fewer worries and restrictions:**
- You no longer have to be concerned about future tax rates or unexpected hikes; you're paid up!
- You don't risk future penalties on your net after-tax distribution.
- Since lump-sum distributions are already taxed, you can use them any way you wish, without restrictions. For example, you could use the cash to buy a retirement home or to buy life insurance to cover the tax on your estate for your heirs (see Chapter 8).

3. **Less hassle for heirs:**
- Once you elect to pay the tax on a lump-sum distribution, you save your heirs from all sorts of complexities involved

in inheriting an IRA or other plan distribution; plus, they have the liquidity to offset expenses.

Not Vulnerable until Withdrawn

Remember that retirement assets aren't vulnerable to the taxman until they're transferred—from generation to generation or from tax-deferred status to a taxable position. Until distribution takes place, the taxman, like the troll under the bridge waiting to jump out and devour the first traveler to come by, must control his appetite. If you haven't taken steps to protect your retirement assets beforehand, it'll be too late to stop the taxman from devouring as much as 90 percent of them—as happened to Ann in Chapter 1.

Always keep in mind too that the longer a retirement account can be kept intact (free of tax erosion), the more it will grow. The more it grows, the bigger the nest egg you get to enjoy in retirement, and the greater the legacy you pass on to family members and other beneficiaries.

My Five-Step Action Plan for Defusing the Retirement Savings Time Bomb

I've given you the three options on *where* to park your retirement plan assets. Now comes the Moment of Truth: doing the parking.

How to begin?

Well, relying on your brother-in-law, your hairdresser, the cab driver, your buddies at the Raccoon Lodge, or any of the other usual "experts" for guidance isn't the way, that's for sure. You have to get down to the nitty-gritty of creating a simple, workable plan you can use to protect your retirement savings from being taxed to death.

This plan will boil down to five steps that are easy to follow and easy to implement.

Step #1: Time It Smartly

By choosing the right time to start taking your money out—and the right amount to take out—you can escape racking up those huge tax bills, plus penalties, which stem from withdrawing too little, too early or too late.

Step #2: Insure It

With a properly set up life insurance policy, you can make sure the funds are there for your beneficiaries to pay any taxes on your retirement distribution so that assets will stay intact. OK, so you'll have to shell out a few bucks for the premiums. Don't be penny-wise and pound-foolish. Spending a few bucks now not only prevents your life savings from being virtually wiped out (as happened to Ann in Chapter 1), but can help keep those assets compounding into a fortune!

Step #3: Stretch It

Keep your assets intact and growing for decades by selecting the right beneficiary—a child or grandchild with 40 or more years of life expectancy ahead. Beneficiaries with long life expectancies can stretch distributions out for decades; by withdrawing the minimum each year, your bequest can build and build. Your choices must be documented on beneficiary forms that your beneficiaries must actually be able to find. This step will show you the way.

Step #4: Roth It

Contribute or convert your current traditional IRA to a Roth IRA, if you're able; it's the tax deal of the century that allows you to stockpile cash in your retirement account income-tax–free for the benefit of generations in your family.

Step #5: Avoid the Death Tax Trap

Create a perfect IRA/estate plan that will curb the taxman's appetite; then save your beneficiaries even more with a little publicized item called the *IRD (income in respect of a decedent) deduction.*

Nothing is certain but death and taxes—neither of which is particularly pleasant to contemplate—although my five-step action plan will diminish much of the dread of the latter (at least where your retirement savings are concerned). But there's always Murphy's Law, not to mention the fact that the unexpected can always be counted on to occur. So, after completing the last step, don't euphorically give this book to a friend just yet. Keep on reading—because s*** will inevitably happen; it always does, and Part 3 will show you how and where to dig yourself out from under it.

That said, let's take the first step on our journey along the yellow (for gold) brick road to success in keeping your retirement nest egg from the maw of the IRS Cookie Monster.

PART TWO

FIVE EASY STEPS TO PROTECTING YOUR RETIREMENT SAVINGS FROM THE TAXMAN

■ FOUR ■

Step #1: Time It Smartly

"I am proud to be paying taxes in the United States. The only thing is—
I could be just as proud for half the money."
—Arthur Godfrey (1903–83), TV and radio personality

Timing Is Everything

You can't let your tax-deferred retirement accounts sit forever without paying tax on them. That's the bargain you made for all those years of receiving those goody-goody tax breaks from the IRS.

It's payback time or soon will be.

And you know what they say about payback!

It's like entering into a deal with the devil. You recognize there'll come a day of reckoning, but for the time being your focus is on the perks instead.

With retirement plan distributions, that day of reckoning (or payback time) has a name. It's called the *required beginning date (RBD)* when you must start taking your *required minimum distribution (RMD)* and pay tax on your long-deferred earnings.

The RBD for IRA holders is the April 1 following the year they turn 70½. For example, even if you turn 70½ in January of 2004, your RBD is not until April 1, 2005. (April 1 is only for the first year's distribution, however; each subsequent year's distribution must be taken by December 31 of that year.)

Don't forget or ignore your RBD date!

If you do, you'll face the worst of all penalties—a 50 percent punishment tax on the RMD you were supposed to take but didn't.

No, that figure of **50 PERCENT** is *not* a typo!

For example, if your RMD is $40,000 and you withdraw nothing from your account by your RBD, you'll get socked with a $20,000 penalty—one-half of the $40,000 you didn't withdraw. Ouch and double-ouch; that's no flesh wound.

On the positive side, the IRS hasn't to date enforced this rule—at least I haven't seen any examples.

"Then what's the big deal?" you ask. "Why worry about it if the IRS won't bother trying to catch us? Think about it, man. If there were no tax audits demanding proof of every deduction, we'd claim a zillion deductions! That's the American way."

You have a good point—except that on the negative side, the party is now over because Congress and the IRS have finally gotten serious about the RMD rule. The rule long had few teeth because the IRS had no way of catching anybody violating it. But that changed as of 2003. Now, the banks, brokers, insurance companies, mutual fund companies, and other financial institutions holding your IRA money are required to alert you that a distribution must be taken (and if you wish, even make the RMD calculation for you).

But that's not all.

In 2004, the reporting requirement goes a mean step farther. Not only must these institutions alert you, they must rat you out to the IRS as well (though they don't have to disclose the required amount—not yet anyway, but you can bet that's in the works, too).

So, if you've been lax about taking your RMD, or figure on being lax when the time comes with the hope that you'll fall below the IRS radar screen, think twice—you're already a blip on that screen and could risk losing a fortune.

Getting It Early (Distributions before Age 59½)

The general rule is that distributions taken before you reach age 59½ are subject to a 10 percent penalty. Don't ask me where Congress came up with the number 59½. Maybe we're being used as guinea pigs in a legislative experiment to see if we can still count after we turn 59. Or maybe the ½ was a typo that never got corrected. Whatever the reason, it's in the Internal Revenue Code, so it's the law.

The early-withdrawal penalty is assessed on the amount that is taxable. For example, if you withdraw $5,000 from your IRA at age 40, you will have to pay income tax on that amount as well as a $500 penalty (10 percent of the $5,000 early withdrawal). If only $4,000 of the $5,000 was taxable because you had, say, $1,000 of nondeductible contributions, then the penalty is $400 (10 percent of the $4,000 taxable amount).

The idea of penalizing us for hurting ourselves is not only ludicrous, but also sadistic. We should not have to pay a 10 percent penalty on money that's ours, just because circumstances compel us to dip into our own retirement accounts early. But that's the reality we face.

Typically people withdraw money early from their retirement accounts because they need it to cover expenses—and they usually withdraw all of it. Then, after paying these expenses, April 15 rolls around, and they find themselves without the money to pay the early-withdrawal penalty plus income tax on top of it. And if they can't fork it over to the government, they get hit with more penalties, plus interest on unpaid taxes and penalties. So, what do they do next? If they haven't already depleted their retirement account, they dip back into it and take out more or all that remains to cover the additional unpaid taxes, interest, and penalties.

Here's another typical scenario: A couple's plan is a 401(k), not an IRA, so they may borrow from it, fully intending to repay the borrowed funds. But then the unexpected happens, and they can't. For example, I know a couple that borrowed from the husband's 401(k) to finance their wedding because they were out of cash from buying a house. Then they couldn't repay the money because the house was a money pit in need of tons of repairs. The funds withdrawn from the husband's 401(k) became taxable and subject to the 10 percent early-withdrawal penalty when they couldn't pay it back in time, so they had to dip into the 401(k) for more. It took this couple almost six years to bounce back from the vicious circle they'd gotten themselves into—and it would have taken even longer if some wonderful friends hadn't stepped in to help out with loans to get Uncle Sam off their backs. But the end result was that this couple paid a fortune in unnecessary penalties and interest, not to mention federal and state income tax, by tapping their retirement savings early. Worse, they decimated their 401(k) nest egg after years of building it up!

Penalty-Free Withdrawals

There are some exceptions to the 10 percent early-withdrawal penalty that make it a little easier now—and, unfortunately, more enticing—to tap our IRA and company plan money early.

These exceptions are sometimes referred to as loopholes, as well. But they are *not* loopholes! You still have to pay income tax when you make the withdrawal, and you are still depleting your retirement money. They are *penalty-free exceptions* that should be used wisely and only as a last resort. Don't see them as a way to beat the system, or you'll only wind up beating yourself.

CAUTION!

Be warned, be *very warned!* It is rarely a good idea to tap your nest egg before its time. The whole concept of saving tax-free for your golden years is lost if you use your savings for purposes other than retirement. Today's liberalized early-withdrawal rules may be welcome, but they may also become an overpowering lure to spend now what should be saved for later.

IRA AND COMPANY PLAN EXCEPTIONS

1. **Death.** This is the ultimate form of early withdrawal and definitely no way to get a tax break! Nonetheless, as ridiculous as it may seem to be stating the obvious, let's make it official: The IRS does not subject the beneficiary of your IRA, or even your corpse for that matter, to the early-withdrawal penalty. But, as always, plan distributions (early or otherwise) are subject to income tax.

2. **Disability.** There is no 10 percent penalty for an early withdrawal if you need the money because you're "disabled"—which the tax code defines as your being "unable to engage in any substantial gainful activity by reason of any medically determinable physical or mental impairment which can be expected to result in death or to be of long-continued and indefinite duration." It's not enough to say that you fit this profile, either; the IRS requires you to prove it with a physical or psychological assessment by a doctor.

3. **Medical Expenses.** Penalty-free early withdrawals can be made if the funds are used to pay unreimbursed medical expenses exceeding 7.5 percent of your adjusted gross income (AGI). Furthermore, you do not have to itemize deductions on your income taxes in order to qualify for this break.

4. **Annuitizing.** This tax break is referred to as the "72(t)" exception. It allows you to escape the early withdrawal penalty by taking your distributions each year in what the tax code calls a "series of substantially equal periodic payments." This process boils down to annuitizing your early withdrawals over a five-year period or until you reach age 59½, whichever is longer. The payout amount is determined by your single life expectancy or by the joint life expectancy of you and your beneficiary, according to IRS actuarial tables. During the payout period, you cannot change the payment schedule formula; if you do, you'll

be hit with the 10 percent penalty, which will be assessed retroactively, as if you never qualified for the 72(t) exception in the first place. For company plans, this exception only applies *after* you have separated from service. For IRAs this exception applies at any time, regardless of whether you are still working. (See Chapter 9 for extensive coverage of the 72(t) exception.)

5. **IRS Tax Levy.** There is no such thing as creditor protection from the IRS. If you can't pay your taxes, the IRS can legally snatch your retirement savings to cover them. This is called an IRS tax levy, and it's serious. If the IRS does levy your retirement account, the withdrawal, if made before you turn 59½, will not be subject to the 10 percent penalty; the seizure itself would still be subject to regular income tax, however. Too bad you can't hire the IRS to collect from people who owe you money. There would be no such thing as accounts receivable.

IRA-ONLY EXCEPTIONS

1. **Education.** Early withdrawals from IRAs (including Roth IRAs) are penalty-free if used to pay expenses for higher education—college, graduate school, vocational school, or any other "post–secondary-educational schooling"—for yourself, your spouse, a child, or a grandchild. Qualifying expenses include tuition, room and board, fees, books, supplies, plus equipment used for enrollment or attendance. If, for example, you're paying tuition bills for a child, he or she does not have to live with you or even be a dependent for you to take an early withdrawal from your IRA penalty-free. This break for education is allowable only for courses being taken now or in the near future. For example, if you withdraw money early from your IRA to cover some old education bills, you'll be hit with a penalty. Also, you can't take advantage of this exclusion under

the following circumstances: (1) your education expenses have already been reduced by scholarships that have been earned, veteran's benefits that have been received, or U.S. savings bonds redeemed for that purpose; (2) you qualify for, and make use of, any other exclusion to the penalty rule for early withdrawals. Furthermore, only distributions up to the amount of the education expenses incurred are exempt from the 10 percent penalty. Amounts paid for education from a Coverdell Education Savings Account (formerly called an Education IRA), tax-free scholarships, employer-provided educational assistance, and any other tax-free benefit cannot be included. For example, if you've got $6,000 of qualifying education expenses and $2,000 will be covered by tax-free funds paid from an employer-provided assistance plan, the remaining $4,000 can come out of your IRA without incurring an early-withdrawal penalty. But if you withdraw more than that amount from your IRA, only the $4,000 would still be exempt from the penalty, if no other exception applied.

CAUTION!

Although taking an early withdrawal from a Roth IRA for school expenses qualifies you for the higher education break too, it's possible to fall into a trap here and wind up paying tax on part of the withdrawal. Here's how: Let's say you're younger than 59½ and have accumulated $15,000 in a Roth IRA as follows: $12,000 in original contributions, $3,000 of earnings. If you just need the $12,000, you don't even have to worry about qualifying for the education break because your original contribution (the principal) can be taken out at any time for any purpose tax-free. However, let's assume you need the whole $15,000; you'd still be able to take out the $12,000 tax-free, but you'd have to pay regular income tax on the remaining $3,000 because that money is made up of earnings, not principal. The same caution flag applies to regular IRAs as well, because even if you escape the penalty, you still pay income tax on the total amount withdrawn early (unless part of that total consists of nondeductible contributions). All in all, this may not seem like a bad deal in order to gain penalty-free early access to your account to defray education costs—but there's a major downside you might not be thinking about: You will, of course, have emptied your entire retirement account in the process!

2. **First-Time Homebuyer.** You can take an early withdrawal of up to $10,000 from an IRA penalty-free to help pay for a first home. Well strictly speaking, not necessarily the *first* home you've ever owned; the tax code defines *first-time homebuyer* as anyone who has not owned a home for two years prior to early withdrawal. In other words (amazing how often one must resort to using this phrase in explaining the tax code), if you sold your last home three years ago and have been renting ever since, then you qualify as a first-time homebuyer under the tax code and are entitled to take an early withdrawal from your IRA penalty-free. The $10,000 is a once-in-a-lifetime maximum, which is why it really doesn't pay to use this exemption to buy a home. Given some of today's home prices, $10,000 would barely cover closing costs. And to get that penalty-free 10 grand, you'll have to pay income tax on it. You'll be lucky to be left with $7,000 of the $10,000 after taxes, but will have probably have spent the entire $10,000 on new home-buying expenses (which never end), thereby digging yourself into a hole—because come April 15, you'll have to cough up the $3,000 you owe that you already spent. So, it's not a good idea to tap your retirement account to buy a home. But if you must, you must. Remember though that what you withdraw from your IRA for home-buying purposes must be used exclusively to "buy, build, or rebuild that first home," which the code de-

fines as your "principal residence." If you're married, your spouse must fit the first-time–homebuyer profile, as well. It may seem like a given that he or she would since you're married and, one presumes, living together, but those little devils who write the tax code think of every possible scenario for grabbing your money. For example, let's say, you owned a home five years, sold it, and moved into an apartment. A few years later, you get married and move into your spouse's house. Then, the two of you decide to buy a new home of your own together, tapping your IRAs early for partial financing. Under this scenario, you and your spouse wouldn't be able to take advantage of the first-time–homebuyer tax break because *both of you must qualify for it individually.*

LOOPHOLE ALERT!

Here's how to double your pleasure with the first-time—homebuyer tax break. If you're a qualifying married couple and you buy the home jointly, each of you can withdraw $10,000 from your IRA, bringing the penalty-free amount you can use to $20,000! So, forget the prenuptial agreement and make sure instead that you marry someone who won't blow this tax break for you!

Here's another hitch to the first-time–homebuyer tax break: You must use the IRA money toward the purchase of that home within 120 days of the withdrawal. If for some reason the deal goes south and the purchase doesn't take place, you can put the money back in your IRA without penalty, as long as you do that within the 120 days. Run that by you again? OK, let's see how this works with some numbers. Let's say you turned 40 this year (2003). Assume you make IRA contributions of $2,000 a year over the next 10 years. It is now 2013, you just turned 50, and your IRA is worth $25,000 ($20,000 from contributions plus $5,000 of earnings). On May 1, 2013, you withdraw $10,000 from your IRA to use as part of a down payment for a home under the first-time–homebuyer provision, and the closing takes place June 1. You'll pay regular tax on the distributed funds but no penalty, as the funds were used for their intended purpose within 120 days of the withdrawal. And under this scenario, the entire $10,000 distribution would be income-tax–free as well if the account is a Roth IRA.

Now here's another example using the same facts, except that the closing takes place September 30. Here, the $10,000 early distribution from your IRA wouldn't qualify for the first-time–homebuyer exception because the funds weren't used within 120 days of their withdrawal on May 1. With a Roth IRA, however, the $10,000 early distribution would still be free of both income tax and penalty because it came out of your original $20,000 in contributions and didn't cut into the $5,000 of accumulated earnings.

3. **Unemployment/Health Insurance.** If you're out of work, you can take an early distribution penalty-free provided you use the funds to pay for health insurance. To qualify as unemployed, the tax rules say you must have received, or be receiving, state or federal unemployment benefits for 12 consecutive weeks. To get the penalty-free break, the early distribution must be used to pay your health insurance in either the year you received unemployment benefits or the year after. Self-employed individuals can also be out of work and need health insurance; if so, they can get this penalty-free break too, even though they generally do not receive unemployment benefits.

COMPANY-PLAN-ONLY EXCEPTIONS

1. **Age 55.** As you'll recall from Chapter 3, if you turn age 55 or older in the year you retire or leave your employer, withdrawals from your company plan are not subject to the 10 percent penalty. The exception does not apply, however, if you retire before age 55 but take no distributions until you reach age 55. For example, if you leave your job at age 52, but take no distributions from your company plan until you are 56, the 10 percent penalty kicks in (unless you qualify for another exception). Also, if you leave your job at age 55 and roll the company plan funds over to an IRA and then withdraw from the IRA before age 59½, you will be subject to the 10 percent penalty—because the age-55 exception only applies to distributions from company plans.

2. **Section 457 Plans.** Early distributions from Section 457 plans (deferred compensation plans) are not subject to the 10 percent early-withdrawal penalty, but they are subject to income tax at distribution time.

SO YOU THINK YOU'VE SPOTTED A LOOPHOLE?

Q. Since withdrawals before age 59½ from Section 457 plans are not subject to the 10 percent penalty, and the new rollover rules from EGTRRA 2001 spelled out in the last chapter say you can roll over your taxable IRA funds to a company plan, including a 457, then why don't I roll over my IRA to my 457? Then I'll be able to withdraw that money from the 457 penalty-free and beat the IRS. This sounds too easy!

A. That's because it won't work. It's true that you can roll over your taxable IRA funds to your company plan, in-

cluding a 457. The plan must accept the rollover, however, and it doesn't have to. But even then, a new section of the tax law [Code Section 72(t) (9)] specifically
states when IRA funds are rolled over to a 457 plan, any
withdrawals of those funds will be subject to the 10 percent penalty (if you are under age 59½ and no other
exceptions apply), the same as if you withdrew those
funds from your IRA. So, rolling them over won't get
you off the hook.

Q: But once the IRA funds are in my 457 plan, how will anyone know which funds I'm withdrawing?

A. The IRS and the plan will know because one of the conditions for the rollover is that the company plan must
keep a separate accounting of the IRA funds you rolled
over. In other words, Big Brother will be watching!

3. **Divorce.** If any part of your company plan is paid to an ex-spouse
as an alternate payee under what is called a qualified domestic re-
lations order (QDRO), this distribution will not be subject to the
10 percent penalty, and if you transfer the funds from your company plan to the exspouse's IRA, the distribution will not be taxable to you (the plan participant). The ex-spouse will pay the tax
when he or she withdraws from the account. IRAs split in a divorce get the same treatment except that a QDRO is not the controlling document; a divorce or separate-maintenance decree
would be used. Once the IRA is transferred to the ex-spouse, the
IRA is treated as if it were the ex-spouse's IRA. The IRA can only
be transferred either by changing the name on the IRA account
from one spouse to the other spouse, or through a direct transfer
(you cannot do a rollover). The funds cannot be withdrawn from
one spouse's IRA and redeposited to the ex-spouse's IRA. If that
happens, the withdrawal is taxable to the spouse who made the
distribution and any funds that are given to the ex-spouse will be
tax-free to the ex-spouse only, but the funds can no longer be
transferred to the ex-spouse's IRA.

THE 60-DAY LOAN

I referred to this in "Talking the Talk" and again in Chapter 3, but let's delve into it more deeply. Once a year, you can take money out of your IRA no matter how old you are, and use it for any reason, with no penalty or tax *provided you return the same amount of money to the account or to another IRA account you may own within 60 days of the withdrawal.* If you don't, the IRS hits you with the 10 percent penalty (assuming it was an early withdrawal) and, unless the account's a Roth IRA, you'll pay income tax on the distribution, as well. In other words, this tax break works only for those who need short-term cash and are absolutely positive they can replace that cash within 60 days—otherwise it could be a very expensive loan. This once-a-year rule does not apply to company plans. You can do as many company plan rollovers as you wish, if the plan allows it.

Although you only take advantage of the 60-day tax-free withdrawal once a year, the rule applies to each IRA you own. So, if you have, say, two IRA accounts, you can take money tax- and penalty-free from both of them within the same year as long as you return it within 60 days to either account, or to another account you may open. You wouldn't, however, be allowed to turn around and tap that new account tax- and penalty-free under the same procedure for another year. This one-year period is not necessarily a calendar year, unless you withdraw from your IRA on January 1. The one-year period starts on the date you receive (withdraw) the funds from your IRA, not on the day you put them back. Be careful about taking the 60-day–loan route. The rules are rigid with little latitude other than the allowable "frozen-deposit" excuse whereby your IRA funds may become frozen as a result of insolvency problems suffered by the bank or financial institution holding them. The IRS has been granted authority to extend the 60-day rule in other special situations. (The 60-day rule also applies to spousal rollovers covered later in this chapter and to Roth conversions; see Chapter 7.)

Getting It Later (Required Distributions)

After 59½ but before 70½

This scenario is easy because there are no rules. It's a free-for-all. You can withdraw any amount you wish any time you wish between the times you turn 59½ and 70½ without incurring an IRS penalty of any kind.

For example, you can take a distribution of $500,000 at age 62 and then not withdraw again until your *required beginning date (RBD)* when you turn 70½. Yes, you'll pay income tax on the $500,000 withdrawal, but there won't be any additional salt poured in that wound.

Think of this period of relatively rule-free bliss as the calm before the storm, as you will soon be entering another dimension, a shadowy dimension of even more shadows—the dimension of required minimum distributions after age 70½ that is otherwise known as "the Twilight Zone of taxation."

LEGISLATIVE ALERT!

As the saying goes, "If it ain't broke, don't fix it." But Congress keeps trying anyway. As this book goes to press, the Beltway crowd is batting around a number of proposals that may affect IRAs and other retirement accounts, among them changing the age for required distributions from 70½ straight to 75, or from 70½ to 73 in 2003–2004, to 74 in 2005–2006, and to 75 after 2006 (soon you'll need a daily reminder of how old you are just to keep up with the agendas of our elected officials). However, even if Congress does legislate such a change and the bill becomes law, all other distribution rules you will read about in this book will remain the same; they will simply apply at a different age.

For up-to-the-minute information you can rely on regarding any potential changes in the tax rules for retirement accounts our legislators spring on us, stay tuned to my website: www. irahelp.com.

After Age 70½ (Lifetime Distributions)

Remember what I wrote at the beginning of this chapter about payback? That after all those years of getting tax breaks, its time will come? Well, it's arrived. You've turned 70½ and as a birthday present Congress has gift-wrapped for you the most complex set of tax rules ever written (assuming they *were* written and didn't just bubble up from a witch's cauldron in the Congressional kitchen) to drive you absolutely bonkers. These are the "IRA distribution rules" for the rest of your life (they apply to most company plans, as well), and sorting them out makes the deciphering of the Rosetta Stone seem like a cakewalk. But you must understand these rules or you will risk the IRS absconding with your retirement savings legally through a combination of draconian penalties, not to mention income and possible estate taxes, as well as your own state's punitive tax measures.

Whether you want to or not, you have to start taking distributions from your retirement account as of your required beginning date (RBD), which is generally April 1 of the year following the year you turn 70½ (there's that ½ again; doesn't Congress have anything better to do than to keep splitting hairs—or, in this case, years?).

The process of how the IRS calculates your RBD is a bit bewildering (I'll "unbewilder" it for you in a moment), but each year thereafter another distribution is required, then another—a sequence of events that won't come to an end until you do . . . unless, of course, you outlive your retirement savings.

Taking the Guesswork Out of RBD

One of the most common questions I get is this: "Ed, when exactly am I 70½ according to the IRS?"

The answer: "The IRS says you're 70½ six months after your 70th birthday."

So far, so good.

But now comes the confusing part.

If, for example, you turned 70 years old on March 10, 2003, you would think that your RBD is April 1, 2003. Not so, says the IRS. It's April 1, *2004*. Here's why:

If you turned 70 on March 10, 2003, that means you're 70½ six months later on September 10, 2003. As your RBD is April 1 after the year you turned 70½, you must start taking your required minimum distributions (RMDs) by April 1, 2004.

Say instead, you turned 70 on August 5, 2003. Then your RBD would be April 1, 2005, a year later than in the previous example. That's because you're 70½ on February 5, 2004, making April 1, 2005, the April 1 after the year you turned 70½ and thus your RBD.

Here's a memory jogger for knowing it's your 70½ birthday. Instead of celebrating turning 70, celebrate turning 70½ instead, and have your birthday party then. Tell everyone it's your IRA/RBD/RMD bash. Your friends will be impressed by your knowledge of IRS alphabet soup, your beneficiaries are sure to attend so the date will be immortalized, and you'll never forget turning 70½.

RBD Exceptions

There are some exceptions to the rules that will allow you to delay taking your RMD after your required beginning date:

- **Still Working.** You first heard about this in Chapter 3; now let's look at the guts of it. If you are still working for a company (and own no more than a 5 percent interest in that company), you can delay required distributions until April 1 of the year following your retirement date. There is no age limit on this exception as long as you are still working. You can even be working part-time. There is nothing in the tax code that says you have to work full-time or a minimum number of hours to qualify for this exception. It just says, "still working." For example, let's assume that you turned 70½ in 2003 and are an employee of, say, Lucent. It's not your company, so you don't own more than 5 percent of it (who would want to?), but are a participant in Lucent's 401(k) plan—referred to by many acid-tongued analysts ever since Lucent took a 50 percent dive in value as its "201(k)" plan. Normally, your RBD would be April 1, 2004, but you figure Lucent's stock price is bound to go up eventually, so you keep working. This means you can delay RMDs until April 1 of the year following your retirement. Fast-forward 28 years. It is now 2031 and you are 98 years old. Lucent's stock price still hasn't moved up and you realize it probably won't (not in your remaining years, anyway), so you hang it up finally and wheeze into your rocking chair. Your RBD will be the following April 1 (2032). This means that you do not have to take any RMDs until that time. Think how much your 401(k) will have grown in the interim, and how much you'll have to live on when you really get old!

CAUTION!

The "still-working" exception does not apply to IRAs or to plans of former employers, only to the plan of the company for which you are still working. Therefore, even though you are, in fact, still working, you must begin distributions from those other plans by your age 70½ RBD. If you do not, you will be subject to the 50 percent penalty on the amount(s) you should have withdrawn from those plans but didn't.

■ **403(b) Plans: Old and New Money.** You can delay taking "old-money" distributions from a 403(b) plan until you turn 75. *Old money* in this case does not mean cash passed down from J. Paul Getty, but money you put into your 403(b) before 1987. Required distributions on this pre-1987 balance can be postponed until you're 75. The remaining balance (i.e., all post-December 31, 1986, contributions, AKA *new money*) must follow the required distribution rules for age 70½. If the 403(b) plan contract is transferred to another 403(b) plan, the exclusion from required distributions for pre-1987 account balances is retained as long as the new 403(b) plan tracks the December 31, 1986, account balance, making it clear which funds are the pre-1987 funds. Old money that is distributed and rolled over to an IRA loses the age-75 exception, however.

CAUTION!

Delaying old-money distributions may save you in taxes in the short run but can cost you a mint down the road if your 403(b) plan beneficiary is not your spouse. How so? If you die before reaching 75 and your beneficiary is a nonspouse (your child, for example), the nonspouse beneficiary will most likely not be able to take advantage of step 3 (see Chapter 6) of my five-step action plan and "stretch" the inherited 403(b) plan over his or her lifetime. This is because most 403(b) plans force the beneficiary to withdraw the entire account balance within five years (or even within one year in some plans) whereas a spouse beneficiary can roll over the 403(b) plan to an IRA and keep it going. Be aware of this pitfall so that you don't fall into it and wind up making your kids pay, as happened to Ann's children in Chapter 1.

- **Grace Period.** For your first-year 70½ RMD, you're allowed a grace period to take your withdrawal. All future distributions, however, must be taken by the end of the distribution year. For example, if your 70½-year is 2003, you can wait until April 1, 2004, to take your 2003 distribution, but you must take your year-2004 distribution by the end of 2004 and so on. There is no grace period for distributions beyond the first year.
- **Penury.** What happens if the market takes such a dive that your retirement account balance won't even cover your required distribution? Well, until recently the IRS never considered the possibility that a retirement account could decline in value, and so it would still impose the 50 percent penalty for nonwithdrawal even if there was nothing in the account to withdraw. But in the 155-page final regulations issued in April 2002, the IRS finally addressed this matter and inserted a single sentence that I call "The Enron Effect Clause," which says that if the value of your IRA or plan has dropped so much that your RMD amount exceeds your entire account balance, then you can simply empty the account without penalty. In other words, the IRS has a heart after all—it won't make you withdraw more than you actually have and penalize you 50 percent if you don't. Your RMD is limited to your account balance. So, if you withdraw the remaining balance in your IRA, that will satisfy your RMD for the year—and future years, since there is nothing left. For example, say that by the time you plan to withdraw your RMD, the balance of your $1 million IRA has declined to almost nothing. The IRS says you don't have to withdraw the RMD calculated on the $1 million that's no longer there, but the RMD will be limited to the balance that's left (if anything), and you will be exempt from the 50 percent penalty forever more. Of course, you will also be broke.

TAX TRAP!

If you turn 70½ in 2003, your RBD is April 1, 2004. If you wait to take your first required withdrawal until 2004 (when you also must also take your second), this will cause a bunching up of your first-year and second-year required distributions into one tax year (because all distributions after the first one must be taken by the end of the distribution year). The result will most likely be an overall increase in your income tax. This double-distribution situation can only happen for the first and second RMDs, and only if you wait until after your first distribution year to take your first RMD. The better route is to take your first required distribution by the end of your 70½-year. This will spread your first two RMDs over two separate tax years and likely result in a lower tax bite each year.

MAJOR TAX TRAP!

Here's the biggest incentive for staying on top of the RBD rules and making sure that you withdraw the right amount at the right time from your plan: *The IRS will take 50 percent of your retirement savings if you mess up.* This is one of the worst tax penalties ever conceived by Congress. It subjects you to a 50 percent penalty on the amount of your RMD that you failed to withdraw in a "timely" manner. By *timely,* Congress means by the RBD of your first distribution year, and by the end of each distribution year every year thereafter. For example, if your RMD is $20,000 and you only withdraw $6,000, you will have to pay a $7,000 penalty, as you were short by $14,000 and 50 percent of $14,000 = $7,000. It's easy to see how you could wipe out a lifetime's worth of savings by falling into this tax trap alone. Even death doesn't erase the 50 percent penalty. It applies to your beneficiaries as well. So, never miss a required distribution.

Calculating Your Required Minimum Distribution

Now that you know *when* you have to start withdrawals after age 70½, you need to know exactly *how much* you'll be required to withdraw. You can always withdraw more each year, but you cannot take less; otherwise you'll play those 50 percent penalty blues. Here's how to make the calculation.

Determine Your Account Balance

RMDs are based on your account balance as of December 31 of the year before you take that first distribution. In order to determine this balance, you must include the combined balances of all the company plans, IRAs, SEP-IRAS, and SIMPLE IRAs you own. For example, if you turned 70½ in 2003, you would determine your plan balance as of December 31, 2002. If you have more than one plan, you would add together the balances of all these plans (except those qualifying for the spousal exception, described on page 103) as of December 31, 2002, to arrive at a *total* balance. IRAs and other plan balances you may have inherited should not be included in this total. You may still be subject to RMDs on inherited IRAs, but they are figured separately and will be covered later in this chapter.

If you own a Roth IRA, the balance is not included in your total either, as Roth IRA owners are not subject to required distributions. Similarly, spouse beneficiaries who roll an inherited Roth IRA into their own Roth IRA, or who treat the inherited Roth as their own, are exempt from required distributions too, but nonspouse Roth IRA beneficiaries are not exempt from taking them.

If you have multiple IRA accounts and the spousal exception applies to any of them, you must compute the required distribution separately for each of them, but the required amount can be withdrawn from any one or a combination of those accounts" (see "Keeping Track of Multiple Account RMDs" toward the end of this chapter). Withdrawing from a beneficiary IRA, however, cannot satisfy the RMD on your own IRA. The RMD on the inherited IRA must be calculated separately and withdrawn only from that account or from another beneficiary IRA that you inherited from the same person. If you have beneficiary IRAs from different decedents, you cannot add those account balances to figure required distributions. Each beneficiary account from a different decedent must be figured and withdrawn separately.

Like IRAs, 403(b) plans can be combined for figuring required distributions, but you cannot satisfy your required IRA distribution by withdrawing from your 403(b) plan or vice-versa.

If you have more than one qualified plan, such as a Keogh self-employment plan and a 401(k), RMDs must be figured for each plan and withdrawn respectively from that account. For example, if you have four different Keogh self-employment plans, you must withdraw the required amount from each plan. You cannot withdraw from one plan to satisfy the RMD on another plan even though they are both Keoghs. That aggregation can only be done with IRAs and 403(b)s. If you have several accounts within a particular Keogh plan, however, you can withdraw the required amount from any one of those accounts.

You cannot satisfy your RMD from a traditional IRA by withdrawing from a Roth IRA or vice-versa. Roth IRA beneficiaries who are subject to required distributions must withdraw from the Roth IRA. They can only aggregate Roth IRAs inherited from the same person.

Determine Your Life Expectancy

Having determined your IRA balance as of the end of the previous year, you must next determine your life expectancy based on your age in the RMD year. The greater your life expectancy, the lower your RMD will be, and the less income tax you will pay. To get your life expectancy, refer to what is known as the Uniform Lifetime Table (Figure 5). This table is used for calculating your (the IRA owner's) RMDs no matter who your beneficiary is—unless your sole beneficiary for an entire year is your spouse and your spouse is more than 10 years your junior. This is the *spousal exception,* and it requires you to refer to the IRS Joint Life Expectancy Tables (see Appendix I) for the combined life expectancy of you and your spouse in calculating the RMD. For example, if Mickey is 75 and his spouse Minnie is 58 as well as his sole beneficiary for the entire year, the spousal exception applies, so Mickey would look up the combined life expectancy of a 75-year-old and a 58-year-old in the IRS Joint Life Expectancy table.

When the spousal exception was first introduced in the proposed Regs, many people questioned what would happen if the spouse and sole beneficiary for the entire year dies or gets divorced during that year. The final Regs answered this question with a provision stating that marital status is determined as of January 1. So, if Minnie dies during the year, and a new beneficiary is named, the spousal exception still applies; Minnie will still be considered the sole beneficiary for purposes of calculating that year's required distribution, *but not the following year's.* If there is a divorce during the year, the spousal exception applies only if the beneficiary is not changed during the year of the divorce.

The Uniform Lifetime Table is a "recalculating" table (the concept of "recalculating" is discussed on page 134). You have to go back to it every year to get your new life expectancy. For example, if you look at the table (see Figure 5), it shows that a 70-year-old has a life expectancy of 27.4 years, but that does not mean the plan balance must be emptied by the time he or she reaches 97.4 years (70+27.4 = 97.4). The 27.4-year life expectancy is for age 70 only. Every year thereafter, a new life expectancy must be calculated. Therefore, at 97, our example still has a life expectancy of 7.6 more years (the lucky dog!). (Even at age 115, there's still 1.9 years of life left in the old codger yet, according to the table.) The theory is that if you only take the required minimum amount each year, you will never run out of IRA money—unless the market tanks, of course, and your retirement account is wiped out—because, as far as the IRS is concerned, you never run out of life expectancy. They want to keep you alive and kicking—kicking in, that is!

As distributions are required after you turn 70½, the question people inevitably raise when looking up their life expectancy in the Uniform Lifetime Table to determine their first-year RMD is "Do I use 70 or 71?" Here's a simple rule of thumb. Use your age as of December 31 in the year you turned 70½. For example, if you're 70½ in February, you'll hit your 71st birthday six months later in August and therefore be 71 on the last day of the year. So, you would look up 71 in the Uniform Lifetime Table for your life expectancy. On the other hand, if you turn 70½ in September, you will not have reached 71 by the end of the year, so you would use age 70 on the Uniform Lifetime Table. After the first-year distribution, there is no more half-year concept to confuse you. Just use your age at the end of each distribution year to look up your new life expectancy.

Make the Calculation

OK, you've determined your account balance for the prior year and you've determined your life expectancy according to the Uniform Lifetime Table (or the Joint Life Expectancy table if the spousal exception applies to your situation). Now, all you have to do to get your RMD is divide your account balance by your life expectancy. For example, let's say you turn 72 in 2003. Your life expectancy according to the Uniform Lifetime Table is 25.6 years. If your plan balance as of December 31 of the prior year (2002) is $400,000, you divide $400,000 by 25.6 years and get $15,625, which is your RMD for that account for 2003. If you have more than one account (and if the spousal exception doesn't apply to any of them), you would divide their combined total balance by 25.6 You can withdraw the entire amount or break it up into several smaller withdrawals, as long as by the end of the year all $15,625 has been withdrawn. You can always withdraw more by the end of the year without paying any penalties, but not less. And if you did withdraw more in 2003—say, $20,000 instead of $15,625—forget about having the extra $4,375 credited to you so that you could take less in 2004. The IRS doesn't work that way. The Regs stipulate that each distribution year stands on its own.

Figure 5. Uniform Lifetime Table

Age of IRA Owner or Plan Participant	Life Expectancy (in Years)	Age of IRA Owner or Plan Participant	Life Expectancy (in Years)
70	27.4	93	9.6
71	26.5	94	9.1
72	25.6	95	8.6
73	24.7	96	8.1
74	23.8	97	7.6
75	22.9	98	7.1
76	22.0	99	6.7
77	21.2	100	6.3
78	20.3	101	5.9
79	19.5	102	5.5
80	18.7	103	5.2
81	17.9	104	4.9
82	17.1	105	4.5
83	16.3	106	4.2
84	15.5	107	3.9
85	14.8	108	3.7
86	14.1	109	3.4
87	13.4	110	3.1
88	12.7	111	2.9
89	12.0	112	2.6
90	11.4	113	2.4
91	10.8	114	2.1
92	10.2	115+	1.9

SO, YOU THINK YOU SPOTTED A LOOPHOLE?

Q: Ed, I think I've figured a way around taking RMDs. You said to base RMD on the prior year's balance, right? What if on December 20 I withdraw the entire amount in my IRA, and then on January 5 of the next year (well within the penalty-free 60-day period) I redeposit all the money back to my IRA? If I go back to the December 31 balance to figure my RMD, guess what? The December 31 balance is ZERO because I withdrew all the money, so there is no RMD! Cool, huh? If I do this 60-day shuffle every year, I'll never have to withdraw from my IRA, right?

A: WRONG! The IRS is way ahead of you—again. There is another little rule that says if you remove any funds from your IRA before year-end and roll them back into your IRA the following year, even within 60 days, you must add the outstanding rollover amount(s) back to your account balance as of December 31 of the prior year for calculating your RMD. For example, let's say that on December 20, 2003, you withdraw your entire IRA balance of $500,000. On January 5, 2004, you redeposit the $500,000 back to your IRA. To calculate your 2004 distribution, you must use your December 31, 2003, IRA balance. That balance is zero, but the Regs say that in this case you must add the $500,000 outstanding rollover back to your December 31, 2003, IRA balance and use that $500,000 to calculate your 2004 RMD.

Test Your RMD Know-How

Here are a few examples of how to calculate your lifetime RMD in a variety of situations. Let's see if you've got the hang of it.

- *The IRA owner is 74 years old in 2003. His beneficiary is his spouse, who is 72 years old in 2003. His IRA balance*

at December 31, 2002, is $425,000. What is his RMD for 2003?
A: $17,857
Q: How did you get that?
A: According to the Uniform Lifetime Table, the life expectancy for a 74-year-old (the spouse's age is irrelevant here because the spousal exception does not apply) is 23.8 years. You then divide the $425,000 IRA balance from the end of the prior year by the 23.8 years: $425,000/23.8 = $17,857.

▪ *The IRA owner is 74 years old in 2003. His beneficiary is his alma mater. His IRA balance at December 31, 2002, is $425,000. What is his RMD for 2003?*
A: $17,857
Q: How did you get that?
A: The situation is exactly the same, except for the identity of the beneficiary, which makes no difference as long as the spousal exception does not apply.

▪ *The IRA owner is 74 years old in 2003. He neglected to name a beneficiary. His IRA balance at December 31, 2002, is $425,000. What is his RMD for 2003?*
A: $17,857.
Q: How did you get that?
A: The same method. The fact that there is no named beneficiary is of no consequence in computing lifetime RMDs. However, as Chapter 6 will show, naming a beneficiary is vitally important in making sure an IRA keeps growing tax-deferred for your beneficiaries.

▪ *The IRA owner is 74 years old in 2003. His 15 children are equal co-beneficiaries. They range in age from 2 to 25 years old. His wife has chosen not to be named a beneficiary because she thinks her children will take care of her. (Obviously she's never heard the adage "A mother can* *take care of 15 children, but 15 children cannot take care of one mother.") His IRA balance at December 31, 2002, is $425,000. What is his RMD for 2003?*

A. $17,857.

Q: How did you get that?

A: Again, the same method; it does not matter how many beneficiaries there are. As long as the spousal exception does not apply (and it does not in this example), the number of beneficiaries and their ages are meaningless to the lifetime RMD calculation. You still use the Uniform Lifetime Table based on the IRA owner's age in the distribution year. The ages and number of beneficiaries will only play an important role in postdeath RMDs (see Chapter 6).

■ *The IRA owner is 74 years old in 2003. His sole beneficiary for the entire year is his spouse, who is 45 years old in 2003. His IRA balance at December 31, 2002, is $425,000. What is his RMD for 2003?*

A: $10,842.

Q: How did you get that?

A: The spousal exception applies because she (or he) is the sole beneficiary and younger by more than 10 years. Therefore, in this situation, the Uniform Lifetime Table would not be used to calculate RMD, but rather the IRS Joint Life Expectancy Table (see Appendix I), where you would look up the joint life expectancy of a 74-year-old and a 45-year-old, which happens to be 39.2 years. You then divide the $425,000 IRA balance by 39.2 and get $10,842.

■ *The IRA owner is 74 years old in 2003. His beneficiaries are his spouse, who is 55 years old, and his son, who is 30 years old in 2003. The spouse will receive 90 percent of the IRA and the son will inherit 10 percent. His IRA balance at December 31, 2002, is $425,000. What is his RMD for 2003?*

A. $17,857.

Q: How did you get that?

A: The spousal exception does not apply here because even though the spouse is more than 10 years younger than the IRA owner and will inherit 90 percent of the account, she is not the *sole* beneficiary—and so the Uniform Lifetime Table is used to calculate the RMD for 2003.

■ *The IRA owner is 74 in 2003. His sole beneficiary is his spouse, who is 53 years old in 2003. His IRA balance at December 31, 2002, is $425,000. His spouse dies in February 2003, and he names his son as beneficiary in May 2003. What is his RMD for 2003?*

A: $13,199.

Q: How did you get that?

A: Even though the spouse died in February of the distribution year and a new sole beneficiary was named, the spousal exception still applies for the distribution year because of the marital-status provision. The joint life expectancy of a 74- and a 53-year-old is 32.2 years. $425,000 divided by 32.2 = $13,199.

■ *Following up on the previous example, assuming the IRA owner does not remarry and keeps his son as his sole beneficiary, what would the RMD be for the next year (2004) when the owner is 75, and the account balance at December 31, 2003, is, say, $450,000?*

A: $19,651.

Q: How did you get that?

A: The spousal exception cannot apply because he didn't remarry, so the Uniform Life Table would be used for 2004. According to that table, the life expectancy for a 75-year-old is 22.9 years. $450,000 divided by 22.9 = $19,651.

Calculating RMDs for "Split IRAs"

For estate planning purposes, it can sometimes pay handsomely to split an IRA into two or more accounts, naming different beneficiaries for each account. It also pays to split IRAs to reduce current income taxes on lifetime RMDs.

For instance, in one of the examples cited previously, if instead of naming his spouse and child as 90/10 co-beneficiaries, the 74-year-old owner of the $425,000 IRA had split the IRA into two IRAs, naming his 55-year-old spouse as beneficiary of one and his son as beneficiary of the other, the spousal exception would have applied to the IRA where the spouse was the sole beneficiary. Thus, the Joint Life Expectancy Table would have been used in calculating RMD on that account, resulting in a lower required distribution.

Uh-oh. You've got a confused look on your face. OK, let's do the calculation using some actual numbers.

The 55-year-old spouse is the named beneficiary on 90 percent of the $425,000 IRA and the son is the named beneficiary on 10 percent, resulting in a total RMD of $17,857. But now the IRA is split 90/10 into two IRAs: one for $382,500 (90 percent of the $425,000) and the other for $42,500 (10 percent of the $425,000). The spouse is the sole beneficiary on the $382,500 IRA and the son is the sole beneficiary on the $42,500 IRA. This split is not set in stone. The IRA owner can change his mind at any time, transfer funds from one IRA to another, or take his RMD from one IRA and not the other if he wishes. But for our purposes here, let's assume the spouse remains the sole beneficiary for the entire year on the $382,500 IRA.

Because the spousal exception applies to the $382,500 IRA, the IRS Joint Life Expectancy Table can be used to determine the life expectancy figure—in this case, the joint life expectancy of a 74- and 55-year old, which is 30.5 years. Divide $382,500 by 30.5 years and you come up with an RMD on that account of $12,541.

However, the spousal exception does not apply to the $42,500 IRA because the son is the sole beneficiary of that account. So, the

Uniform Lifetime Table would be used instead to determine the single life expectancy of a 74-year-old, which is 23.8 years. Divide $42,500 by 23.8 years and you get an RMD on that account of $1,786. The total RMD for the two IRAs is $14,327 ($12,541 + $1,786 = $14,327), which is the minimum that can be withdrawn from any one or both of the accounts.

To sum up: Before the $425,000 IRA was split, the RMD was $17,857. After the split, it is $14,327. Subtract $14,327 from $17,857 and you get a difference of $3,530. That's how much less the owner is required to take out for the year by having split his one IRA into two and naming different beneficiaries for each. And, as a result of taking less out, the owner's income tax on that distribution will be lower. This is the main benefit of splitting accounts in situations where the spousal exception applies. But there are benefits to splitting IRAs even in situations where the spousal exception may not apply, such as when your spouse is a beneficiary and wants to treat the IRA as his or her own or wants to take advantage of the special option if he or she chooses to remain a beneficiary (see Chapter 6, page 189), "Stretching with Multiple Beneficiaries on One IRA Account," and page 194, "Stretching by Splitting Accounts with Different Types of Beneficiaries.") So, it is generally a good idea to split accounts if you have multiple beneficiaries. This can even be done by beneficiaries themselves, but it's better that you do it, so as not to open the door to a family feud and other potential problems. (Chapter 6 tells more on splitting accounts with multiple beneficiaries after the death of the IRA owner.)

CAUTION:

Don't mix different kinds of beneficiaries—for example, a person (or designated beneficiary) with a nonperson such as an estate, charity, or trust—as co-beneficiaries on one IRA; it won't affect calculating RMD, but it may close the door to stretching the account later on because the stretch IRA is not permitted after the owner's death in cases where one of the co-beneficiaries is not a person and the account is not split by the end of the year after death. So, for example, instead of naming your favorite charity and your three children as co-beneficiaries on one IRA, split the IRA into two IRAs naming the charity as sole beneficiary on one of them and your three children as co-beneficiaries on the other. You might even want to split the IRA that names your three children into three different IRAs so that they don't have to split the account after death.

Calculating RMDs for Inherited IRAs

This gets a little funky because there are so many variables.

IRA beneficiaries are subject to RMDs and to the 50 percent penalty for not taking an RMD. Calculating the RMD depends on which kind of beneficiary you are. There are different kinds (I don't mean good and evil), and in some cases the payout rules will differ depending on when the plan participant died—either before or after the required beginning date (RBD).

A *designated beneficiary* enjoys the special status of having a life expectancy—though not necessarily a "life" (even the IRS can't guarantee that). For calculating their lifetime RMDs on an inherited IRA, designated beneficiaries do not look to either the Uniform Lifetime Table or the IRS Joint Life Expectancy Table used by plan owners. They must use the Single Life Expectancy Table for Inherited IRAs (see Figure 6), which is a recalculating table as well, but only a spouse beneficiary who is the sole inheritor can go back to this table each year for recalculating life expectancy. A nonspouse beneficiary cannot recalculate and would only use this table to compute the first year's required distribution for the inherited IRA. The life expectancy will then be reduced by one year for each succeeding year.

A *beneficiary* on the other hand is an estate, a charity, or a trust, for example, and therefore has no life expectancy. Postdeath pay-

Figure 6. Single Life Expectancy Table (for Inherited IRAs)

Age of IRA or Plan Beneficiary	Life Expectancy (in Years)	Age of IRA or Plan Beneficiary	Life Expectancy (in Years)	Age of IRA or Plan Beneficiary	Life Expectancy (in Years)
0	82.4				
1	81.6	41	42.7	81	9.7
2	80.6	42	41.7	82	9.1
3	79.7	43	40.7	83	8.6
4	78.7	44	39.8	84	8.1
5	77.7	45	38.8	85	7.6
6	76.7	46	37.9	86	7.1
7	75.8	47	37.0	87	6.7
8	74.8	48	36.0	88	6.3
9	73.8	49	35.1	89	5.9
10	72.8	50	34.2	90	5.5
11	71.8	51	33.3	91	5.2
12	70.8	52	32.3	92	4.9
13	69.9	53	31.4	93	4.6
14	68.9	54	30.5	94	4.3
15	67.9	55	29.6	95	4.1
16	66.9	56	28.7	96	3.8
17	66.0	57	27.9	97	3.6
18	65.0	58	27.0	98	3.4
19	64.0	59	26.1	99	3.1
20	63.0	60	25.2	100	2.9
21	62.1	61	24.4	101	2.7
22	61.1	62	23.5	102	2.5
23	60.1	63	22.7	103	2.3

Figure 6. Single Life Expectancy Table (for Inherited IRAs) (*cont.*)

Age of IRA or Plan Beneficiary	Life Expectancy (in Years)	Age of IRA or Plan Beneficiary	Life Expectancy (in Years)	Age of IRA or Plan Beneficiary	Life Expectancy (in Years)
24	59.1	64	21.8	104	2.1
25	58.2	65	21.0	105	1.9
26	57.2	66	20.2	106	1.7
27	56.2	67	19.4	107	1.5
28	55.3	68	18.6	108	1.4
29	54.3	69	17.8	109	1.2
30	53.3	70	17.0	110	1.1
31	52.4	71	16.3	111+	1.0
32	51.4	72	15.5		
33	50.4	73	14.8		
34	49.4	74	14.1		
35	48.5	75	13.4		
36	47.5	76	12.7		
37	46.5	77	12.1		
38	45.6	78	11.4		
39	44.6	79	10.8		
40	43.6	80	10.2		

outs to beneficiaries follow a separate, less favorable set of rules that will be explained later.

Get used to the two terms. When I use *beneficiary,* I am referring to the inheritor of an IRA or plan that may or may not be a designated beneficiary, whereas when I use the term *designated beneficiary,* I am referring to a person who was named a beneficiary by the IRA owner or company plan participant on the beneficiary form.

Spouse or Nonspouse Makes a Difference Too

Another distinction among IRA inheritors is whether the beneficiary is a spouse or a nonspouse. A *spouse* is the wife or husband of
the deceased IRA owner or plan participant. *Nonspouse beneficiaries* are divided into two more groups: *persons* and *other*. The
former is defined as an individual who is not the wife or husband
of the IRA owner or plan participant, such as a son or daughter.
Other is defined as an estate, charity, trust, or entity that, without
a life expectancy, can never be a designated beneficiary (unless,
perhaps, it's Pinocchio. You may recall, he becomes a real boy!).

Incorrect "Titling" Will Destroy Your Inherited IRA

Before a nonspouse beneficiary begins RMDs, the deceased IRA
owner's account must be titled correctly. The IRS stipulates that
the deceased's name must stay on the account. Nonspouse beneficiaries cannot retitle inherited accounts in their own name—otherwise, the account becomes taxable immediately, and *poof* . . . it
disappears. Often the beneficiary, let's say a son, will say, "I inherited the account, so it's mine now; I may as well put it under my
name." Sounds logical; after all it does belong to him. The IRS,
however, deems this action to be a rollover, even though no money
is actually withdrawn from the account, and subjects the entire
balance in the account to income tax. To avoid this costly mistake,
make sure the deceased owner's name remains on the account
forever.

Here's a tale that might have turned into another of the horror
stories I spooked you with in Chapter 1, but fortunately I was able
to save this inherited IRA from becoming taxable before its time.

When her mother unexpectedly died in a tragic car accident, a
client of mine, age 40, and her brother found out that they were
the named beneficiaries on their mother's $500,000 IRA account.
My client and her brother live in New York State (near my office,

in fact), but their mother was living in Florida, so they retained their mother's Florida attorney to handle the estate. Luckily for them, they asked the estate attorney to check with me on any tax issues. The attorney dutifully touched bases and, figuring it would be the same as deeding the mother's house to the children, suggested casually, "Why don't I just go ahead and put the IRAs in the beneficiaries' names and get that out of the way."

I rocketed up in my chair with a thundering "NOOOOOOO!" Then I explained in a quieter tone that an IRA is a completely different kind of animal from a house. It is loaded with unforgiving tax traps if not handled properly; changing the name on the inherited IRA would make it a rollover and the $500,000 would be fully taxable to the children this tax year.

"But if the law denies rollovers for inherited accounts, how is it that a spouse can roll over? That's an inherited account, isn't it?" the attorney asked.

"No, it isn't," I said. "At least for tax law purposes, it isn't. Under the Tax Code, an inherited account means a retirement account inherited by someone other than a spouse. That's because when a spouse—a wife, say—rolls the IRA over to her own IRA, it becomes *her IRA* and is no longer inherited."

The attorney asked for the specific tax law so she could brush up on it, and I gave it to her. For you Code junkies out there who may be wondering, "Yeah, Ed, where does it say that?" here's where to look: IRC Section 408(d)(3)(C), "Denial of Rollover Treatment for Inherited Accounts." Doesn't beat around the bush, does it?

Satisfied, the attorney then asked, "Well, how should the account be titled?"

The IRS offers no official titling language. So, let's assume that the name of the deceased IRA owner was Roberta Smith and the named beneficiary is Elizabeth Smith. Here's what other advisors and I would recommend as an acceptable way to title an inherited IRA: **"Roberta Smith IRA (deceased May 12, 2003) F/B/O (for the benefit of), Elizabeth Smith, Beneficiary."** If there were more than one beneficiary named on the IRA, then the IRA would be

split and the other beneficiaries' names would go at the end of the
account set up for them. If the account were left to Elizabeth Smith
and her brother James Smith, then James Smith's beneficiary IRA
would be titled: **"Roberta Smith IRA (deceased May 12, 2003)
F/B/O, James Smith, Beneficiary."**

Keep each inherited IRA separate. Typically, each financial institution has its own verbiage for this, but the important thing is
that the account is identified as a "beneficiary account" and that
the deceased IRA owner's name stays on it. The financial institution may use the words *inherited IRA* instead of *beneficiary account*. That's OK too. The "FBO"—which, as just noted, means
"for the benefit of"—is sometimes written out rather than abbre-
viated.

It is not unusual for a financial institution to make the uninformed
(to put it mildly) mistake of transferring the title of a nonspouse
beneficiary's inherited IRA to the beneficiary's name in the honest
belief that it is doing the right thing. If this is suggested by your
bank or brokerage, persuade the uninformed employee you're
dealing with—or, even better, the employee's superiors—that the
account must stay in the deceased owner's name or you'll get
robbed. If you have to, cite the section of the Tax Code section I
gave. Remember, the money you save is now your own.

Although the IRA owner's name must remain on the account,
the Social Security number must be changed from the deceased's to
the beneficiary's. The IRS goes by the Social Security number on
the account to determine who will pay tax on any distributions
and it frowns upon having to collect from beyond the grave.
Therefore I recommend changing the Social Security number on inherited accounts for tax reporting purposes as soon as possible after the owner's death. Then it won't later slip your mind and incur
the IRS's wrath.

If I hadn't alerted the Florida attorney to the grave (no pun intended) mistake she was about to make, my client and her brother
would have found themselves paying tax on the $500,000 instead
of being able to grow the account tax-deferred and spread distributions over another 40 years. They may even have slapped the at-

torney with a lawsuit for costing them a bundle. But there were smiles all around instead.

While the Tax Code considers retitling an inherited account to be the same as a taxable withdrawal of the entire account balance, this doesn't mean a nonspouse beneficiary can't change the account's investments via a direct transfer from one bank to another without being taxed if, say, the investments are performing badly. The IRS rules allow this. The transfer can actually be made for any reason, not just to change investments. The bank holding the account must be willing to do the transfer to the receiving bank, however, and some banks aren't. They will say, "We don't do trustee-to-trustee transfers, but if you are unhappy, here's your money." So, you're stuck—because once funds are distributed, they're taxable. Thus, an uncooperative financial institution can hold your inherited IRA hostage. Of course, depending on the size of the account, you may have greater leverage than you know because the bank will not want to lose such a valuable customer.

What if you take the check and, within the allotted 60-day period for tax and penalty-free withdrawals, transfer it to a correctly titled inherited IRA account at the mutual fund company where you want it? No good. The 60-day rule applies only to rollovers, and a nonspouse beneficiary cannot roll over an inherited IRA without killing the account taxwise. I cannot emphasize this enough.

Postdeath Distributions

Now that you know the kinds of beneficiaries there are, plus the ins and outs of beneficiarydom, the next move is to determine what the payout period will be to these beneficiaries when postdeath RMDs must begin. The payout period is based on life expectancy—the maximum years over which the inherited IRA can be withdrawn. Here is where we get into a lot of tricky variables, so I'll break my discussion of the postdeath distribution rules for beneficiaries on inherited IRAs into three separate parts. There's a lot at stake, so keep reading!

POSTDEATH DISTRIBUTIONS

1. **The IRA owner dies before his (or her) RBD.**
- Nonspouse designated beneficiary.
- No designated beneficiary.

2. **The IRA owner dies on or after his (or her) RBD.**
- Nonspouse designated beneficiary.
- No designated beneficiary.

3. **The beneficiary is a spouse.**
- Spouse elects to roll the IRA over to his or her own IRA (or treat it as his or her own IRA).
- Spouse chooses to remain a beneficiary.

The IRA Owner Dies Before His or Her RBD

An IRA owner's required beginning date is April 1 following the year of his or her 70½ birthday. Even if the IRA owner dies on the eve of that date, the death is viewed as occurring before RBD even though the IRA owner is, in fact, past the required minimum distribution age of 70½. So, for example, if the IRA owner is 70½ in 2003, his RBD would be April 1, 2004. If he dies on March 30, 2004, he will be treated as having died before his RBD, and his beneficiaries will follow those distribution rules.

Nonspouse Designated Beneficiary

If an IRA owner names an individual (a son or daughter, for example) who is not the spouse as beneficiary, it will generally not matter whether the owner dies before or after the RBD because nonspouse designated beneficiaries get to use their own life expectancies to calculate postdeath RMDs on inherited IRAs, the first of which must be taken by the end of the year after the year of the IRA owner's death. This is the first distribution year, meaning the first year for which the designated beneficiary has a required distribution. Each year thereafter, an RMD must be taken by the end of the year. For example, if Sam (the IRA owner) dies in 2003 at either 65 or 75 (i.e., either before or after his RBD) and names his son Brad beneficiary, Brad must take his first RMD by December 31, 2004. If an RMD is missed, the 50 percent penalty applies the same as it does for lifetime distributions missed by IRA owners.

How much must be withdrawn each year? The method of calculating is not all that different from the method used by IRA owners discussed earlier in this chapter, except that here the designated beneficiary looks up his or her age in the year after the IRA owner's death from the Single Life Expectancy Table (Figure 6) for the life expectancy factor. The IRA account balance (as of the end of the prior year) is then divided by the life expectancy factor to get the RMD for the first distribution year. For the next year, the designated beneficiary simply reduces that factor by 1 because the first year's life expectancy factor is a set (nonrecalculating) term of years over which the RMDs can be extended that will not change, so there is no need to go back to the table each year to look up a new life expectancy factor.

For example, Barry (the IRA owner) dies in 2004 at 66 years of age (obviously well before his RBD), and his daughter Jennifer inherits. She is 40 years old in 2005 and is a designated beneficiary because she was named as such on the IRA beneficiary form. Her first distribution year is 2005 (because that is the year after her father's death), and the balance in the account as of the end of the prior year (December 31, 2004) is $300,000. According to the Single Life Expectancy Table, Jennifer's life expectancy at 40 in 2005 is 43.6 years. Divide $300,000 by 43.6 and you find that her first-year RMD is $6,881. For the second-year (2005) RMD, she simply subtracts 1 from the first-year (set-term) life expectancy factor and divides the account balance at December 31, 2005, by that number (43.6 − 1 = 42.6). So, if the account's balance as of that date is, say, $310,000, then Jennifer's second-year RMD on the inherited IRA is $7,277 (or $310,000/42.6). She repeats this process each year until the original 43.6-year set term is completed or until the account is emptied, whichever comes first. She can always withdraw more than the minimum if she wishes; in fact, she could withdraw the entire account balance her first distribution year. But it's to her benefit to stretch distributions over the longest time period allowed, which in this case is 43.6 years, so that her inherited IRA can keep compounding tax-deferred the whole time.

No Designated Beneficiary

What if there is no designated beneficiary on an IRA or company plan inherited from an owner who dies before his or her RBD? Remember (for the zillionth time) that having a beneficiary named does not mean the same thing as having a designated beneficiary. If your account doesn't have a designated beneficiary and you're reading this, then you still have time to name a beneficiary so that no one will be left with a problem. All you have to do is fill out a beneficiary form for the account. Sounds easy, and is easy, but most people don't do it—just as most people know they should quit smoking and go to the gym, but they don't do that either.

If the IRA owner dies before his or her RBD, then the beneficiary named (notice I did not say "designated beneficiary") must withdraw from the account under what is called the *five-year rule*. One would guess this means that the inherited IRA must be emptied within five years, but this is tax law where nothing is ever simple. The five-year rule requires the entire inherited IRA or company plan to be fully distributed by the conclusion of the fifth year following the IRA owner's death. It does not matter how much the beneficiary withdraws yearly during the five-year–rule period as long as the account is emptied by end of that period. Any balance remaining in the inherited IRA after that time is subject to the 50 percent penalty.

For example, Mike dies in 2004 at age 57 (again, well before his RBD) and names his estate beneficiary of his $500,000 IRA. The estate is not a person and therefore not a designated beneficiary. Mike's brother Max inherits through the estate. Since Mike died before his RBD and there was no designated beneficiary, the five-year rule applies. This means the entire $500,000 balance must be distributed by December 31, 2009, which is the fifth year after Mike's death. No distributions are required for 2004 through 2008. But if nothing is withdrawn by the December 31, 2009, end date, the IRS will assess a 50 percent ($250,000) penalty on the remaining balance, ending the tax deferral as well. (The 10 percent penalty never applies to a beneficiary. Just reminding you.) So, you see, the five-year rule is not a good thing. No one should be stuck with this treatment, but many are because they neglect to name a beneficiary.

The five-year rule only applies when the IRA owner dies before his RBD. I want to emphasize that fact until it's coming out of your ears because there is so much confusion over the five-year rule. I hear too many stories of beneficiaries and designated beneficiaries being told by their banks and advisors that they must withdraw the account over the five-year–rule period, and for most of them it is simply untrue. Say, for example, a beneficiary inherits through an estate of an IRA owner who died at 75. Will the five-year rule apply? NO! Even if there is no designated beneficiary (as is the case here because the estate is the beneficiary), the five-year rule can never apply when the IRA owner dies at 75, well after his RBD.

But what if there was a designated beneficiary on the inherited IRA and the IRA owner died before his RBD? Can the five-year rule ever apply in that case? Yes and no. Under the old rules it happened all the time, and as a result many designated beneficiaries withdrew their entire inherited account in five years when they did not have to. But, under the new rules, that should never happen anymore.

Part of the confusion over the five-year rule was that under the Proposed Regulations (1987–2000), even if you were the designated beneficiary, you had to know to elect the life expectancy method of calculating RMDs with the Single Life Expectancy

Table over the five-year rule. But you had to elect that by taking your first RMD as a beneficiary by the end of the year after the IRA owner's death. Almost nobody knew this. There was also no official election form or place to state that you want to use the life expectancy method. You just had to know, somehow, that it was available. If you did not know, the default was the five-year rule. Since the five-year rule was written in all the paperwork and books on IRAs as being the default, most banks and advisors assumed and told beneficiaries that it applied. Since under the five-year rule, you did not have to take any RMDs in the year after death or for three years after that (all you had to do was empty the account by the end of the five-year term), many beneficiaries waited until the last year to withdraw and pay the tax. By not taking a required distribution in the year after death (because the beneficiaries did not have to under the five-year rule), they blew the election of the life expectancy method and defaulted to the five-year rule. This is why so many designated beneficiaries who could have used the life expectancy method never did. All of that was changed in the 2001 Proposed and 2002 Final Regulations when the IRS brilliantly switched the default to protect beneficiaries from themselves and ill-informed financial institutions. This was a great provision from the IRS, truly helping so many beneficiaries hold on to their inherited accounts for the rest of their lives instead of being dumped in five years.

Beneficiaries no longer have to elect the life expectancy method. It is now the default and every designated beneficiary gets the life expectancy method. The five-year rule is still there, but you'd have to be stupid to elect it. No one should elect it. That's why if you are a designated beneficiary of an IRA owner who dies before his RBD, you automatically get to take your RMDs under the life expectancy method. Don't let anyone tell you the account has to be withdrawn in five years. That's not true anymore. If there is no designated beneficiary, however, and the IRA owner dies before his RBD, then the five-year rule is the only rule. The life expectancy method only applies to a designated beneficiary—because only a designated beneficiary has a life expectancy.

The IRA Owner Dies on or after His or Her RBD

Nonspouse Designated Beneficiary

Regardless of when the IRA owner dies, if there is a designated beneficiary, that person can stretch the postdeath RMDs over the beneficiary's own life expectancy using the Single Life Expectancy Table—just the same as if the IRA owner died before the RBD. If the IRA owner took no year-of-death distribution (or just a portion of it), then the designated beneficiary would have to take it (or the rest of it) by the end of the year of the owner's death and pay the income tax. The year-of-death RMD that the IRA owner did not take is paid directly to the beneficiary and the beneficiary, pays the income tax. The distribution is not paid to the estate of the IRA owner.

Regardless of when the IRA owner died, RMDs to the designated beneficiary must begin by the end of the year after the IRA owner's death. If the IRA owner died in 2005, the designated beneficiary must take the first RMD by the end of 2006, the year after the IRA owner's death.

There is one exception to the general rule that a designated beneficiary must use his or her own life expectancy to calculate RMDs if the IRA owner dies after the required beginning date. It is this: If the designated beneficiary is older than the IRA owner, then the designated beneficiary can use the age of the deceased to calculate postdeath RMDs. This is a nice break from the IRS that provides a rare opportunity for a designated beneficiary to stretch distributions over a life expectancy longer than his or her own. But it is only permitted when the IRA owner dies after the RBD and is younger than the designated beneficiary.

Let's look at a couple of examples of how to calculate postdeath RMDs if the owner dies after the RBD. The first example will show how to make the calculation in a situation where the general rule applies; the second will show how it's done when the exception applies.

EXAMPLE 1: GENERAL RULE SITUATION

A man dies in 2005 at age 76 (well after his RBD, but before taking his year-of-death RMD), leaving his $180,000 IRA to his designated beneficiary, a son, who is 28 and must take that year-of-death RMD. The year-of-death RMD is the RMD the IRA owner would have taken had he lived, so it is based on the IRA owner's life expectancy factor for his age in the year of his death. For a 76-year-old, the life expectancy factor, according to the Uniform Lifetime Table, which is what the IRA owner would have used, is 22.0 years. At December 31, 2004 (the end of the year prior to his death), the IRA balance was $180,000. So, the IRA owner's year-of-death RMD ($180,000 / 22.0) is $8,182. This is the amount the son will have to withdraw and pay tax on in 2005. And what about next year? Since the son, the designated beneficiary, was 28 the year his father died, he will look up the life expectancy factor from the Single Life Expectancy Table for a 29-year old—because that will be his age in the year after the IRA owner's death. That factor, according to the table, is 54.3 years. So, he will divide whatever the account balance is at December 31, 2005, by 54.3 to calculate his RMD for 2006. Thereafter, the son never has to refer to the Single Life Expectancy Table again as 54.3 years is his set-term withdrawal period. He will just reduce that number by 1 each subsequent year to calculate his RMD for 2007, 2008, and so on until the term is over or the account is emptied, whichever comes first.

EXAMPLE 2: EXCEPTION APPLIES

A man dies in 2005 at age 71 (after his RBD), leaving his IRA to his designated beneficiary, an uncle who is 88. Assume that the nephew took his year-of-death RMD before he died. The uncle therefore only has to deal with his own post-death RMDs on the inherited IRA, which will begin in 2006. Since the uncle is older, he can use the nephew's age in the year of death to calculate his own RMD. According to the Single Life Expectancy Table, the life expectancy of a 71-year-old is 16.3 years. That factor is reduced by one year for each future year RMD. The uncle then divides the December 31, 2005, IRA balance by 15.3 years (the 16.3 years less one year) to get a first-year RMD for 2006 (the first year after the IRA owner's death). The uncle will drop the set-term life expectancy factor of 15.3 years by 1 (to 14.3 years) to make the 2007 calculation, to 13.3 years for 2008, and so on.

No Designated Beneficiary

Unlike when an IRA owner dies before his or her RBD, if the IRA owner dies on or after that date and there is no designated beneficiary, then the IRA will be paid out over the IRA owner's remaining single life expectancy based on the IRA owner's age in the year of death—less 1 for each future year's distribution. (The five-year rule only applies when the IRA owner dies before his or her RBD.) If the IRA owner did not take a year-of-death distribution (or just a portion of it), then the beneficiary must take it (or the rest of it) and pay tax on it.

EXAMPLE

A man dies in 2004 at age 78 with no designated beneficiary. The IRA must be paid out over 10.4 years. The first distribution year is 2005, the year after the IRA owner's death. The first distribution must be taken by December 31, 2005, and then by each December 31 thereafter until the 10.4-

year term is up (unless the account is emptied before then). Where did I come up with a 10.4-year set term? The life expectancy factor of a 78-year-old (from the Single Life Expectancy Table) is 11.4 years. For 2005, the first distribution year, you would reduce the 11.4 factor by 1, yielding 10.4. You then divide the December 31, 2004, IRA balance by 10.4 to arrive at the RMD for 2005. For the 2006 distribution the factor will be 9.4 years. You then divide the December 31, 2005, IRA balance by 9.4 to arrive at the RMD for 2006. For 2007 it will be 8.4 years, for 2008 it will be 7.4 years, and so on.

The Beneficiary Is a Spouse

Now we're in variable Heaven—or Hell, depending upon one's point of view.

When you name a spouse (and I mean your spouse, not someone else's) as your IRA or company plan beneficiary, the spouse has great freedom of choice. But each choice may have ramifications:

Roll Over

The best option is called the *spousal rollover.* It does not mean your spouse has to physically roll over or play dead to inherit your retirement money. The spousal rollover provision allows your spouse to transfer your IRA to his or her IRA after your death. Your IRA then becomes your spouse's IRA, and he or she follows the rules for calculating RMDs based on the Uniform Lifetime Table the same as any IRA owner. The Single Life Table is used to calculate RMDs on inherited IRAs, but if the spouse rolls over or elects to treat the account as his or her own, the IRA is not treated as an inherited IRA. Under the tax code, an inherited IRA is an IRA inherited by someone other than the IRA owner's spouse.

When the spouse inherits, the IRA is treated as if it were always the spouse's IRA, so the spouse uses the Uniform Lifetime Table to calculate RMDs, the same as any IRA owner. The spousal rollover can be accomplished in two ways:

1. Rollover—where your spouse withdraws the balance from your IRA or company plan and deposits it in his or her IRA within 60 days.
2. Direct transfer—(also known as a trustee-to-trustee transfer)—where the funds go directly from your retirement account to your spouse's without your spouse touching the money in between. This is the preferred method for transferring funds from your IRA or plan to his or her IRA.

Under a provision in EGTRRA 2001, your spouse could roll over your IRA or plan to his or her own company plan—provided the company the spouse works for agrees to accept the funds in its plan.

Elect to Treat the IRA as His or Her Own

In this case, instead of moving the money from your IRA to his or hers, your spouse can simply put his or her name on your account. Now it's the spouse's IRA and is treated the same as if it were rolled over, subjecting the spouse to RMDs when he or she reaches his or her RBD. If the spouse is already past his or her RBD when the account is inherited, the spouse, whether treating the account as his or her own or rolling it over, must begin distributions on the IRA by the end of the year after your death. Treating an inherited IRA as his or her own IRA is the same as a rollover since in either case the spouse becomes the IRA owner and is no longer considered the beneficiary. The spouse must be the sole beneficiary to elect to treat the IRA as his or her own. But if he or she is one of several beneficiaries, the account can be split and the spouse can still be the sole beneficiary of his or her share of the account. The only difference is that with the spousal rollover, the funds must be

physically moved from the deceased IRA owner or plan participant's account to the spouse's IRA. By electing to treat the IRA as
their own, spouse beneficiaries do not have to move the money.
They can just retitle the account in their name as their own IRA.
Nonspouse beneficiaries can never retitle an account into their
own name. The spouse can be deemed to make the election to treat
the account as her own by not taking a required distribution or by
making an additional IRA contribution to the account. The IRS
figures that these two actions mean that the spouse beneficiary is
treating the account as her own IRA.

Remain as Beneficiary

The spouse can choose to neither roll the account over nor treat it
as his or her own.

Spouse Rolls Account Over or Treats It as His or Her Own

A spouse beneficiary rollover or a spouse's decision to treat the inherited IRA as his or her own without rolling it over yields the
same outcome: The spouse is no longer the beneficiary but is instead the *owner* of the account and treated by the IRS as if he or
she had *always* been the owner.

For example, if Peter dies in 2004 at age 66 (before RBD), des-
ignating his 62-year-old spouse Blanche beneficiary of his IRA,
and Blanche rolls the IRA over (or elects to not roll it over but to
treat the account as her own), she becomes the owner of the account. But as she is 62, she can delay taking her first-year RMD
until April 1, 2013, which is the April 1 after the year—2012—she
turns 70½ (although she would probably be better off taking her
first RMD by the end of 2012 to avoid paying tax on both first-
and second-year RMDs in 2013).

OK, let's use the same example but make Blanche 72. She can
roll the entire IRA account balance over to her own IRA (or elect
to treat it as her own) as before and not have to take any RMD for
Peter's year of death because he died before he was subject to

RMDs. As she herself is past 70½, however, once she rolls over, her first distribution year will be 2005 when she's 73. As the IRA is now hers, she'll look to the Uniform Lifetime Table for her life expectancy factor at age 73, which is 24.7 years. She then divides the December 31, 2004, IRA balance by 24.7 to arrive at her RMD for 2005. For 2006 and later years, she will simply repeat the process of looking at the Uniform Lifetime Table to determine the new life expectancy factor for each year's RMD.

Now, let's look at a couple of "after-RBD" scenarios where the spouse is beneficiary of the inherited IRA:

Ralph dies in 2004 at age 76 (after his RBD), leaving his IRA to his 62-year-old wife Sheila. If Sheila rolls the IRA over (or elects to treat the account as her own), she becomes the IRA owner. Just as in the first "before-RBD" example I gave you, since she is 62, she does not have to begin RMDs until she reaches her RBD at 70½, which will be in 2012 (although, again, she could delay to April 1, 2013, if she wanted).

In our new scenario, however, Ralph, at 76, was past his RBD and already taking his required distributions. If he died without taking his 2004 RMD, however, Sheila, even though she is not subject to RMDs until her own first distribution year of 2012, must take and pay tax on the distribution he would have taken had he lived. She cannot roll that amount over too because rolling over a required distribution is disallowed. So, if the IRA balance at December 31, 2003, were $400,000, then Ralph's RMD for 2004, based on the Uniform Lifetime Table life expectancy factor for a 76-year-old of 22.0 years, is $400,000/22.0 = $18,182. If he died before taking it, Sheila would have to take it. If he withdrew only part of it, she would only have to withdraw the remainder. If he only withdrew $10,000 in 2004, she would have to withdraw the remaining $8,182 after which she could roll the remainder of the IRA account balance over to her own IRA.

Now, let's make Sheila 72 years old instead of 62. Otherwise, the facts are the same: Her husband Ralph dies in 2004 at 76 (after his RBD) and leaves his IRA to her. As before, he went to his great reward before taking his 2004 distribution, so she must take it, and then she can roll the remainder of the IRA into her own account. Since she's over 70½, however, she must begin RMDs the year after Ralph's (the IRA owner's) death; in this case she must begin in 2005. Once rolled over, however, she becomes the IRA owner and so she will use the Uniform Lifetime Table for calculating her first-year (2005) RMD. In 2005, she'll be 73, so that's the age she will use to get her life expectancy factor, which is 24.7 years. Then she divides the December 31, 2004, IRA balance by 24.7 to arrive at her RMD for 2005. For later-year RMDs, she just repeats the process.

TIP!

As soon as a spouse rolls over or redesignates the account as his or her own, the Social Security number on the account should be changed to the spouse's number because it is now his or her account and the spouse will pay the income tax on distributions. Often, making that change is neglected and a 1099-R is issued with the deceased IRA owner's Social Security number. This should be addressed immediately after death. Even if the spouse chooses not to roll over and instead remains a beneficiary, the Social Security number on the IRA account should be changed to his or her number.

Spouse Chooses to Remain a Beneficiary

A rollover is generally the best move for a spouse who inherits, but the spouse can choose instead to remain a beneficiary and be subject to the same general rules as nonspouse beneficiaries. Why would a spouse want to do this instead of going the more advantageous rollover route? One situation where it pays off is if the spouse is much older than the deceased. But the main reason why a spouse would choose to remain a beneficiary would be when the spouse beneficiary is younger than the 59½-year eligibility age for withdrawing penalty-free.

For example, if Sadie, the footloose widow, is 40 when she inherits the IRA and does the rollover, the account then becomes hers, and she is no longer treated as a beneficiary but as an owner. If she wants to take any money out then, she must pay the 10 percent penalty assessed to retirement plan owners who tap into their retirement plan accounts before age 59½. (This 10 percent penalty does not apply to company retirement plan or IRA beneficiaries, only to owners, which Sadie has become.) And so, in cases like Sadie's, where the spouse beneficiary is much younger than 59½, it could pay to remain as beneficiary. This way, if she needs some of that IRA cash to live on, she can tap it penalty-free. Furthermore, choosing to remain a beneficiary does not restrict her from being able to roll over later on. Therefore, when she does hit 59½, the rollover option, with its attendant advantages, is still available.

If the spouse is the sole beneficiary and chooses to remain so rather than rolling over, then he or she must begin taking RMDs by whichever is later: December 31 of the year the IRA owner would have turned 70½, or December 31 of the year following the IRA owner's death.

This is an interesting provision because it can be used to delay RMDs when the IRA owner dies before reaching 70½. But it can only be used if the spouse is the sole beneficiary. If not, RMDs must begin the year following the IRA owner's death. If there are multiple individual beneficiaries, the account may be split so that each beneficiary is the sole beneficiary of that share. In such situations, the spouse would again qualify as a sole beneficiary—but only of his or her cut.

The real benefit of this provision is when the IRA owner dies before reaching 70½, especially if it's well before. In such cases, if the spouse chooses to remain as beneficiary instead of rolling over, he or she does not have to begin RMDs until the year the deceased would have turned 70½. That means if the deceased died at age 50, for example, the spouse could delay RMDs—and keep growing the account tax-deferred—for more than 20 years! (If the surviving spouse were younger than the deceased IRA owner, he or she could roll the IRA over just before the year the deceased would have turned 70½ and delay distributions even longer—because once the rollover occurs, the spouse beneficiary is deemed to be the IRA owner and can therefore wait until he or she reaches 70½ to begin RMDs under the rules.)

Once the spouse beneficiary hits his or her required beginning date, however, the spouse is better off rolling over than remaining a beneficiary. Why? Because the spouse will be able to use the longer life expectancy factors in the Uniform Lifetime Table (for IRA owners) for calculating RMDs instead of the Single Life Expectancy Table (for beneficiaries). The longer (or higher) the life expectancy factor, the lower the RMD and the lower the tax on that RMD.

Calculating RMDs When the Spouse Remains a Beneficiary

If a spouse—let's call her Rachel—chooses to remain a beneficiary (instead of rolling the IRA over or treating it as her own), she will have to take beneficiary payouts based upon her life expectancy using the Single Life Expectany Table. (She only uses the Uniform Lifetime Table when she rolls over because then she is deemed to be the IRA owner.) Though she uses the Single Life Expectancy Table to compute her RMDs, she still gets an advantage that other (i.e., nonspouse) beneficiaries don't: *She is permitted to recalculate.* This means that she gets to go back to the Single Life Expectancy Table each year and use the life expectancy factor for her age in the distribution year (just as IRA owners go back to the Uniform Lifetime Table each year to look up the figure for their ages). This is called *recalculating.* And it's an advantage because your life expectancy is always increasing, allowing you to stretch out your RMDs over a longer period of time. This will cut the tax bill each year and extend the life of the IRA. All IRA owners who are taking lifetime RMDs get to recalculate their life expectancy, but not all beneficiaries can recalculate. Only a spouse beneficiary who is the sole beneficiary can do that. A nonspouse beneficiary uses a set-term method where he looks up the term for his age from the Single Life Table only once (in the year after the IRA owner's death) and that is the payment period for the inherited IRA.

A WORD TO THE WISE

Whether the spouse beneficiary elects to roll over the inherited account or remain beneficiary, he or she should name a beneficiary and a contingent beneficiary on the account immediately! As you'll see in Chapter 6, neglecting to do this is the number-one mistake made by spouses who inherit because it is the key to the survival of the account after the spouse's death, and it's the key to keeping it in the family.

Recalculating vs. Not Recalculating (Using a Set Term)

To illustrate the difference between recalculating and not recalculating, here's an example:

Linda, 49, inherits an IRA from her husband Sy, age 72. She does not roll over. The year after her husband's death, she turns 50 and uses the life expectancy of a 50-year-old from the Single Life Expectancy Table to calculate RMDs. It is 34.2 years. For the next year, when she is 51 years old, she goes back to the table (she gets to recalculate) and uses a life expectancy for a 51-year-old of 33.3 years. She can do this every year. In 40 years if she's still kicking, she will be 91 years old and will go back to the Single Life Expectancy Table as she has done every year and will look up her life expectancy. The life expectancy for a 91-year-old is 5.2 years. (In fact a 111-year-old still has a life expectancy. It's one year!)

Let's compare this to a nonspouse beneficiary—a son, say—who is the same age as Linda was when he inherits. He is 50 years old in the year after the IRA owner's death, so he goes to the same Single Life Expectancy Table and looks up his life expectancy. For the first year it is the same 34.2-year life expectancy as Linda's. But that is the last year it will be the same because, as in this case, a nonspouse beneficiary cannot recalculate. Therefore, he cannot go back to the Single Life Expectancy Table each year the way Linda did. His life expectancy for calculating his RMDs is set at 34.2 years. For future years' distributions, he reduces that by a factor of 1 each year. For the next year, his factor is 33.2 years, then 32.2 years for the year after that and so on until the 34.2-year schedule has expired (unless the entire account balance has been withdrawn before then). This means that he would have to withdraw the remaining account balance when he is 84 years old, whereas Linda, who could recalculate, would have an additional 8.1-year life expectancy when she turns 84. But that does not mean that her account has to be emptied 8.1 years after she turns 84 years old. Remember, she gets to goes back to the table and recalculate a new life expectancy each year.

How Will RMDs Be Calculated When the Spouse Dies?

Let's say a Clara, age 55, is the sole beneficiary and chooses to remain a beneficiary (no rollover). But in 2010 she dies at age 61 before her husband Steve (the IRA owner) would have reached 70½ (he passed away at 57 in 2004).

The postdeath payout depends on whom Clara named as her beneficiary and whether she (Clara) dies before or after her husband would have reached age 70½. Most spouses who choose to remain a beneficiary either neglect or don't realize that even though they did not roll the IRA over to make it their own, they should immediately name a beneficiary. You'll see the difference it makes in this example.

If Clara had named her son Ken her beneficiary and in 2011 (the year after her death) he was 35 years old, Ken could use his life expectancy from the Single Life Expectancy Table to calculate his RMDs even though, technically, he is not the beneficiary. *He is the beneficiary's beneficiary.*

Under the general rules for inherited IRAs, a beneficiary's beneficiary cannot use his or her own life expectancy. Except in the case of this other special rule . . .

"Ed, not another rule! My head is going to explode!"
I hear you. Take two aspirin and call me in the morning.

OK, the sun's up. Back to work.

Here is that special rule. And if you're ever a beneficiary, you'll be glad that it exists.

Even though sonny boy Ken inherited the account from his mom (his dad's beneficiary), he can still use his own life expectancy because Mom chose to remain a beneficiary and died before Dad would have reached age 70½. Wow . . . that's a mouthful. But it fully describes the situation here.

The IRA owner (Dad) died at 57 in 2004 before his RBD and named his wife Clara (Mom) as beneficiary. Mom was under 59½ so she elected to remain a beneficiary in order to avoid the 10 percent penalty on any distributions taken before she reached age 59½. She was also smart enough to right away name a beneficiary, her son Ken. Then she died in 2010, well before her husband would have reached 70½. So, the special rule applies in this case, allowing Ken to use his own life expectancy based on his age of 35 in 2011 (the year after his mother's death) to calculate his RMDs with the Single Life Expectancy Table. This is the rule only when a spouse beneficiary has named a beneficiary and dies before the year the IRA owner would have reached age 70½.

But what if Ken's mom dies before his dad would have reached 70½ and she hasn't named a beneficiary? Ken will still inherit through her estate, but now the five-year rule applies. Why? Because Mom remained a beneficiary (instead of naming one) and died before Dad would have reached 70½, she is now treated as the IRA owner and deemed to have died without a designated beneficiary. Thus, Ken must empty the account of every penny no later than 2015 (the fifth year following Mom's death) and pay income tax on the distribution.

"What's the difference?" you ask.

The difference is 43.5 years. By naming Ken beneficiary rather than letting the IRA pass to him through her estate, Mom enabled Ken to extend the life of the IRA over his life expectancy of 48.5

years as opposed to being forced to empty it in five years after her death. The tax-deferred compounding on this kind of difference is exponential! So, looking at it the other way, Ken would have lost over 40 years of additional tax deferral if his mom had neglected to name a beneficiary.

OK, now let's look at what happens if a spouse beneficiary chooses to remain a beneficiary and dies after the IRA owner would have reached 70½. Then the IRA will be paid out over the spouse's own remaining life expectancy based on the spouse's age in the year of death using the Single Life Expectancy Table. The life expectancy would be reduced by 1 for each future year RMD.

For example, Andrew (the IRA owner) dies in 2004 at age 67, leaving his wife Beth, age 55, as the sole beneficiary of his IRA. She chooses to remain a beneficiary (no rollover) and dies in 2010 at age 61, neglecting to name a beneficiary.

Since Andrew would have been older than 70½ when his wife died, the five-year rule does not apply. Because Beth was 61 when she died, the life expectancy of a 61-year-old from the Single Life Expectancy Table (24.4 years) will be used to determine the payout period. The first distribution year is 2011 (the year after Beth's death). To arrive at the payout period in years, reduce 24.4 by a factor of 1 to get 23.4 years. For the second postdeath RMD (in 2012), reduce 23.4 by a factor of 1 to get 22.4 years. For 2013 it's 21.4 and so on until the original 23.4-year term expires (unless the IRA is withdrawn in full before then).

If Beth had named a beneficiary, the result would have been the same because she remained a beneficiary and died after her husband would have reached age 70½. In this case, Andrew (the IRA owner) would have reached age 70½ in 2007 and once Beth (the spouse beneficiary) lives into 2007, the special rule allowing her named beneficiary to use his or her own age is no longer available.

If Beth chooses to roll over the IRA to her own IRA, however, we have a different scenario. Once she rolls over, she is the IRA owner; any individual beneficiary she names is a designated beneficiary, and that person can spread distributions over his or her own life expectancy whether or not Beth reached 70½ by the time of her death. If she rolls the IRA over to her own IRA and neglects to name a beneficiary (or names her estate or other nondesignated beneficiary), then the IRA is paid out depending on when she died, the same as all IRA owners. If she died before her RBD with no designated beneficiary, the IRA will be paid out over the five-year rule. If she died on or after her RBD with no designated beneficiary, then the IRA will be paid out over her remaining life expectancy based on her age in the year of her death from the Single Life Table reduced by one year for each postdeath distribution.

Got it? Good.

Keeping Track of Multiple-Account RMDs

Staying on top of RMDs for one account is pretty easy, but if (like most people today) you have more than one IRA, 401(k), 403(b), or any other type of retirement account, including inherited IRAs, this task can easily become a confusing, tricky, time-consuming ordeal, especially if a person is at all disorganized (no, not you!).

To avoid headaches in dealing with multiple-account RMDs that could lead to making a costly mistake (such as missing an RMD on one account and getting hit with the 50 percent penalty for the error), take these four simple action steps:

Action Step 1: Make a List

Compile a complete list of all your retirement accounts, including company plans, 401(k)s, 403(b)s, 457 plans, Keogh plans, traditional IRAs (including SEP- and SIMPLE IRAs), and inherited IRAs or inherited Roth IRAs. This list should only include retirement accounts that are subject to required distributions. For example, you would not include your company plan if you are still working for that company (and you do not own more than 5 percent of it) because you are exempt from required distributions on that account until after you retire. You also would not include a Roth IRA since Roth IRA owners are not subject to required distributions. Roth IRAs inherited from someone other than your spouse, however, are subject to required distributions even though the required distributions may not be taxable.

When writing down your list of accounts, include the name, age, and relationship of the beneficiary to you on each account, so that you can ascertain whether the spousal exception applies; then you can separate that account from the others.

Another good reason for writing this information down is that it forces you to check that you have named a beneficiary on each account. You might find that you neglected to name a beneficiary in some cases. While not naming a beneficiary has no effect on *your* lifetime distributions, it's key to the "stretch-it" step I'll be covering in Chapter 6.

Action Step 2: Group Accounts by Category

Once you have accounted for all your retirement plans subject to RMDs, group them together by category. For example, all traditional IRAs, including SEP-IRAs and SIMPLE IRAs, go together. All inherited IRAs from the same person go together, but those inherited from a different person should be separated. Likewise, group all Roth IRAs inherited from the same person together, but keep Roths inherited from others separated. And if the spousal exception applies to any of your accounts, separate them from the pack too—because you will be using a different table for calculating RMDs. With the exception of Section 403(b) plans, company retirement plans stand individually. Do not group them with other company plans. Multiple accounts in one company plan, however, can be grouped together, but here again you must keep any spousal exception plans separate.

Action Step 3: Figure RMDs for Each Group

Use the Uniform Lifetime Table (Figure 5) or the IRS Joint Life Expectancy Table (Appendix I) to calculate the RMD for each group other than IRAs and Roth IRAs you have inherited; to do the

RMD calculation on these inherited accounts, you need your life expectancy figure from the Single Life Expectancy Table (Figure 6). Each group will produce a different RMD. This is why you need to figure RMDs separately for each group.

Action Step 4: Take Your RMD

You can take the entire distribution from one account or take several distributions equaling the entire amount from a combination of accounts within that same group. What you can't do, for example, is take a required IRA distribution from a 403(b) account or from a Roth IRA. Whichever account or combination of accounts within the same group that you decide to withdraw from, make sure that your total withdrawal at least equals your RMD; otherwise there's a 50 percent penalty. Also, if you have more than one group or category of plans, make sure that you have withdrawn the minimum from each group. You cannot satisfy one group's required distribution by taking more from another group.

Now that you've gotten the idea of how to keep track of multiple-account RMDs, let's go through the four actions using a real-world example—although if you have this many different accounts with all the bells and whistles, my hat's off to you because you're that rare bird with too much money!

Assume that you turned 70½ in July 2003. You won't be 71 by the end of the year, so you will use age 70 to figure required distributions. You have decided to take your first required distribution by the end of 2003 so that you won't have to take your first two RMDs in 2004. Your first RMD will be based on the balance in your retirement accounts as of December 31, 2002.

Action Step 1: Make a List

    1. IRA
    Your account balance at December 31, 2002 $100,000
    Your beneficiary: spouse, age 67 in 2003

2. IRA
Your account balance at December 31, 2002 $250,000
Your beneficiary: 3 children, ages 42, 40, and
34 (⅓ each)

3. IRA
Your account balance at December 31, 2002 $50,000
Your beneficiary: charity

4. SEP-IRA
Your account balance at December 31, 2002 $70,000
Your beneficiary: spouse, age 67 in 2003

5. Roth IRA
Your account balance at December 31, 2002 $65,000
Your beneficiary: spouse, age 67 in 2003
Note: Not subject to required distributions.

6. 401(k) from former company
Your account balance at December 31, 2002 $340,000
Your beneficiary: spouse, age 67 in 2003

7. 401(k) plan from company (still working)
Your account balance at December 31, 2002 $26,000
Your beneficiary: spouse, age 67 in 2003
Note: You don't own more than 5 percent of the company
so this plan is exempt from required minimum distribu-
tions until you retire.

Action Step 2: Group the Accounts by Category

Group the four IRA accounts, even though each has a different beneficiary, because the spousal exception does not apply; therefore,
the Uniform Lifetime Table will be used for life expectancy. Do not
include the Roth IRA in this group because Roth IRA owners are

not subject to RMDs. Include only one 401(k) company plan since there is no RMD on the other 401(k) because you are still working.

Group 1: My IRA(s)	Balance at December 31, 2002
Account # 1 IRA	$100,000
Account # 2 IRA	$250,000
Account # 3 IRA	$ 50,000
Account # 4 SEP-IRA	$ 70,000
Group 1 total:	**$470,000**
Group 2: My Company Plan(s)	**Balance at December 31, 2002**
Account # 6 401(k)	$340,000
Group 2 total:	**$340,000**

Action Step 3: Figure RMDs for Each Group

Group 1

Total balance, December 3, 2002	= $470,000
Life expectancy, age 70	= 27.4 years
RMD ($470,000/27.4)	= $17,153

Group 2

401(k) balance, December 31, 2002	= $340,000
Life expectancy, age 70	= 27.4 years
RMD ($340,000/27.4)	= $12,409

Action Step 4: Take Your Required Distribution

RMD for group 1 is $17,153. The $17,153 can be taken from any account or combination of accounts in group 1. RMD for group 2 is $12,409. The $12,409 must be taken from the 401(k) of the company you are retired from but not from the second 401(k) or from any other retirement account.

Now, let's tweak the example a bit by trading your spouse in for a younger model. Everything in the example remains the same except that your new spouse is 25 years old (don't you wish!). It's just an example so it's OK to dream.

To save space, I won't bother repeating the list of accounts since nothing will have changed except the age of the beneficiary spouse on accounts # 1, #4, and #6. So, let's move on.

Action Step 2: Group the Accounts by Category

As before, group the four IRA accounts, but now separate the IRAs naming your 25-year-old spouse as beneficiary from the other IRAs. Since the spousal exception now applies to the two accounts in group 1(a), the IRS Joint Life Expectancy Table (Appendix I) will be used to calculate RMDs. The Uniform Lifetime Table will be used to calculate the RMD for the remaining two accounts in group 1(b).

Group 1(a): My IRA(s)	Balance at December 31, 2002	
Account # 1 IRA	$100,000	Spousal exception applies
Account # 4 SEP-IRA	70,000	Spousal exception applies
Group 1(a) total:	**$170,000**	

Group 1(b): MY IRA(s)	Balance at December 31, 2002
Account # 2 IRA	$250,000
Account # 3 IRA	50,000
Group 1(b) total:	$300,000
Group 2: My Company Plan(s)	Balance at December 31, 2002
Account # 6 401(k) $340,000	Spousal exception applies
Group 2 total: $340,000	

Action Step 3: Figure RMDs for Each Group

Group 1(a)

Total balance at December 31, 2002	= $170,000
Life expectancy, ages 70 and 25	= 58.3 years
RMD ($170,000/58.3)	= $2,916

Group 1(b)

Total balance at December 31, 2002	= $300,000
Life expectancy, age 70	= 27.4 years
RMD ($300,000/27.4)	= $10,949
Combined total, groups 1(a), 1(b)	= $13,865

Group 2

Total 401(k) balance at December 31, 2002	= $340,000
Life expectancy, ages 70 and 25	= 58.3 years
RMD ($340,000/58.3)	= $5,832

Action Step 4: Take Your Required Distribution

The $13,865 RMD for groups 1(a) and (b) can be taken from any account or combination of accounts in group 1, but not from group 2. Similarly, the $5,832 RMD for group 2 must be taken from that account, not from your other company plan.

A WORD TO THE WISE

Don't wait until the last minute of the last day of the distribution year to take your RMDs. There could be a delay at the financial institution holding onto your money because of a landslide of other last-minute RMDs, or an emergency situation may occur on the homefront that temporarily knocks all thoughts of RMDs from your mind until it's too late to take it without incurring a 50 percent penalty. I recommend taking your RMD before Thanksgiving. That way, you know that you've taken care of it in time, and you can enjoy the holidays.

You're probably wondering at this point how you could ever have taken a distribution safely before reading this book.

Well, guess what? You're not home free yet.

There's more.

Keep reading.

FIVE

Step #2: Insure It

"I've got all the money I'll ever need—if I die by four o'clock."
—Henny Youngman (1906–98), comedian

Hall of Shame

If you're not a baseball fan, then the name Bill Buckner probably doesn't ring a bell. But if you follow the game, you'll recognize it as one of the most ignominious names in the history of baseball.

Bill Buckner was the first baseman for the Boston Red Sox in the 1986 World Series when the Sox were matched against my favorite team, the New York Mets. It was Game 6. The Red Sox were an out away from winning a World Series for the first time in 68 years. The ball was pitched. The Mets batter swung and connected with a thunderous *c-r-a-c-c-k-k-k*, sending the ball straight to first base and the outstretched arms of Bill Buckner, who flubbed the catch before the stunned but elated crowd in New York's Shea Stadium, letting the ball roll between his legs!

Thanks to this colossal error, the Mets were able to pull their fanny from the fire, win the game that night, and go on to win Game 7 and the World Series title. The city of Boston has never forgiven Bill Buckner. Last I heard, he'd moved to Idaho, which apparently still wasn't far enough for Boston fans, who use epithets such as "loser" and "through-the-legs Bill" (and others that are even worse) rather than let his name pass their lips. To Boston Red Sox fans in particular, and to baseball fans in general, Bill Buckner remains but one thing: the Man Who Dropped the Ball.

Now, what if I told you that Bill Buckner was also one of the best players ever to play the game of baseball? Would you be shocked? Disbelieving? I know I was when I heard that exact statement made in a recent show about Buckner called "Beyond the Glory" on the Fox Sports Network. Being an accountant by trade, I decided to do my own audit of Buckner's statistics to see if the show was right.

But how would I find those statistics? Easy. I went to a local baseball card store and asked the owner if he had any old Bill Buckner cards for sale. He looked at me like I'd sprouted two heads. "Why would you want a Bill Buckner card?" he asked. "*Nobody* wants them. That's why I don't carry any. We'd never sell them." But I persisted, and he said he'd check around the baseball card grapevine to see if he could come up with one.

I went back in a few weeks and, lo and behold, he'd managed to dig up a few old Bill Buckner cards for me.

"How much?" I asked.

He said, "They're worthless. You can have 'em for free."

I thanked him, took the cards home, and quickly checked Bill Buckner's statistics. Fox was right. The numbers were astounding!

Bill Buckner played 22 seasons. Only 25 players in the history of baseball have played more games than he did. He'd scored more hits than 70 percent of the players currently in the Baseball Hall of Fame, including such superstar names as Mickey Mantle, Ernie Banks, Reggie Jackson, Johnny Bench, and even Ted Williams (pre-thawed). He had 500 more hits than Joe DiMaggio!

When Buckner played for the Chicago Cubs, he won a National League batting title. In fact, if you visit Wrigley Field, the home of the Cubs, his star is embedded in the concrete walk of fame outside the stadium. Throughout his career, Buckner also was an exceptional fielder. He genuinely was one of the greatest players the game of baseball has ever had. And yet he will be forever locked in the Baseball Hall of Shame for that one slip-up at the end of his career that cost the Red Sox the World Series.

As I pondered the ill-fated career of Bill Buckner, I found myself thinking, "He's a lot like an IRA. He had such a brilliant career, accumulated so much, but in the end lost it all due to one error, and now his name is mud."

Is that how you want your family to remember you? As the guy (or gal) who dropped the ball?

How Retirement Accounts Are Lost

Most people don't think about it much, but the combination of estate and income taxes can easily consume an IRA of any size. Even though the latest tax law (EGTRRA 2001) repeals the estate tax in 2010, it comes back in 2011, which is ridiculous and likely to change (probably for the worse) many times before 2010. Therefore, assume that when you die, an estate tax will be levied on your retirement account, especially if it's a large retirement account. By *large,* I mean an account that, combined with the value of the rest of the property in your estate, will exceed the year-of-death estate tax exemption. Currently that exemption is $1,500,000 per person, which means that you get to leave this earth and know that the first $1,500,000 in your estate will go to whomever you wish, free of estate tax—except for your spouse, who can inherit an unlimited amount from your estate completely free of estate tax, provided he or she is a U.S. citizen. For nonspouse beneficiaries, all bets are off after the exempted first $1,500,000; your IRA is then subject to estate taxes on all the rest, plus the income tax on the IRA, which means that they'll pay and pay BIG—upwards of 90 percent in combined tax! Outrageous? You bet, but unfortunately not impossible—because estate tax currently runs at 49 percent, and the top federal and state income tax bracket can total 40 percent. Combined, that's a possible 89 percent tax on a large inherited retirement account. If your state income tax and/or state estate tax rates are higher, then the total erosion of that account you worked so hard to build up and leave to your children and grandchildren could easily exceed 90 percent.

If you think 90 percent is an appallingly high number, you'll be even more appalled to learn that it's actually an improvement! It wasn't all that long ago that the combined tax was 95 percent—because federal estate tax was running at 55 percent on top of the 40 percent income tax rate. Our legislators were so shocked when they realized this that they exclaimed, "That's not enough! A combined 95 percent tax on retirement accounts? We can't have that! We're leaving people with too much of their own money!" So, they added a third tax, called the excise or excess accumulations tax, of 15 percent on top of the 95 percent so the combined tax to nonspouse beneficiaries on an inherited retirement account could have exceeded 100 percent! I called this the "taxation trifecta!" All it took was one taxpayer to hit this triple and the laws got changed. Here's how.

A young man inherited a very large IRA and got socked with all three taxes. Finding himself having to kick in 103 percent in combined income, estate, and excise tax (thus becoming, in effect, a negative beneficiary), he screamed to the IRS, "I didn't even know the guy!" "But he's your father," the IRS replied.

In a landmark case, the young man took the IRS to court, where he found a sympathetic judge who ruled in his favor. "No longer can you take more than 100 percent of what a person has!" the judge instructed the IRS with mathematical as well as legal precision, and by 1996 the 15 percent excise tax was repealed. But until then, it was literally possible to lose more in taxes on an inherited retirement account than was actually even in the account! So, the fact that today you can only lose up to 90 percent if you don't follow the precepts of this book is good news (I guess).

When it comes to retirement accounts, it's not enough to earn great investment returns. Yes, that's important in building the account, but even if you earn 30 percent a year, every year, for 30 years, what good is it if, at the end of the line, up to 90 percent of the account's value is lost—which can happen if the funds aren't there to pay the combined estate and income taxes on an inherited IRA, and so the IRA itself must used to pay those taxes. Remem-

Figure 7. The Death of an IRA

Column 1	Column 2	Column 3	Column 4
Amount Withdrawn to Pay Estate Tax	Income Tax Owed on Amount Withdrawn to Pay Estate Tax	Funds Left to Pay Estate Tax	Estate Tax Actually Paid
$ 4,900,000	x 40% = $1,960,000	$2,940,000	$2,940,000
1,960,000	x 40% = 784,000	1,176,000	4,116,000
784,000	x 40% = 313,600	470,400	4,586,400
313,600	x 40% = 125,440	188,160	4,774,560
125,440	x 40% = 50,176	75,264	4,849,824
50,176	x 40% = 20,070	30,106	4,879,930
20,070	x 40% = 8,028	12,042	4,891,972
8,028	x 40% = 3,211	4,817	4,896,789
3,211	x 40% = 1,284	1,927	4,898,716
1,284	x 40% = 514	770	4,899,486
514	x 40% = 206	308	4,899,794
206	x 40% = 82	124	4,899,918
82	x 40% = 33	49	4,899,967
33	x 40% = 13	20	4,899,987
13	x 40% = 5	8	4,899,995
5	x 40% = 2	3	4,899,998
2	x 40% = .80	1.20	4,899,999.20
.80	x 40% = .32	.48	4,899,999.68
.32	x 40% = .13	.19	4,899,999.87
.13	x 40% = .06	.07	4,899,999.94
Totals	**$3,266,666**		**$4,900,000.00**

This chart shows how a $10,000,000 IRA can shrivel immediately due to the interplay of estate and income taxes. Every time a withdrawal is made to pay estate taxes (column 1), then income tax is owed at an estimated 40 percent federal and state rate (column 2). Column 3 shows how much is left to cover estate taxes after the income tax on the original withdrawal is paid. Column 4 shows how much estate tax is actually paid. The total combined estate and income tax ($3,266,666 + $4,900,000) is $8,166,666—that's 81.67 percent of the IRA lost immediately if there are no other funds but those in the IRA to pay the estate tax. The IRD deduction (see Chapter 8) can reduce the overall tax somewhat, but the major damage is irreversible.

ber the Bill Buckner story? It's the score at the end of the game that counts (see Figure 7).

Who Is Most at Risk?

People who don't have much else in the way of assets other than their retirement accounts, as well as those with million-dollar IRAs, are most in danger of losing their savings due to the combination of taxes I've described.

If an IRA must be tapped to pay tax when the IRA owner dies, the result is a cycle of taxation that doesn't stop until the beneficiaries are so punch drunk that they don't know what's happened to them, let alone to their IRA.

Why do IRA owners let their life savings fall into such an abyss? The reason can be summed up in a single word: *admiration*.

Rather than doing whatever is takes (even—oh, horror of horrors!—spending some money) to keep their accounts from being sacked and pillaged by the IRS after they're gone, they just sit there admiring how much the balance is.

For example, I have a client with a $16 million IRA (no, he's not a crooked inside trader or an absconding CEO; hard to believe, but he made it the old-fashioned way: honestly). When he shows me his account statements with such prideful admiration, mesmerized by the mushrooming size of this single most valuable asset he owns, I have to snap him out of it with a harsh dose of reality. "This isn't your money in these statements," I tell him. "You're not going to keep any of this. This money is only temporarily attached to your letterhead. If you just sit there looking at it without taking any measures to protect it, it'll be lost after you die. Do something now while you are still alive and options to protect that money for your heirs still exist."

Many people with retirement accounts, especially those with large ones, believe the money in these accounts is sacred and should never to be touched until you're absolutely forced to at age 70½.

That's wrong. You can, and should, touch it. Real wealth is built by leveraging what you have to prevent an ultimate loss.

Life Insurance—Your Retirement Account's Best Defense

The single best, most cost-effective yet amazingly underutilized strategy for protecting retirement account balances, especially large ones, from being decimated by the highest levels of combined taxation is buying life insurance to offset the tax burden beneficiaries may face.

TIP!

There are some offsetting income tax deductions available to beneficiaries as well, but even these IRD (income in respect of a decedent) deductions, which will be explained in detail in Chapter 8, can only lower the overall carnage from a potential high of 90 percent to about 70 percent—at best.

As a tax advisor I'm always helping families to sort out their postdeath tax filings after the loss of a loved one so they can move ahead with their lives. And all too frequently I run into situations where families are financially devastated by taxes because of what was left undone. This should never happen—because it can almost always be avoided. That's why life insurance exists. And yet so many people ignore it, put it off, see it as an unnecessary expense, or are just too cheap to buy—only to wish they had when the day comes that The Biggest Check They'll Ever Get arrives, and they watch the taxman snatch most of it away.

Don't get me wrong. I'm not a shill for the insurance industry. I don't sell life insurance. But I believe in the concept as the best defense against confiscatory taxation for your family. In fact, not only am I believer, but I practice what I preach by carrying a substantial amount of life insurance to provide for my family in that critical area. And you should too!

If the only money available to pay the life insurance premiums is in the IRA, then you should withdraw from the IRA to make those premium payments. Since withdrawals at age 70½ are mandatory, why not begin the beguine early, take out the money that will have to be withdrawn then anyway, pay the income tax on it now, and use the rest to leverage your IRA into a fortune by buying life insurance?

To be absolutely clear about this in case you read the preceding paragraph with blinding enthusiasm, you cannot actually buy life insurance with IRA money. Tax law prohibits this. When I say, "Use the IRA to buy life insurance," I mean you must withdraw first and pay the income tax due on the withdrawal. Then you are free to use the after-tax amount to pay the insurance premiums. If this is your only option, take it—because the results in the long run will be worthwhile. Don't just sit there admiring your balance, afraid to touch it, or go cheap on me here, like the fellow in this true-life horror story from my file drawer marked "Penny-wise and Pound-Foolish."

Rob and his wife Sue came to me five years ago for some estate planning. Rob's estate consisted largely of an IRA (about $6 million) plus some other assets. My advice was straightforward: Buy life insurance to protect the IRA from estate tax. I recommended $3 million worth (approximately half the value of the IRA).

"Absolutely, positively, categorically NO," Rob said, putting his foot down literally and figuratively.

"Why not?" I asked.

"First, because I hate insurance companies. They're thieves," he answered. "And second, because it isn't necessary. I'm leaving the entire IRA to my wife, and you told me spouse beneficiaries are exempt from estate tax."

True enough, I replied. "But what if Sue dies first?"

He had no answer to that except that statistics were on his side, and he remained adamant about "not spending a dime extra that can be saved."

Sue on the other hand could see what I was driving at; she realized that the insurance was necessary to protect what they had earned for their four children. So, she decided she would buy her own policy, about $2 million worth, even though she knew the premiums would be high because she was not in the best of health at the time. But she had the money and went ahead on my recommendation, correctly setting up the policy outside her estate so that none of the insurance money would be subject to estate taxes. It could be used instead by her children to offset the estate tax bill on the $6 million IRA and other assets she inherited from Rob (assuming he did die first) that would be due when she passed away.

As things turned out, however, Sue did die first, and her four children inherited the $2 million worth of life insurance she'd bought, each receiving a $500,000 check estate- and income-tax–free.

No longer hating insurance companies, Rob opted to heed the advice I'd given him when he and his wife first came to me five years ago. He tried to get that $3 million life insurance policy I'd recommended.

Unfortunately, it was too late.

Had he applied five years sooner, he would have had no problem, but Rob had become quite ill in the meantime, and no insurance company would cover him at any price.

All I could do was advise his four kids to hold on tight to the $2 million they'd received from their mother's death because when Rob dies and his IRA passes to them, they will need every cent of it—and more!—to pay for his mistake.

Poor Rob. He thought he was saving money.

Keeping Life Insurance Estate-Tax–Free

Life insurance money is already income-tax–free, but if you're not careful, it will be subject to estate tax. You should set up the policy, as Sue did, so that it is not included as an asset of your estate. If it is included, its value is effectively cut in half. Here's how:

If you own the policy yourself and it is worth, say, $1 million, then when you die, that $1 million will be included in your estate, entitling Uncle Sam to roughly half of it, with the remaining $500,000 going to your beneficiaries (e.g., your family). Not only is that highway robbery, it's inefficient. Nevertheless, that is how most people set up life insurance—but only because they do not know any better.

The better strategy is *not to own your own life insurance*. Think about it. Why would you want to own your own life insurance, seeing as how it pays off only after you die? What are you going to do with it then? Why own a policy you can't benefit from? Just to control where it goes? That can be done without owning it!

OK, if you shouldn't own it, who should?

Your beneficiaries!

Have them own the policy and pay the premiums from money you gift to them. If your beneficiaries are young, or if you want some postdeath control on how the money is spent, you can set up an irrevocable life insurance trust (ILIT). That's what I have for my family. The trust owns the policy and my trustee pays the premiums from money I deposit into the trust.

Whether you choose beneficiary direct ownership or an ILIT, the main point is that you do not own the insurance when it pays off; therefore the proceeds will be excluded from your estate. Your goal is to keep all or as much as possible of your retirement account intact. Sufficient insurance money to cover the estimated estate tax will avoid having to invade the account for that purpose, and will give your beneficiaries the maximum to work with in stretching the account over their lifetimes, turning it over several decades or more into a tax-sheltered fortune (see Chapter 6). If the account is lost to taxes before your beneficiaries get it, there'll be nothing left to stretch, so the key to retaining retirement account money for the next generation is to make sure that it stays whole when you're gone.

What if There Is No Estate Tax?

After all, the estate tax is supposed to get repealed in 2010, right?

Never assume anything.

Proper planning should always include the probability that there will be some cost of dying. After all, the government needs money. If it can't be gotten from estates, it'll be gotten from taxing something else. So what if estate taxes are slated for repeal? The year 2010 is a long way off. Anything can happen. Besides, a tax never really gets repealed, you know. Its name is just changed so you'll think it's been repealed. That's what gets votes. So, don't start canceling your policy or scratching life insurance from your "to-do" list just yet.

Even if there is no estate tax, your beneficiaries may have to deal with tax on the capital gains buildup of appreciated assets in your account. Life insurance can be used to pay that tax. It can also be used to provide tax-free money for beneficiaries so they do not have to withdraw amounts in excess of their required minimum distributions. This will keep their income taxes lower, since the excess IRA distributions would have been taxable. It will also allow them to stick to the schedule they've set up to stretch the account (see Chapter 6), instead of having to deplete the account before its time. If you have no retirement account, the life insurance can also serve as a pension alternative, providing your beneficiaries with a tax-free stream of cash for the rest of their lives. And if you are young and have not yet built up a substantial retirement account, life insurance can provide instant cash for your family. That can be essential if you have small children—because even a small life insurance policy can be a big help when the worst happens.

Life insurance has many other uses beyond the scope of this book,

---

TIP!

I have a credo: *"Don't shop for bargains in parachutes, toilet paper, or life insurance. They're too important for cutting costs."* Forget about the latest cut-rate deals at "Policies-to-Go.com." Find yourself a living, breathing, professional insurance agent on the other end of the phone to work with you and your family to advise and guide you.

He should represent a brick-and-mortar insurance company with a solid reputation (Think about it: Who will your family call when they have to collect on a dot-com policy—especially if the dot com is dot gone by then?) Ask friends or business associates to refer an agent they trust and respect. That's the best way to find someone. But if that doesn't pan out, look for an agent who is a member of the Million Dollar Round Table (MDRT), a top-of-the-line insurance industry group made up of the finest insurance professionals in the world. Check out the group's web site at www.mdrt.org.

so I'll leave it at this: Tax-free cash is always the best source of money and solves a lot of nontax problems, as well as tax problems.

How Much Life Insurance Should You Have?

You should have enough to cover the taxes and other expenses that must be paid on your estate after you're gone. To do that you will need to know the balance in your account at the time of your death, which means you will have to project that balance. You cannot go by today's market or values—because if you have an IRA that's worth, say, $1 million right now and you are only 60 years old, that IRA could easily be worth $5 million or more over the long term given today's long life expectancies.

A good rule of thumb is to buy enough life insurance to cover at least 50 percent of the projected value of your estate at your death. This may seem like a lot of insurance to buy now, but remember what happened to Rob. As you and your account grow older and fatter, not only will purchasing more life insurance become an increasingly expensive proposition, but if your health deteriorates, you may become uninsurable.

A quick way to estimate the value of your IRA (without taking withdrawals or taxes into account) is to use the "rule of 72." This is a little math trick that shows how many times over the years your retirement account money will double at a given interest rate. Don't panic. You don't have to be Good Will Hunting to do the calculation. Just divide 72 by an estimated average interest rate. For example, if you use a conservative interest rate of, say, 6 percent, that means your money will double every 12 years (72/6 = 12). An 8 percent rate would double your money every 9 years (72/8 = 9), and so on.

Let's use the rule of 72 with some dollar figures, and say your IRA isn't a million but $300,000, and you're not 60 years old but 50 (with a life expectancy of 86).

Using an average 8 percent interest rate for the rest of your life (that may not seem like a very conservative average to you, but over the long haul it is), the value (straight growth excluding withdrawals or taxes) of your $300,000 IRA will double every nine years (72/8 = 9), so that by the time you reach 86, your $300,000 IRA will have doubled four times and be worth $4.8 million! The first time it doubles, it will go to $600,000, then, after another nine years, to $1.2 million, then to $2.4 million, and finally to $4.8 million. If you start with a $500,000 IRA at age 50 and use the same 8 percent interest rate, your IRA would grow to $8 million by the time you reach 86. And a $1 million IRA would grow to a staggering $16 million!

It is absolutely astounding what compound interest can do, especially in a tax-deferred account such as an IRA. This is why I am so insistent that even people with modest retirement accounts need life insurance. Through the magic of compounding, even the smallest accounts can well exceed the estate tax exemption (currently at $1 million) come inheritance time.

What Kind of Life Insurance Should You Buy?

OK, this is where I draw the line, or I will start sounding like a shill for the insurance industry. You must rely on your own professional insurance advisor for guidance here.

Whatever kind you buy, though, what I can tell you is this: The policy should be set up so that it pays off when funds are needed after death.

"But don't all insurance policies pay off at death?" you ask.

No, they don't, because some people buy survivorship life insurance (also known as second-to-die insurance), which insures both spouses at the same time but only pays off when both spouses are deceased.

A second-to-die policy is usually much less expensive than a single-life policy, but it may cause problems if you need cash after the first death. Here's why:

When one spouse dies and leaves everything to the other spouse, there is generally no estate tax regardless of how much the spouse inherits. But even if there is no estate tax due, when the first spouse dies, the second spouse will still need cash to continue the premiums on the second-to-die policy which does not pay off until he or she dies. If there is no other cash available, the surviving spouse may not be able to maintain the policy. So, if you buy a second-to-die policy, it might be best to couple it with a single-life policy on each spouse for a smaller amount. That way, there is at least enough cash available at the first death to continue the premiums on the larger second-to-die policy.

In addition to being less expensive, second-to-die policies do have this advantage over single-life policies though: If one spouse is uninsurable, insurance can still be purchased since qualifying for coverage is based on two lives.

If you want to protect an IRA for your children so they can stretch it out over their own life expectancies after you die, then you are better off with a policy on your life alone, as you will see in the next chapter.

Leverage It or Lose It

It is important to look at life insurance not as an expense that must be suffered to achieve a desired end, but as a solution to a problem. You can set it up in any number of creative ways to provide the funds needed to protect your retirement account from the taxman, leaving it free to grow tax-deferred for years.

Consider this scenario that shows how life insurance can be set up to provide leverage and tax-free cash for a surviving spouse.

Ralph and Sadie, a married couple, have a $1 million IRA but few other assets besides their home, which is worth $500,000. The IRA belongs to Ralph. They have a 40-year-old daughter, Ruby.

I suggest to Ralph that he leave the $1 million IRA not to his wife Sadie, but to their daughter Ruby instead. This way, when Ralph dies, Ruby will receive the $1 million IRA estate-tax–free because it passes under the estate tax exemption (currently at $1 million, but that ceiling could always change), and by naming Ruby rather than his wife, Ruby gets to stretch distributions over her longer life expectancy, adding potentially another 40 years of tax-deferred growth to the IRA (see Chapter 6) that could turn into millions!

"Hey, wait a minute, Ed," Sadie says, looking steamed. "I see our daughter getting rich on this suggestion, which is OK by me, but what the heck am I supposed to live on?"

Yes, that is a problem, I tell her. "How much do you need?"

"Well, I need the $1 million IRA, don't I?" she replies.

I make another suggestion. "How would you like $1 million tax-free instead? There would be no age-70½ distribution rules; anytime you need money, you just withdraw it, tax-free. That's better than a tax-infested IRA, isn't it?"

"Of course! But where do I find that pot of gold at the end of the rainbow?" she asks.

"Life insurance," I answer.

I advise Ralph to buy a $1 million life insurance policy and name Sadie as beneficiary. He can set it up as a plain vanilla policy and even own it himself with no need for a trust. There will be no estate tax since it will pass to his spouse, Sadie. The premiums will be paid from the IRA.

After Ralph's death, their daughter Ruby will receive what's left in the IRA free of estate tax (up to the existing estate tax exemption, of course, at the time of her father's death) as before and be able to stretch required distributions over her lifespan if she wishes, turning it into millions.

Meanwhile, Sadie receives Ralph's $1 million tax-free life insurance policy to spend as she wishes—a much better alternative than inheriting and paying income tax on the IRA. So, together Sadie and Ruby wind up with more than the family started with, and their cash needs are solved for life, estate-tax–free.

But it gets better.

I now suggest that Sadie use some of that tax-free life insurance money to buy a $1 million policy of her own, and set it up outside the estate, naming her daughter Ruby as beneficiary. During Sadie's lifetime she will have unrestricted use of the tax-free life insurance money she inherited from her husband, so she can gift enough each year to Ruby to pay the premiums on the new policy. After Sadie's death, Ruby will receive her mother's life insurance policy, inheriting potentially another $1 million of tax-free money.

When all is said and done, this family will have both protected and leveraged a single IRA into a tax-free family fortune. How? With plain old life insurance, that's all!

The "Rollback" Strategy

Remember at the beginning of this chapter where I wrote that you can't use IRA money to buy life insurance—how you must first withdraw the funds, pay the income tax on the withdrawal, and then use what's left to pay the insurance premiums? Well, nothing's changed since you read that part. It's still true. But wouldn't it be great if you could use the IRA money to buy the life insurance without having to withdraw it first and pay the income tax? Imagine how much more money you'd have available to buy life insurance with if you didn't first have to pay that pesky income tax on the withdrawal?

Well, check this out.

That crazy tax law EGTRRA 2001 features a provision that does let you buy life insurance that way! You still cannot use money within your IRA to buy the life insurance, but as you'll recall from Chapter 3, taxable IRA funds can be rolled over to a company plan—and company plans can purchase life insurance!

Are you thinking what I'm thinking?

If your company plan (your Keogh plan, for example) allows you to purchase life insurance and you have lots of cash in your IRA, then you can roll the IRA funds over to your Keogh plan and use that money to buy the life insurance without paying the income tax. No, you're not hallucinating. This is a legitimate strategy, called a *rollback*. Not every company plan will allow it (most big company plans won't), but if you have your own company, or are a partner in a law firm, medical practice, accounting firm, or other business where you can customize your own plan, the rollback strategy is doable.

In effect, what you're doing is using your IRA money to buy life insurance, but it's not prohibited in this case because the insurance is actually being purchased with company plan funds rolled over from your IRA.

You cannot play games with this strategy, though. There are rules to follow. For example, you cannot create a dummy company just to have a vehicle to roll the IRA funds to for buying insurance. That's a sham and against the law.

So, there you have the "Insure It" step. It really is amazing to see how powerfully a creative but simple life insurance plan can build tax-free wealth, isn't it? Can you imagine choosing up to 90 percent taxation on your retirement account when this alternative exists? And yet many hundreds of thousands continue do just that, even with professional advice.

But you're not going to be one of them, are you?

You've seen the light!

And now that you know how easy it is to insure it . . . wait'll you see how much fun it is to strrretch it.

SIX

Step #3: Stretch It

*"There's no reason to be the richest man in the cemetery.
You can't do any business from there."*
—Colonel Harlan Sanders (1890–1980),
founder, Kentucky Fried Chicken

A Process, Not a Product

The term *stretch IRA* is an invented one; perhaps that's why many people think of it as a product they can buy off the shelf. It goes by other names as well—the *legacy IRA*, the *super IRA*, the *multigenerational IRA,* the *dynasty IRA,* the *hundred-year IRA,* among others. But I like *stretch IRA* because it tells it like it is. Nevertheless, when I inform my clients about it, I invariably get a phone call a few days later that goes something like this:

"Ed, I'm at the bank. I asked for a stretch IRA. They don't have one! Where can I pick one up?"

I'm tempted sometimes to say, "Have you tried Home Depot or Staples?" But I never do because I realize that where taxes and money are concerned, people assume the worst. Even a simple and straightforward concept such as the stretch IRA *must* be complicated because it has to do with finances, and so they let themselves become confused. Of course, some advisors and financial institutions don't help; many of them make it sound like something so involved that only they can do it for you.

There are no stretch IRA stores at the mall. You can't get a stretch IRA online or via mail order either. There are no sales at your local bank. A stretch IRA is a process, not a product—and every IRA can be stretched, regardless of the age of the owner.

To "stretch" is to keep your inherited account growing tax-deferred (or tax-free if it's a Roth IRA; see Chapter 7) by your beneficiaries for as long as is legally possible. That's it. And under the latest version of the IRS rules, it's easier than ever. You can also change beneficiaries anytime you like without increasing required distribution amounts.

You might say, as many of my clients have, "Let my kids deal with this stretching business after I'm gone." But that may never happen—because in order to gain the best possible stretch option, all the pieces have to be put in place by the IRA owner while he or she is still breathing. You cannot leave this to your beneficiaries because there is little they can do to change things if they were not planned out properly by you. They can't go back and undo your decisions (or lack of them) after you're dead. That's like playing the home movies of your wedding backwards in the belief that you'll become single again. What's done is done. And if you don't make the right choices now, your beneficiaries will be stuck.

The stretch option isn't mandatory, of course. Your beneficiaries can always withdraw more than the yearly minimum and empty the account fast if they wish. But they have to be aware of the option first in order to know whether they want to take advantage of it. So, make sure they read and absorb this chapter . . . after you do.

Stretch 401(k)s Too? Yes and No

You may be wondering why I use the term *stretch IRA* but never *stretch 401(k)*, *stretch company plan*, or *stretch 403(b) plan*.

That's because they generally don't exist.

Many times throughout this chapter I will say that if you do everything right, your beneficiaries are guaranteed the option of

STEP #3: STRETCH IT ■ 165

stretching required distributions from your IRA over their lifetime. But the same is not true if they inherit from your company retirement plan. They may be able to get a stretch from the plan but that is unlikely.

Even though the tax rules allow the stretch for beneficiaries, most company retirement plans do not permit it. After your death, the plan will generally cash out your beneficiaries in five years at best. Even if your spouse is the beneficiary, he or she will be cashed out. But your spouse has the advantage of being able to roll the inherited company plan over to his or her own IRA, then name new beneficiaries on the IRA (for example, the children); when the spouse dies, the beneficiaries get the stretch, but they get it from the inherited IRA, not the 401(k).

As you'll recall from Chapter 4, as well as from the story of Ann and her kids in Chapter 1, a nonspouse beneficiary cannot roll over an inherited company plan or IRA to his or her own IRA. In Ann's case, her children were the beneficiaries of their mother's 403(b) plan, so they couldn't do a rollover. And even though the IRS rules would have allowed the plan itself to provide the stretch option to Ann's children, the plan, like most company retirement plans, would not permit it. So, Ann's children had to cash out in five years and lose a substantial amount of their inheritance to taxes.

"But why would a company plan not allow this option?" you ask. "Isn't it something all employees would want for their beneficiaries?"

Any logical person would think so. But we're talking about companies here—especially big companies—and the sad truth about them is this: You may have been a good and loyal worker for however many years, but once you leave or retire from that company, you aren't making any more money for it anymore, and so it wants as little to do with you or your family as possible. You're just one of the pain-in-the-neck reasons why the company had to hire a Human Resource Department in the first place, and add more employees just to handle your annoying company plan questions. (I wonder why Human Resources is called that? I've never gotten a human being on the phone. Have you?) This is why I recommend rolling over your 401(k), 403(b), and 457 plan money to an IRA as soon as you retire. You'll be better off looking out for yourself or hiring a financial advisor to do it, as most companies today do not look out for the long-term interests of their current hard-working employees, let alone retirees. They don't permit the stretch, even though the IRS does, because they don't want the cost and the administrative problems associated with paying out distributions for another 40 to 50 years. Heck, they don't want you pestering them, let alone your beneficiaries!

So, when I use the term *stretch IRA,* I am referring only to inherited IRAs, not to inherited company plans.

Building Family Wealth through Tax-Sheltered Compounding

The stretch concept is what will turn your retirement savings into the most powerful family wealth-building device available to you. Nothing beats tax-deferred growth. Well, nothing except tax-free growth—and you can have that as well, with a stretch Roth IRA because the same concept also applies, except that with Roths the distribution taken by your beneficiaries will be income tax free (see Chapter 7 for the whole scoop on Roth IRAs).

Do you recall when the $2,000-per-year IRA was first created years ago? The press and the banks enthused, "If you begin contributing a maximum of just $2,000 per year to your IRA at age 15, and keep that up for the next 50 years, you could wind up a millionaire!"

They were right. At an 8 percent interest rate, the $2,000-per-year maximum contribution over a 50-year period would grow tax-deferred to $1,239,344. Today, the contribution limit for an IRA is $3,000. If that amount were contributed each year at the same 8 percent, it would grow to $1,859,015 over a 50-year period. That's almost $2 million!!

OK, now think about this: If that's what an initial balance of $3,000 could turn into over 50 years, what would your IRA turn into if you started out not with a $3,000 balance but a $200,000,

$500,000, or $1 million balance or whatever figure you have in your retirement savings? The potential is incredible, and it's attainable for your beneficiaries. Einstein called this potential "exponential notation," but we mortals know it as "compound interest." Add compound interest to tax-deferred growth and the buildup is exponential.

I can hear you thinking, "But what about required minimum distributions? Won't they stall growth?"

It's true beneficiaries must take RMDs on their inherited IRAs every year, but what is so amazing is that mathematically the accounts will still continue to grow until those beneficiaries are well into their dotage. Even if they begin withdrawals in their early 40s, each year they will only be withdrawing 1/40, 1/39, 1/38, 1/37, and so on. That comes to an average of about 3 percent. If the IRA is growing at, say, 8 percent per year during that time, then you've got a 5 percent spread of pure, untaxed growth building for decades within the IRA. And if the average investment return is higher, then the spread is also higher.

In this example (assuming that the beneficiaries withdraw only the minimum each year, and that investment returns average the same as they have for the past 50 years), the inherited IRA account balance will not begin to decline mathematically until what they must withdraw exceeds 8 percent of the account value. That won't happen until the beneficiaries are in their 70s. So you see, even after taking RMDs into consideration, an IRA will grow and grow sheltered from taxes. Also, because the beneficiaries are withdrawing so little each year, the income tax they pay on each distribution is significantly lower than if the entire IRA had to be withdrawn in a few years rather than being stretched.

The benefit of compounding is even more powerful with younger beneficiaries, such as grandchildren who may, for example, start taking required minimum distributions at rates of 1/70, 1/69, 1/68, and so on each year. And if the inherited account is a Roth IRA, the untaxed growth within the IRA is mathematically the same but remains tax-free when withdrawn!

RMDs won't reduce the tax-free buildup of an inherited IRA in the hands of inheritors if they withdraw only the minimum each year. And you can see that they don't by making sure they don't have to. As discussed in Chapter 5, leave them the extra cash in the form of life insurance to cover estate taxes and other expenses relevant to inherited property.

"OK, Ed," you say, "You've convinced me. I worked hard for my money and would love to see it last for years after my death. What do I have to do to accomplish that?"

"Make sure your IRA account has a designated beneficiary," I answer.

"Is that all?"

"You don't need to do anything more. *That's it.*"

The IRS pretty much says that if you have a designated beneficiary on your retirement account, you're guaranteed the stretch option. This means that your named beneficiary can stretch (spread out) his or her postdeath RMDs over his or her life expectancy according to the IRS Single Life Expectancy Table (see Chapter 4, Figure 6). The IRS does not set a dollar limit on how much your stretch IRA can grow to, it only sets a time limit on when the account must be completely withdrawn.

For example, if the named beneficiary is a 40-year-old daughter, once the IRA owner dies, the daughter can stretch the inherited IRA over her life expectancy of 43.6 years. She only needs to use the life expectancy table once—to look up her age in the year following the year of the IRA owner's death (her first required distribution year). As you'll recall from Chapter 4, to calculate her RMD for each succeeding year, she will subtract one year from her 43.6-year life expectancy until that set term has expired or she's withdrawn everything from the account (a beneficiary can always withdraw more than the required amount), whichever comes first.

If the beneficiary dies before the 43.6-year term has expired and there is still a balance in the IRA, then the beneficiary's beneficiary can continue the stretch for the remaining years left on the original 43.6-year schedule. That's why it's so important to the stretch concept for every beneficiary to name his or her own beneficiary as soon as he or she inherits so that there will be someone designated to continue the schedule if the beneficiary dies early. When a beneficiary names his or her own beneficiary, the remaining IRA balance will go directly to that beneficiary with no probate, claims, or other legal obstacles.

I probably could end this chapter right here, because the "stretch concept" is that simple. But the fact is, most IRA owners and plan participants will never get even 10 percent of the stretch on their IRAs that the IRS allows. And the reason almost always comes down to one of two things: lack of planning or poor advice (although sometimes it's good advice but people don't listen or don't take care of the simple details in order to lock in the stretch for their beneficiaries).

"Ed, are you telling me that all I have to do is name a beneficiary and my children get the stretch over their lives?"

The key is not a beneficiary, but a *designated beneficiary*. As you'll recall from Chapter 4, there is a difference—and that difference is critical to the survival of your retirement account after you die.

If you do not have a designated beneficiary, your beneficiaries won't get the stretch opportunity, and they won't be able to do anything about it.

Who Is the Designated Beneficiary?

In the best of all possible worlds, I would be able to say that whomever you name on your IRA beneficiary designation forms (see Appendix III) will be the one who inherits your IRA. But here again, the IRS has added some twists and turns to keep us on our toes by making this process more complex—and for good reason. You see, the IRS realized that nothing is constant (except the IRS); things change and IRA owners need the opportunity to change with them by being able to amend and update their plans as events in their lives warrant. So, the IRS came up with an improved, albeit somewhat more involved, system to give IRA owners and their beneficiaries the maximum flexibility in beneficiary planning.

As you know from Chapter 4, to have a designated beneficiary, you must name an individual (a person) as your beneficiary on your IRA beneficiary form. (You could also name a trust, even though a trust is not a person, but let's leave that discussion for Chapter 8.) The IRS has gone the extra mile by allowing limited changes in beneficiaries to be made even after you're dead, however.

"Oh, come on, Ed. You're pulling my leg! A beneficiary can be changed after I'm dead? By whom?"

"By you."

"*Me?* Where from? The grave?"

"In a way, yes. You see, the changed beneficiary must come from a list of candidates pre-approved by you."

It's like allowing your daughter to marry only from a group of candidates pre-approved by you—although if she's still single after your death, she can, and probably will, marry anyone she likes whether he's on your list or not. But with an IRA, no other non-approved person can be a designated beneficiary. Beneficiaries can be changed after the IRA owner's death, but only to beneficiaries named by the IRA owner during his or her life (from the owner's pre-approved list). No beneficiary can be added to the list who wasn't named by the owner—otherwise that would undermine the whole goal of leaving your money only to the people you want to have it.

In most cases, the designated beneficiary will be the person you named on the IRA or company plan. But in other cases it may not be. So, in fact, the actual designated beneficiary won't be known until after you're dead!

Determining the Designated Beneficiary

The designated beneficiary on your IRA or company plan will not be determined until September 30 of the year following the year of the IRA owner's death. *Say what???*

For example, if the IRA owner (that's you) dies in 2003 (let's pray not), then the designated beneficiary will be determined on September 30, 2004. On that date, there will only be one designated beneficiary left standing and that person (hopefully the one you named) will officially become *the* designated beneficiary.

"Could someone besides the beneficiary I name end up the designated beneficiary on September 30 of the year after my death?"

"Easily." You see, the period between the IRA owner's death—say, June 10, 2003—and September 30, 2004 (the September 30 of the year after the owner's death) is what is commonly known as the "gap" period (see Figure 8) during which a variety of things can happen. A beneficiary can be changed during the gap period (but only to some other beneficiary actually named by the IRA owner). The change can be to another primary beneficiary or a contingent beneficiary (terms I'll get to shortly), but it cannot be

Figure 8. The Gap Period IRA Timeline

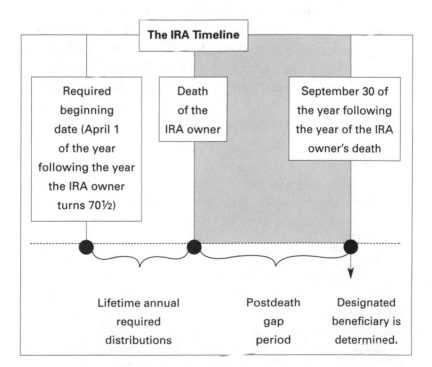

The IRA Timeline		
Required beginning date (April 1 of the year following the year the IRA owner turns 70½)	Death of the IRA owner	September 30 of the year following the year of the IRA owner's death
Lifetime annual required distributions	Postdeath gap period	Designated beneficiary is determined.

changed to anyone whose name was not put on the IRA beneficiary designation form by you. So, your designated beneficiary could wind up being a different person than you may have had in mind, but no *new* designated beneficiary can be introduced after your death.

Eligible Players

Here's a baseball analogy to illustrate what I mean by "no new designated beneficiary can be introduced." Let's go out on a limb and assume that the Boston Red Sox somehow find themselves in the World Series. The Boston Red Sox have not won a World Series since 1918 and aren't likely to in my lifetime (and I say that not because I'm a Mets fan, either). But let's humor (or tease) the Boston crowd and assume that this earth-shaking event has occurred.

It's the seventh inning of the deciding game. If the Red Sox win this game, they win the Series. But it's late in the game and they are losing. They need a clutch hitter *right now.* Can they bring in a ringer to sew up the game—say, Barry Bonds, Sammy Sosa, or Mike Piazza to bat for them and pitching ace Randy Johnson to pitch for them, even though these great players are not Red Sox?

No, they cannot.

To be eligible to play in the World Series, players must be named on the team roster in the regular season. They cannot be added in the postseason.

It's the same with IRA beneficiaries. To be eligible to play in the postseason (after the death of the IRA owner), they must be named in the regular season (during the IRA owner's lifetime).

Primary and Contingent Beneficiaries

This brings us to the importance of naming contingent (also known as secondary) beneficiaries in addition to the primary (or first-named) beneficiary, who has first dibs on the account.

The primary beneficiary will inherit the account as long as he or she is still alive when the IRA owner or plan participant dies. The primary can also decide not to accept the inheritance and disclaim any right to it. This disclaimer (also called a "renunciation" in legal parlance) is a written statement that says the beneficiary does not want the account he or she is to inherit, and so the IRA would pass to the contingent beneficiary (if there is one).

For example, Bill is the primary beneficiary on his father's IRA, and Bill's son, Jim, is the contingent beneficiary named by his grandfather.

Bill's father dies in 2004. Bill is 55 years old and his son Jim is 25 years old in 2005, the year after the IRA owner's death. Bill is legally entitled to the IRA. But since Bill doesn't need the money; he would rather see his son Jim inherit it, so Bill disclaims his interest in the IRA and Jim, formerly the contingent beneficiary, now becomes the primary beneficiary.

In order to change the designated beneficiary, a disclaimer must be considered valid under Section 2518 of the IRS Code. A valid disclaimer is defined as a written refusal to accept property you are legally entitled to; this disclaimer must be filed with the court within nine months of the date of the IRA owner's death (unless the person disclaiming is a minor, in which case the nine-month period would begin upon the minor's 21st birthday). Also, the person disclaiming cannot accept any of the benefits of the property (e.g., spend some of the money and then say you don't want it) or direct who will get the property as a result of the disclaimer. This means that you also cannot say, "I don't want it. Give it to my buddy Joe." You can only say, "I don't want it." Then the property goes to the next in line (usually the contingent beneficiary) based on the wishes of the decedent. You can disclaim part or all of your inheritance.

If the disclaimer does not qualify under Code Section 2518, then it is not considered to be a valid disclaimer; thus, the designated beneficiary cannot be changed, and the transfer will be treated taxwise as a gift.

Had Bill not disinherited himself, he would have been the designated beneficiary and used his own life expectancy to calculate RMDs from the Single Life Expectancy Table. This would have allowed him to stretch the account over his 29.6-year life expectancy period based on his age (55) in 2005, according to the Single Life Expectancy Table. But instead Jim inherits and gets the nod as designated beneficiary when that is determined on September 30, 2005. As a result, it is Jim whose life expectancy will be used to calculate postdeath RMDs. Based on his age (25) in 2005 from the Single Life Expectancy Table, Jim can stretch the IRA over a 58.2-year life expectancy period—a full 28.6 years longer than Bill could have. So, the IRA stays in the family, growing tax-deferred for another generation.

This result was only possible because the IRA owner (Bill's father) was smart enough to name a contingent beneficiary (his grandson, Jim). You should name a contingent beneficiary (or several as the case may be) on every retirement account you have. By naming a contingent beneficiary, you will have made that person an eligible player in the postseason. Once that person is eligible, he or she can become the designated beneficiary after your death even though that person was not the primary beneficiary originally.

But in the example I cited, if Jim hadn't been named contingent beneficiary, couldn't Bill, in disclaiming the inheritance, just have instructed the bank to turn the IRA over to Jim instead of him?

The answer is no. Bill can name Jim as his own beneficiary, but he has no right to name Jim as beneficiary of the inherited IRA; only the IRA owner can do that. If Bill had such a right, he could instead name Spike, Jim's stupid twin brother, who runs through money faster than Kansas can whip up a cyclone—which would have been totally against the wishes of the IRA owner. Remember, Bill can only disclaim or refuse the inheritance.

If there were no contingent beneficiary named by Bill's father, and Bill disclaimed his interest in the inheritance, then the IRA would pass to whomever was to receive it next under the terms of the IRA agreement, and then the IRA owner's will—or, if there is no will, through intestacy, a legal procedure where the state decides where and to whom the asset will go.

Assuming Bill's father did not name a contingent beneficiary and Bill disclaimed the inheritance, over whose life expectancy would the inherited IRA then be paid out? To find out, we would have to wait until September 30, 2005, when the designated beneficiary is determined. But, of course, there is no contingent beneficiary named, and Bill disclaims, so guess what? On September 30, 2005, the envelope is opened, and oops . . . **there is no designated beneficiary!**

"But wait a minute, what if under the terms of the will, it says Jim is to receive the disclaimed account? Won't he be declared the designated beneficiary on September 30, 2005?"

Nope. And if you've been paying close attention, you know why.

Jim can *never* be a *designated beneficiary* because his grandpa, the IRA owner, didn't *name* him as such. Jim is only a *beneficiary* because he has inherited through the will. When someone inherits through the will, the estate is the beneficiary. The estate is not a person and, therefore, cannot be a designated beneficiary. It makes no difference that Jim receives the IRA through the estate. The estate is still the beneficiary on the date that the designated beneficiary is determined. When that happens in this case, there is no designated beneficiary and the IRA will be paid out to Jim, but under the rules applied to a situation in which an IRA owner has died without naming a designated beneficiary. Those rules, which are explained in detail in Chapter 4, require you to know whether the IRA owner died before or after his required beginning date (RBD).

So, the bottom line is this: *Always* name a contingent beneficiary in addition to a primary beneficiary on your beneficiary form to keep your plan going.

Where There's a Will . . . It Still Won't Help Your IRA

When I ask people, "Who'll get your IRA after you die?" what typically pops out of their mouths is "I don't know. But it's in my will." They figure it *must* be covered their will. "Isn't that what a will is for? To say who gets what?" That's true—of property that is meant to pass through the will. But . . .

Most couples own their home jointly. They have joint investment, bank, and brokerage accounts. They also have life insurance, pensions, and IRAs or other retirement accounts. That list of property is the typical estate of every American couple. Well, guess how much of that typical estate is typically covered by every typical American couple's typical will (assuming the will is perfect in all respects)?

None of it!

People are shocked when I tell them this. They react with "I just paid thousands of dollars for a will, with trusts and a complete estate plan, and you're telling me it hardly covers any of the assets I own?" For many people, indeed most, that's right.

Most property today passes *outside the will*. In other words, the will is overridden. For example, if you own your home jointly with your spouse and one of you dies, the house goes to the surviving spouse who is the joint owner, regardless of what the will says. It passes by operation of law and trumps any conflicting provision in your will.

The same is true of property that passes by beneficiary designation, such as an IRA, a company retirement account, or an insurance policy. All of these items are spoken for, so to speak. They have assigned destinations and are transferred according to the designated beneficiary form, not the will. The form overrides the will. So, if your IRA or other retirement account is one of the larger assets in your estate, as it is for many people, then your beneficiary form is the essential document as far as your beneficiaries are concerned. It controls the distribution of the money you worked and saved for all your life. It is, in effect, the will for your IRA that guarantees the stretch option for your beneficiaries.

You can use the designated beneficiary form supplied by your bank, brokerage, or mutual fund company—in fact, some insist upon this—but if the form doesn't provide enough space to fit all the pertinent information about your beneficiaries that should be there, then attach a separate sheet. Here's why:

When you have many beneficiaries and contingent beneficiaries, it is unlikely they will all fit in the small amount of room the typical beneficiary forms give you to write in your beneficiary's name, share, relationship, Social Security number, etc. Most beneficiary forms give you room for two or three beneficiaries and that's it. If this is not enough space, don't write smaller to cram the information in, or include some names but not others. Write, "See attached list of primary and contingent beneficiaries" or "See rider attached listing all beneficiaries" and clip the list(s) to the form. The idea is to *force* the reader (the financial institution) to look elsewhere for the complete list of beneficiaries rather than assume that the only beneficiaries are those listed on the front page of the form. Therefore, both your "See attached" note and your attached lists of names and information should appear to be obviously part of the document. This is an important tip. Be careful to follow it, or else . . .

If the financial institution will accept your own customized designated beneficiary form (see Appendix III), better yet.

Items you will want to make sure to ask your financial institution about, or will want to make sure are covered by your own customized form, include:

- Your beneficiary's ability to name a beneficiary. In some cases a stretch IRA can be lost or severely curtailed if a beneficiary is not given this permission. Also, when the estate is the beneficiary, the IRA will have to go through probate, resulting in possible delays plus additional fees and expenses, and it may end up with someone you never intended.
- Your nonspouse beneficiary's ability to move the inherited account to another financial institution via a trustee-to-trustee transfer. This is important because a nonspouse beneficiary cannot roll over.
- A "per stirpes" payout in case your beneficiary dies before you do. *Per stirpes* means that if a beneficiary is one of several beneficiaries on an inherited account and dies, then that

person's share goes to his or her beneficiaries and not the other co-beneficiaries.

- The default provisions of your IRA agreement (more about this later in the chapter).
- Procedures for keeping track of beneficiary forms. You don't want to use a bank that has none or won't reveal what its procedures are.
- Your designated beneficiary's ability to stretch the IRA over his or her life expectancy as the IRS allows. Unbelievably, some financial institutions do not allow the stretch IRA because they are afraid of making a mistake that might incur a liability—and so they create ultraconservative IRA agreements that are more restrictive than what the IRS itself allows. If so, move your IRA money to a more cooperative financial institution that will serve your family's long-term needs.
- The ability of your beneficiary's beneficiary to keep the stretch going if your beneficiary dies before the account is emptied. Or will the bank force the remaining funds in the account to be withdrawn immediately? For example, if your beneficiary has a 40-year life expectancy but dies after three years, the next beneficiary should be able to continue RMDs over the remaining 37 years. But if the bank forces the account to be emptied after your beneficiary's death, the remaining 37-year stretch will be lost.
- Whether the financial institution will provide you with an "acknowledged copy" of your designated beneficiary form. By an "acknowledged copy" I mean a copy signed by someone at the bank so that in the event that the bank loses the form after your death, your beneficiaries can present this acknowledged copy and know that it will be accepted. Who at the bank or financial institution should sign the acknowledged copy? Anyone with a title, even if it's "chief janitor" (who is probably a vice-president in disguise anyway). This is a precautionary measure, but one that could spell the dif-

ference between a 50-year stretch or a 5-year payout, as well as settle any potential family feuds.

Who Gets What?

There is another important but obvious item that should go without saying, but I'll say it anyway because I take nothing for granted. You have to spell out who gets what—in other words, clearly state each beneficiary's share. I know this sounds like a no-brainer, but it isn't. Most beneficiary forms get no respect (not to mention time or attention) and are filled out carelessly. If you have four children and want them to inherit equally, then say that. Use the term *equally* or *25 percent each* or *¼ each* so that it is clear what percentage or fraction you want to go to whom. The same goes for contingent beneficiaries. Say who gets what, or there could be big problems ahead for your beneficiaries.

For example, a 60-year-old beneficiary came to see me for tax advice on the IRA she just inherited from her 80-something mother. She was one of six co-beneficiaries, all sisters, and she was the oldest. There was about $600,000 in the mother's IRA account. Most of this was from a rollover that her deceased father left to her mother. She told me she was having a problem with the bank. She knew her mother's intention was that all six sisters share equally in the IRA. However, there was no indication on the bank's form as to who was to get what amount. As a result, the bank would only pay sister number one (the one who came to see me—the oldest and the first beneficiary listed). Absent any instructions to the contrary from the deceased, the bank took the position that sister number one was the primary beneficiary, and sisters two through six were all contingent beneficiaries. This meant that sister two could only inherit if sister one died prior to the IRA ower, sister three could only inherit if sisters one and two died prior to the IRA owner, sister four could only inherit if sisters one, two, and three died prior to the IRA owner, and so on.

If she'd been a creep, sister number one could legally have taken the entire $600,000 with the bank's blessing, left the other sisters high and dry, and gone off on a hell of a vacation somewhere. But she wasn't that type. She wanted the account divided equally among all six sisters as her late mother wanted—but unfortunately, Mom had never spelled this intention out to the bank, which took the position that it could not assign shares based on what the sisters *said* their mother wanted.

The only way to uphold the mother's wishes to have the IRA equally shared was for the sister deemed primary beneficiary to withdraw the entire $600,000 IRA, pay the income tax on it, and then divide the remainder equally among the sisters as gifts. (Of course, she could also have gone through the disclaimer process, but she and the other sisters were already disgusted with having to deal with so many legal complexities arising from their mother's death, and they didn't want to go through more.) The income tax turned out to be over $240,000 and had to be paid only by the oldest sister because she was the only one who could take the distribution. As the distribution was reported on one tax return instead of six different tax returns, the tax was much higher than it would have been if all six sisters were able to report one-sixth of the distribution on their individual tax returns. Under our graduated tax rate system, six people who report $100,000 of income each will pay less tax than one person reporting $600,000.

Although an even split was ultimately achieved as the mother wanted, almost half the IRA was lost to taxes, which might easily have been avoided if the mother had put just two words in the designated beneficiary form—"equal shares."

Use a Beneficiary *Information* Sheet, Too

As is obvious by now, the biggest IRA nightmares occur because of neglect. Not naming a beneficiary and not being able to find the designated beneficiary form when it is needed are the most common blunders that kill beneficiaries' chances of getting the maximum stretch on their inherited IRAs. So, don't leave your beneficiaries without a clue as to where your IRA beneficiary designation forms are.

Fill out a *stretch IRA beneficiary information sheet* (see Figure 9 and Appendix III) for each account you own, sign it, date it, and make copies. I have designed this form to be as simple as possible to use, but at the same time to include enough key IRA information to both alert you to potential IRA problems and make your beneficiaries aware of your IRA accounts and where the accounts are located. If you make changes, update the respective information sheet right away. Give a copy of each information sheet to each of your IRA beneficiaries, your financial advisor, your estate attorney, and/or your accountant. This simple piece of paper could turn out to be worth millions to your IRA beneficiaries . . . *but only if you use it*!

Estate as Beneficiary

The last thing you want is for your IRA to pass through your estate. Once the IRA is paid to your estate, there cannot be a designated beneficiary on your IRA and if there is no designated beneficiary, there is no life expectancy, which means the stretch IRA opportunity is lost for your beneficiaries. This seems obvious, but even the best and brightest have trouble understanding it. Here's what I mean:

A few years ago, I gave a lecture at the Wharton School of Business alumni dinner in New York City. Before I spoke, the person running the event told me that this was an extremely intuitive and intelligent audience, so I should not be hesitant to speak on a highly advanced level. He made his point. They weren't dummies.

I reached the part of the lecture where I said that if you want to stretch your IRA for your beneficiaries, don't let it pass through your estate because the whole idea of stretching is to have a life ex-

Figure 9. Sample Stretch IRA Beneficiary Information Sheet

IMPORTANT—DO NOT LEAVE THIS BLANK
Location of beneficiary designation and distribution election forms:
_____

Dated: _____

Type of Retirement Account (use a separate form for each account)

IRA (traditional)	❑	401(k)	❑
Roth IRA	❑	403(b), TSA, or TDA	❑
SEP-IRA	❑	Keogh	❑
SIMPLE IRA	❑	Other Company Plan _____	❑

Name of Financial institution (bank, broker, mutual fund co., etc.)

Name _____
Address _____
Telephone number _____
Contact person _____
Account number _____

Primary Beneficiary(s)

Name	Relation	Share (% or Fraction)

Secondary (contingent) Beneficiary(s)

Name	Relation	Share (% or Fraction)

If you make any changes, be sure to update this form.

WARNING: This is NOT an IRA designated beneficiary form and should not be confused with one. It is an IRA beneficiary information sheet (see Appendix III for a full-size clip-out version). Use it to provide your beneficiaries with key information about your retirement accounts, your beneficiary selection on each account, and, most important, where your designated beneficiary forms are and when they were last updated.

pectancy for the inherited IRA distributions to be stretched over. Then I asked the audience, "What's the life expectancy of your estate?" The response was a flurry of activity as everybody reached for a calculator! Since an estate is not a person, it cannot have a life expectancy, but I guess that was too simplistic a concept for this highly intelligent crowd.

When you name your estate as your beneficiary, you are turning your retirement plan into a probate asset like anything else that passes through a will. So, in addition to the tax ramifications, which can be expensive, there are the probate costs to contend with, as well. If you have a large retirement plan, the combination could add up to a substantial amount of money, depending on lawyer and court filing fees. And if the will were contested, even more—perhaps most—of the IRA could get eaten up.

But the worst thing of all about naming your estate the beneficiary of your IRA—which you should never, NEVER do—is that your heirs lose the ability to stretch it.

Even if a living, breathing human being inherits through your estate, the IRA distribution rules say that an estate cannot be a designated beneficiary because it is not a person. **And if the estate becomes beneficiary, for whatever reason, the option to stretch your IRA is lost.**

Point made. Let's move on.

How Does the Estate Become a Beneficiary?

When you open an IRA with a bank, broker, mutual fund company, or insurance company, one of the forms you sign is an IRA agreement. You'll know which form is the IRA agreement. It's the document with the smallest possible writing and the most pages. Only the people who write them actually read them . . . maybe.

This document can kill your IRA, but only with your help. If you do not name a beneficiary, or if your beneficiary (or the financial institution holding the account) cannot find the beneficiary form, then you are subject to the default provisions of the IRA agreement, whether you read them or not. Generally, the default provisions will do your beneficiaries in because they say that if no beneficiary is named, then the IRA will be paid to your estate. That's how your estate becomes the beneficiary. And once that happens, out the window goes the opportunity for stretching your IRA.

Your IRA may also get a second crack at life if the financial institution is one that believes most people are their own worst enemies when it comes to naming beneficiaries and offers IRA agreements that can create a designated beneficiary in spite of your forgetfulness and neglect.

For example, The Fleet Private Clients Group's IRA agreement states that if you die without a beneficiary named on your IRA, then the beneficiary will be your spouse. If you are single or divorced or your spouse is dead, then it goes to your children. If there are no children, then it goes to your estate. This creates two lines of defense before your estate can ever become the beneficiary. If your institution has an IRA agreement like Fleet's, that's great, but it's not the bank's job to name your beneficiaries. You should do that—because the people named by the bank may not be the beneficiaries you would want your IRA to go to. Here's such an example:

John was married to Mary for 40 years and they have three children. Mary died recently and John remarried. John's understanding with his new wife is that after he dies, his IRA will go to his children and not to her. John dies and his children cannot locate his IRA beneficiary form. They go to the bank, but the bank does not have a copy of the form. The IRA will therefore be treated as if there were no beneficiary named. Next, the IRA agreement must be checked to see what the default options are when there is no beneficiary named. In this case, the IRA agreement is one that seeks to protect the inheritance by naming a person instead of the estate. But that's bad news here because the designated beneficiary will be the spouse, not the children, which was not John's intent. This situation could easily have been avoided if John had named his children as his IRA beneficiaries. But even if he did, if the beneficiary form stating that cannot be found, then the result is the same as not naming a beneficiary.

Where's the Designated Beneficiary Form?

If at this very moment you had to put your hands on the beneficiary form for every IRA or retirement account you own, could you? For most people, the answer is "No," followed by "It's OK, though; the bank will have them." Sorry, but the chances of that are about equal to the chances of the IRS's closing up shop. The bank may simply have lost the forms. Or it may have destroyed them for any number of reasons—including making space for more forms—or purged them in the latest merger.

Think I speak with jaundiced tongue? Consider this true story then:

A few years ago a local bank teller who is a tax client of mine asked if I would prepare her son's tax return. She said that he was a student and had only one W-2 from a summer job, so the return would be easy. (All clients say that . . . and I fall for it every damn time.) I examined her son's W-2 and saw that his summer job was at the same bank where she worked, so I asked her what type of work he'd done at the bank. She explained that the bank had been taken over by another bank, requiring a change in the old bank's name. So, a crew of people—her son among them—was hired to destroy bank documents with the old letterhead on them.

"What kind of bank documents?" I asked suspiciously.

"Blank forms, stationery, beneficiary forms, and other old or unimportant items like that," she answered.

Trust me on this. Anyone with an IRA in a bank (including me!) better have a copy of his or her IRA beneficiary forms because the likelihood is the bank won't.

OK, so maybe you can't count on banks, but since you have your IRA with a broker, not a bank, the firm will certainly have copies, right? Probably not. Brokers move around a lot, and when they switch to a different firm, their old paperwork often gets lost in the shuffle.

Should you look for missing beneficiary forms? No! Don't waste your time. All prior choices can be changed now anyway. The old forms no longer lock in any elections as they did under the old rules. Fill out new beneficiary forms, keep them in a safe place, and let your beneficiaries know where that safe place is, so they don't have to have your home bulldozed after your death in hopes of finding them. I'm not exaggerating; I actually had a case where this almost happened. Two sisters called me. They were 50-ish and their parents were in their 80s. The sisters were worried because all their lives their father was hiding things in the house—literally in the walls, under the floors, in false panels, or under the property. Their father had somewhat of a checkered past during which he'd accumulated lots of cash and other assets, including bearer bonds, as well as numerous retirement accounts that he'd stashed, along with other important documents, at his home. (No, I won't tell you the address because I'm buying the house as soon as the parents pass away so I can go on a treasure hunt!) The sisters called because they wanted to have an updated estate plan for their parents. It was an emergency, they said, because their father (the only one who knew where all the gems were buried) was losing his memory and deteriorating fast. We were able to track down most of the investments and contacted the various banks and brokers to obtain new beneficiary forms, but most of the banks had nothing on file as far as beneficiary forms were concerned. So, we had new forms filled out. We also had the parents fill out powers of attorney allowing the daughters to handle their financial affairs. Fortunately the daughters had enough of a heads-up and were prepared enough to eventually find most of the financial information they needed. But that is not the case with most beneficiaries.

The mutual fund companies have a pretty good record on beneficiary forms. Some even print the beneficiary and contingent beneficiary names right on the quarterly or annual statements. But again, it's your job to check that these beneficiary designations are current.

What do I mean by *current?*

Even if the financial institution has a beneficiary form on file, it has no way of knowing if your beneficiary has died unless you update your form with this news. That's what I mean by keeping the form current. Most of the beneficiary forms I see list dead beneficiaries because the form hasn't been touched since the account was opened in, say, 1978. Having a dead beneficiary is the same as having no beneficiary, which is almost always the same as naming your estate as beneficiary.

Under the IRA rules, you can change your beneficiary any time you wish, at any age, but you cannot change it once you're dead. I mention this because for some strange reason there is so much confusion based on old rules that people cannot get out of their heads. The IRA rules that were in effect between 1987 and 2000 made the current rules look like "See Spot Run." We won't touch the old rules in this book except for a few references that could help you understand the new rules.

Under the old rules, many key choices were locked in at the RBD. Your choice of beneficiary though was not one of them, but many people mistakenly thought that it was. There were so many irrevocable rules at age 70½ that people also thought they could not change their beneficiary after 70½ either. The problem was not that the beneficiary could not be changed after 70½, but that the distribution method could not be improved after 70½ and many older IRA owners were locked into irrevocable and often poor decisions they had made at 70½ without understanding the full consequences of those decisions. Many of them didn't even know they were making irrevocable tax elections. As far as they were concerned, they were just filling out the necessary IRA forms.

But today all that has changed for the better. Under the rules in effect now, nothing is locked in until you die.

When I tell this to my older clients who were locked into poor unchangeable choices they made at 70½, they are absolutely thrilled. They love the fact that they can make changes any time they want. One client told me he calls this new freedom of choice his "IRA leverage." I asked him what he meant by that. And he explained, "Well, it's like this. I can change my IRA beneficiaries any time and as often as I want now. Last week I had my 80th birthday party and two of my kids didn't show up. So, they're out!"

Now I know what he means by IRA leverage. Attention, prospective IRA beneficiaries: Better be good to your parents. They can and will eliminate you in a heartbeat.

Life Events

Pay attention to what I call *life events* that may require appropriate changes on all your beneficiary forms.

By "life events," I mean the following:

- Changes in the tax laws seem to occur every time Congress meets. (Stay up-to-date on how these laws could affect your IRA by visiting my web site, www.irahelp.com, or with my monthly IRA newsletter, *Ed Slott's IRA Advisor*, see page 370.)
- The birth of a new grandchild may lead to your wanting to add that child as a beneficiary.
- If you're getting married, you may not want your spouse-to-be to inherit your IRA, or maybe you do. Whichever the case is, make the appropriate changes immediately after the nuptials (although if you want your spouse-to-be to get your IRA and he or she is 30 years younger than you are, maybe waiting until after the honeymoon to make the changes is a safe move).
- A divorce would certainly require beneficiary changes (if your ex-spouse was your beneficiary)—unless you are out of your mind and *want* to leave your retirement savings to your ex!

- You may have named your spouse, but now your spouse has died and probably won't need your retirement account wherever he or she is headed.

Keep your antennae tuned for any such events that would necessitate a change in the beneficiary form for each retirement account you have. And make the change right away. Don't leave the updating to next week or next month to be forgotten about until you die and your beneficiaries realize the changes went unmade, at which point there is no designated beneficiary and your heirs will have to empty the inherited account much quicker than if they had gotten to stretch.

So, don't think of this form as a stale old document to be filled out once and never looked at again. Think of it as something that needs constant attention, just like you.

Stretching with Multiple Beneficiaries on One IRA Account

Many IRA owners name several beneficiaries on a single IRA account. For example, a father may name his three children. That's fine. But how will the stretch IRA work when the father dies?

Because there can only be one designated beneficiary on a retirement account, the general rule is that the beneficiary with the shortest life expectancy is the one who will be used to calculate postdeath RMDs.

This is probably not a big deal if the beneficiaries are your children, who are probably all within a few years of each other. But what if, say, Aunt Edna, age 87, your son Chip, age 46, and your grandchild Rachel, age 11, are the co-beneficiaries? That's quite a spread. Using the Single Life Expectancy Table, their life expectancies would be, respectively, 6.7 years for Aunt Edna, 37.9 years for Chip, and 71.8 years for Rachel. Following the general rule, the postdeath payouts would be based on a life expectancy of the oldest, Aunt Edna, whose life expectancy would the shortest, 6.7 years. Poor Rachel, who would have otherwise been able to stretch her portion over 71.8 years, will instead have to empty her account in 6.7 years too. Some "Sweet Sixteen" birthday party that will be!

Recognizing the inequity here, the IRS has come up with a solution that makes everyone happy yet sticks to the same general rule. Now, the IRA owner can split the IRA into several IRAs so that each beneficiary will be the *sole beneficiary* of his or her share. Therefore, when the IRA owner dies, each beneficiary can now use his or her own life expectancy for calculating his or her postdeath RMDs.

So, in the previous example, if the IRA owner splits his IRA into three IRAs and names Aunt Edna, Chip, and Rachel as sole beneficiaries on each IRA, they can each use their own age to compute their RMDs after the IRA owner's death. The general rule still applies. The age of the oldest beneficiary is still used for calculating, but as each is now the sole beneficiary on the IRA he or she inherited, each now is also the oldest beneficiary on that account!

Splitting IRAs is a useful technique when you have more than one beneficiary. But some IRA owners do not want to bother.

They ask why they should have to maintain three separate IRA accounts, tripling their paperwork. Or why worry about making sure that each account is generating equal returns so that each beneficiary gets an equal inheritance? For example, what if you've got Enron stock in the IRA you are leaving to Chip, and Microsoft stock in the IRA you are leaving to Rachel? That would require some shifting around of funds between IRAs to get that score even.

You can always move money between your IRA accounts via a rollover or trustee-to-trustee transfer, of course, but what if instead of 3 beneficiaries you had 12 beneficiaries? Would you want to split your IRA into 12 separate IRAs and face the prospect of drowning in a sea of paper and record keeping? You'd probably forgo the split account.

Once again, the handy and ever-helpful IRS has come up with a solution. The rules state that you or your beneficiaries (after your death, of course) can request the financial institution holding your IRA to split it into several IRAs at *any time*. Your beneficiaries can still each use their own life expectancies to calculate their stretch IRA period, provided they split the accounts into their separate shares soon after your death. In this way, each beneficiary can be the designated beneficiary on his or her separate share. In tax talk, this is called the "separate share" or "separate account" rule, and it is the exception to the general rule requiring beneficiaries on one IRA to use the age of the oldest beneficiary for calculating RMDs.

Generally though, even with all the paperwork, it still may be best for the IRA owner to split the IRA into separate IRAs for each beneficiary, rather than hope that it all goes as planned after death—because if the account is not split "on time" after your death, the stretch IRA could be reduced or lost.

And what exactly does *on time* mean?

The Regs require that an inherited IRA be split into separate accounts by the end of the year (December 31) following the year of the IRA owner's death. If the IRA owner died in 2003, the account would have to be split by the end of 2004. This poses an inconsistency in interpreting the rule that the IRS is grappling with as of this writing.

As you know, tax law states that the designated beneficiary is determined on September 30 of the year following the year the IRA owner dies. This would seem to indicate that the account must be split by that date, as well. But the Regs say beneficiaries have until December 31. If the September 30 rule says you should look to see who the designated beneficiary on the account is as of that date, but the account is not split yet, then there will likely be several beneficiaries, which could mean that only the elder among them could be deemed the designated beneficiary and the others could be stuck with the elder's shorter life expectancy for calculating RMDs!

Read that paragraph again. Then read on for a refreshingly clarifying example.

OK, here's the example: Bob Reilly, the IRA owner, dies in 2004 at age 75 (after his RBD). His beneficiaries are his two children, David and Debra, and his granddaughter Ilana. In 2005, David is 50 years old, Debra is 47, and Ilana is 14. David and Debra are each listed as 40 percent beneficiaries and Ilana will inherit the remaining 20 percent. The IRA balance at December 31, 2004, is $480,000. Bob took his RMD for 2004 before he died.

If Bob had split the account into three separate IRAs during his\ lifetime, then his beneficiaries would each be the sole beneficiary of their respective share and would use their own life expectancy from the Single Life Expectancy Table based on their age in 2005, the year after Bob's death. Here's what the result would have been:

Beneficiary	Age in 2005	Life Expectancy	Share of Inherited IRA
David	50	34.2 years	40% ($192,000)
Debra	47	37.0 years	40% ($192,000)
Ilana	14	68.9 years	20% ($96,000)

Now, let's assume the account was not split by Bob while he was alive. If they want to be able to use their own life expectancies to calculate RMDs, David, Debra, and Ilana have until December 31, 2005, to split the account. If they do not split it by the December 31 deadline, they will all be stuck using the shortest life expectancy, which is David's. That won't make any difference to David, and not much difference to Debra either, since they are close in age. But Ilana, who would have otherwise been able to stretch distributions on her share over a 68.9-year life expectancy, will be stuck withdrawing based on David's 34.2 years, thereby cutting the life of her share roughly in half. Also, Ilana's RMDs will be higher each year, and so will the tax she'll pay—her first RMD (for 2005) will be $2,807 ($96,000/34.2 years = $ 2,807).

My advice is to split the account by September 30 (the date the designated beneficiary is determined), 2005, so she'll be able to use her own life expectancy. Thus, she can withdraw $1,393 ($96,000 /68.9 years = $1,393). That's less than half the amount she would have to withdraw using David's life expectancy, so her inherited IRA will stretch longer.

MEMORY JOG

Remember that each inherited IRA must be correctly titled (as discussed in Chapter 4) after the IRA owner dies or risk being immediately taxed as a complete distribution. Here is how each of the inherited accounts would be titled after the split in the case of Bob Reilly's IRA:

Acct # 1: Bob Reilly IRA (deceased August 20, 2004) F/B/O David Reilly, beneficiary
Acct # 2: Bob Reilly IRA (deceased August 20, 2004) F/B/O Debra Levine, beneficiary
Acct # 3: Bob Reilly IRA (deceased August 20, 2004) F/B/O Ilana Slott, beneficiary

---

Until the IRS resolves the September 30/December 31 confusion, my advice to any beneficiary who is one of several on a single IRA account is to not wait beyond September 30 of the year following the year of the IRA owner's death to split the account because there is no guarantee you will be able to each use your own life expectancy for the first year's RMD. So, even though the rule says the account can be split as late as December 31 of the year following the year of death, don't play it close to the wire. Split the account as early as possible after the IRA owner's death. If for some reason there are delays or problems and the account is not split by December 31 of the year following the year of death, then the co-beneficiaries will be stuck with the life expectancy of the oldest forever, even if they split the account up later. Don't let this happen to you.

> ## TIP!
>
> If you're an IRA owner, you're probably thinking, "The heck with leaving it to my kids to do the split on time. I'll just split it now and deal with the extra paperwork. At least I will know for sure that the stretch is in place and after I die each will be entitled to use his or her own life expectancy to keep the stretch going." You're right. That's probably the best course of action—especially if the co-beneficiaries don't get along or have different ideas and goals. By splitting the account before they inherit, you turn your wishes into a sure thing.

Stretching by Splitting Accounts with Different Types of Beneficiaries

What happens if one of the co-beneficiaries on your IRA is a spouse and another is an entity such as an estate, trust, or charity? The same general rules apply as when co-beneficiaries are all of the same type. The IRA can still be split either before or after the IRA owner's death. But when one of the co-beneficiaries is not a designated beneficiary (a charity, for example), the account must be split by September 30 of the year following the year of the IRA owner's death. If the split is done after that time (even if it is before December 31 of the same year), there is a question as to whether there can be a designated beneficiary. If not, the stretch will be lost.

The problem when co-beneficiaries are different types (a spouse, say, and children) is that splitting the account is not as easy after the IRA owner dies. Mechanically, it is, but not emotionally. In the real world I find that spouse beneficiaries are slow to act after their spouse dies; they don't want to talk about financial issues, and often put things off until it's too late—in this case, too late, perhaps, to avoid sticking the nonspouse co-beneficiaries (the children) with the spouse beneficiary's age for calculating their RMDs. Thus they lose the benefit of using their own ages for the stretch, which diminishes in elasticity.

As with splitting an account where the co-beneficiaries are all the same type, it is best if the IRA owner takes care of this during his or her lifetime. Thus, the surviving spouse has little to do after the IRA owner dies—because she or he will already be the sole beneficiary of one of the inherited IRAs. The children will also benefit by not having to hope that the account will be split in time. They will already be entitled to the full stretch based on their own ages.

The same advice holds true when co-beneficiaries are nonspouse individuals (say, children) and entities (an estate, charity, or trust). These are not good bedfellows for co-beneficiaries. Although the account still can be split after death, there is even more real world opportunity for delay than when a co-beneficiary is a spouse. For example, if there are problems in the estate, the postdeath split may be delayed beyond September 30 of the year following the year of the IRA owner's death; then there will be no designated beneficiary on the account, and the stretch will be lost for the nonspouse individual beneficiaries (the children) who, if they were not co-beneficiaries with an estate, could have been designated beneficiaries and stretched the IRA.

The Postdeath Cash-Out Provision

When there are several beneficiaries on one IRA, the account does not always have to be split. One beneficiary can cash out (meaning take his, her, or its share out) and pay income tax on the withdrawal. For all concerned, this might be better than a split because the co-beneficiary who cashes out is out of the picture for good.

But what type of co-beneficiary would opt to cash out if the taxman's outstretched hand was waiting? An estate might cash out if all the co-beneficiaries wanted all their money fast, the withdrawal tax notwithstanding. Or a charity might—because charities pay no income tax on withdrawals from an IRA. Nor would a charity care about the stretch option since it's not a person with a life expectancy. The charity wants all its money *now*, not extended over 50 years.

For example, let's say a daughter is a co-beneficiary with a charity on her father's IRA, with 95 percent going to the daughter and 5 percent to the charity. The rules say that if the charity takes its share out before the September 30 date when the designated beneficiary is determined, the daughter in this case would be determined the sole beneficiary of her 95 percent share—and thus would be able to stretch her RMDs over her life expectancy based on the Single Life Expectancy Table.

How Long Can an IRA Be Stretched?

There are limits. It cannot go on forever, unless you marry right.

For example at age 20 Ed begins contributing to an IRA. He's 100 years old when he dies. His beneficiary is his 25-year-old fifth wife (Ed remarried after his fourth wife died—at age 30, under mysterious circumstances, just like the previous three). Ed's 25-year-old wife rolls the IRA over to her own IRA and she lives to be 100 too. When she dies, she leaves her IRA to her 30-year old husband, Pierre. Pierre lives to 100 and leaves the IRA to his young wife Maria and then . . . well you get the point. Through marriage the IRA can last forever.

Realistically though, there does come an end because the general rule is that a beneficiary cannot stretch the IRA longer than his or her own life expectancy. The longest life expectancy a beneficiary can have is 82.4 years, which is the life expectancy from the Single Life Expectancy Table of a zero-year-old, a newborn. No beneficiary can stretch out RMDs on an inherited IRA longer than that. But if you consider the complete time the IRA is growing tax-deferred (or tax-free as is the case with a Roth IRA), in the hands of both the IRA owner and the designated beneficiary, then, depending upon how long the former and the latter live, the IRA could live on for more than 100 years! This is why some companies are marketing the stretch IRA concept as the "hundred-year IRA."

Take the same example, except that Ed is single when he dies. After growing his IRA for 80 years (from age 20 to age 100), he dies and his great-granddaughter Linda is the named beneficiary. Linda is 21 years old. If Linda takes only the required minimum distributions each year, she will be able to stretch the inherited IRA over her single life expectancy of 62.1 years. Add that to the 80 years Ed saved and you have an IRA growing tax-sheltered for 142 years! If, however, Ed left the IRA to his daughter Ilana, who is 65 when Ed dies, Ilana could stretch the IRA over her own single life expectancy of 21.0 years. Added to the 80 years Ed saved, that's still more than 100 years.

Distribution Rules When an IRA Beneficiary Dies

What happens if a beneficiary dies before his or her life expectancy is up and there is still a balance in the IRA?

I was hoping you wouldn't ask that, because there are, of course, another set of RMD rules for that situation.

Ed, no more rules!! Please, I beg you. Just one more RMD rule might put me over the edge.

Then you'd better make sure to take your medication and see that all your IRA beneficiary forms are in place.

Actually, these rules aren't too bad, and they'll preserve your IRA for as long as legally possible without your having to keep finding 20-year-olds to marry.

First things first. Although I've already said this, I'll say it again (and again, probably) until it sinks in: **As soon as you inherit an IRA, you should immediately name a beneficiary.** That person will be *your* beneficiary. If it's a nonspouse, the maximum postdeath stretch on the RMDs will be based on *your* life expectancy, not your beneficiary's. If your beneficiary is your spouse (your wife, say), she can roll the IRA over to her own IRA and name her own beneficiaries, who would also follow these rules. For the most part, it will be the nonspouse beneficiary who gets the longest stretch IRA.

The general rule is that when a beneficiary dies during his or her payout term and there is still a balance remaining in the inherited IRA, the beneficiary's beneficiary can complete the remaining term of the deceased's life expectancy. A beneficiary's beneficiary cannot tack on his or her own life expectancy to this, however.

For example, Tom, the IRA owner, dies in 2003 at age 75 (after his RBD). His beneficiary is his daughter Lucy. In 2004, the year after Tom's death, Lucy is 50 years old and begins taking her RMDs. Tom took his 2003 RMD before he died. Upon inheriting Tom's IRA, Lucy immediately names her son Mike as her beneficiary. Lucy dies in 2009. Mike is 30 years old in 2009. Over what term will Mike take RMDs? 28.2 years. That is Lucy's remaining life expectancy in 2009 (34.2 years less the 6 years that she took RMDs before she died = 28.2 years remaining). Even though Mike is much younger than Lucy, he cannot use his life expectancy because he is not the original beneficiary. He is the beneficiary's beneficiary and he can only stretch his RMDs over the deceased beneficiary's remaining life expectancy. Therefore, Mike's age is meaningless (except to him) because his RMDs will not be based on his age.

If instead of naming Mike as her beneficiary, Lucy named her Aunt Ethel as beneficiary, and Aunt Ethel is 92 years old in 2009 when Lucy dies, over how many more years could Aunt Ethel stretch RMDs? The answer is the same: 28.2—even though Aunt Ethel may not live that long. Again, Aunt Ethel's age has no effect on the payout term because she is the beneficiary's beneficiary and continues the original beneficiary's (Lucy's) remaining 28.2-year term.

Now, if Aunt Ethel dies during the 28.2-year remaining term, what is the payout to her beneficiary? Whoever inherits from Aunt Ethel will still be able to withdraw over the remaining payout schedule (or sooner). It does not matter who ends up inheriting

from Lucy, the remaining payout term is fixed at 28.2 years—even
if Lucy neglected to name a beneficiary.

"But if that's the case," you begin with a puzzled look on your
face, "why then is it so important for a beneficiary to immediately
name a beneficiary if the payout is the same?"

The IRA owner names a beneficiary *to secure the stretch IRA*
for his or her beneficiary. But once that is done and the IRA owner
dies, the stretch is secured regardless of who inherits from the beneficiary. A beneficiary does not name a beneficiary to secure the
stretch IRA. That is already done.

The reason you want to immediately name a beneficiary is to
make sure the inheritance goes to that beneficiary and does not go
through your estate, where it's anybody's guess who might end up
with it. By naming Mike as her beneficiary right away, Lucy en-
sured that her IRA will pass directly to him with no questions
asked, no costly probate, and no delays.

Another Exception

Remember my telling you (the beneficiary) that your beneficiary
cannot use his or her own life expectancy to continue postdeath
RMDs, that only your remaining term can be used? Well, as with
almost all of the IRA distribution rules, there is an exception. And
that exception applies when a spouse chooses to remain a beneficiary and dies before his or her RBD. In such cases, the beneficiary's beneficiary is allowed to use his or her own life expectancy
to compute postdeath RMDs.

For example, Marvin, the IRA owner, dies in 2003 at age 62
(before his RBD). His beneficiary is his wife Lynn, who is 54 in
2003. Lynn needs to withdraw some of the IRA for living expenses, so she elects not to roll over but chooses instead to remain
a beneficiary (thereby avoiding the 10 percent early-withdrawal
penalty). Lynn does not have to withdraw anything until the year
Marvin would have reached 70½ years of age.

Now let's assume Lynn dies at 57 in 2006, having named her

son Greg as the beneficiary of the IRA she inherited from her husband. Lynn, therefore, is the designated beneficiary of her husband's IRA, and Greg, their son, is the "beneficiary's beneficiary." Greg is 28 years old in 2006, the year of his mother's death. In this case, he can use his own life expectancy even though he is the beneficiary's beneficiary.

What if Lynn had neglected to name a beneficiary?

That would spell bad news. The entire IRA would have to be paid out under the five-year rule, in other words emptied by the end of 2011, the fifth year after the year of Lynn's death. That's because under this special exception, Lynn is treated as the IRA owner and since the IRA owner (Lynn) died before her RBD, which would not have been until 2011, the five-year rule applies since there is no designated beneficiary.

And what if Lynn had lived past 2011, the year that the IRA owner would have reached 70½, and died, say, in 2015 at 66 years old? Then Greg would be able to continue Lynn's remaining 19.2-year term, even if he was not named as Lynn's beneficiary, but inherited through Lynn's estate.

Death in the Gap Period

What happens if a beneficiary dies before becoming the designated beneficiary—that is to say, during the so-called gap period referenced earlier in the chapter?

In this case, the deceased beneficiary is deemed the designated beneficiary, even though he or she did not live to be officially appointed as such. It is the deceased's life expectancy that will be used to calculated postdeath RMDs, and the deceased's beneficiary will take those payments. Even if the deceased beneficiary neglects to have named a beneficiary, the IRA can still be stretched over the deceased's life expectancy, based on his or her age in the year of death.

Disaster-Proof Your IRA
with These New Year's Resolutions

What's great about these resolutions is that they're easy. They don't involve going to a gym and working out, eating food you don't like just because it's fat-free, or cleaning out 30 years worth of junk from the garage. All you have to do to achieve these resolutions is be a bit organized when it comes to your retirement accounts. Everything else can stay a mess—because that's how we like it, right?

THIS NEW YEAR'S I WILL . . .

- Name a primary beneficiary for each IRA I own.
- Go a step further and name a secondary or contingent beneficiary (in case my primary beneficiary dies before I do), and be able to take advantage of postdeath estate planning and disclaimer opportunities available under the IRA rules.
- Obtain copies of the beneficiary forms outlining my wishes for each IRA I own.
- If there are multiple beneficiaries on one IRA, make sure that each beneficiary's share is clearly identified with a fraction, a percentage, or the word *equally* if that is applicable. Otherwise some beneficiaries may be left out or it may be unclear what their portion is. There should be no question as to who gets what. This includes contingent beneficiaries as well.
- Make sure that the financial institution has my beneficiary selections on file and that their records agree with my choices.
- Keep a copy of all my IRA beneficiary forms and give copies to my financial advisor and attorney.
- Let my beneficiaries know where to locate my IRA beneficiary forms. I will give them a beneficiary information sheet so they know how many accounts I have and where the beneficiary form for each is located.

- Review my IRA beneficiary forms at least once each year to make sure that they are correct and reflect any changes due to new tax laws or major life events such as a death, birth, adoption, marriage, divorce, or *somebody forgetting my birthday!*

SEVEN

Step #4: Roth It

> *"The point to remember is that what the government gives it must first take away."*
> —John Strider Coleman (1897–1958),
> American business executive

The Big Picture

The Roth IRA is the single best gift Congress has ever presented to the American taxpayer. It allows us to build retirement accounts that, over the long haul, will grow to incredible size—and remain free of income tax forever. There is only one catch: You have to pay the income tax up-front. Many people run screaming the other way when they hear that. But when it comes to retirement planning and account protection, keep your eye on the Big Picture.

The Roth IRA works the opposite of the traditional IRA and other tax-deferred retirement accounts such as the 401(k). With tax-deferred accounts, you get a tax deduction when funds are put into the plan and you pay the tax when you withdraw later, usually at retirement. With the Roth IRA, however, you pay the income tax when you put in the money and get no tax deduction—but after that, all future growth and withdrawals are tax-free to you and your beneficiaries.

I prefer the Roth IRA approach hands down. Here's why:

While a current tax deduction will save you money now, withdrawals on earnings from a deductible IRA are eventually subject to tax. Many people believe that they will be in a lower tax bracket in retirement so the tax on withdrawals from a traditional IRA will be less. But that's a myth. Most people are in a higher tax bracket in retirement given their retirement income, Social Security, and investment income. Therefore, a Roth IRA can save even more money over the long run because withdrawals of earnings are completely tax-free and remain tax-free to your beneficiaries. And all you have to do to get this marvelous tax break is have the account a minimum of five years and avoid taking distributions until after age 59½. As with a traditional IRA, you can withdraw before 59½, but you may face a 10 percent penalty for doing so—unless the following same exceptions apply: the early withdrawal is for death, disability, education, medical expenses, or first-time home-buying expenses, etc. (see Chapter 4).

Unlike with a traditional IRA, Roth IRA owners are not subject to a required beginning date (RBD) or required minimum distributions (RMDs). That's right. You *never have to take the money out* if you don't want to, not even after you turn 70½. You can just let it grow and grow and grow. In fact, with a Roth IRA, you can keep making contributions (if you qualify and have the earnings) even after age 70½. You can't do that with a traditional IRA. Only when you die and the money is left to a nonspouse (child) must withdrawals begin—because beneficiaries are subject to RMDs; but with a Roth, the RMDs are almost always income-tax–free to beneficiaries, as well!

Paralysis by Analysis

Anyone eligible to start a Roth IRA (I'll get to the requirements shortly) should do so. Now!

So, why isn't there a stampede?

Is the Roth IRA too good to be true?

Is it that we don't trust Congress to keep its mitts off the Roth?

Is it that you still aren't sure that it really, truly, absolutely, positively pays to take the tax hit now with a Roth rather than later with a traditional IRA?

I'm not being flip here. These concerns have been expressed by millions of Americans as the primary reasons they've yet to hop on the Roth IRA bandwagon. Are these concerns legit? Let's look at these concerns and others that people have, and separate truth from baloney.

- **It's too good to be true; Congress will water it down or snatch it away.**

    Don't worry about Congress—it certainly isn't worrying about you! This fear is wholly without foundation. Not only would such a move be a politically unpopular one at the present time, even if it occurred in the future, Roth IRA participants would be grandfathered into the new rules, as happens whenever the tax law changes to repeal a former tax benefit.

- **But I'll be paying the tax now!**

    True. And you've had it drummed into you that tax deferral is the name of the retirement game, haven't you? Well, I have to face the fact that my profession is largely to blame for such arbitrary thinking. We accountants are virtually taught to tell our clients never to pay a tax before they have to. But that's wrongheaded—if paying tax now will lead to your prospering later, which is the case with a Roth IRA where you'll be paying **zero percent** tax on withdrawal! How much better can you do than that? Take my word. It's true. I'm an accountant. Would I lie?

- **But I'll get no tax deduction!**

    True again. So what? Big deal! A tax deduction on a $3,000 traditional IRA contribution, even if you are in the 30 percent federal and state income tax bracket, is worth only $900 a year to you. That's barely more than 17 bucks a week. You probably blow more than that going to the movies . . . alone. On the other hand, if you give up the $17, and instead stay home and wait for the movie to be out on cable in about two weeks, you're trading up to a much better deal, wouldn't you say? In addition, you can participate in a Roth IRA even if you are active in a 401(k) or other company plan—where deducting your traditional IRA contribution may not be possible anyway, due to income limits. And if you can't deduct contributions to your traditional IRA, you'll be stuck with a nondeductible traditional IRA, which, as you'll recall from Chapter 4, is one big pain in the neck when it comes to figuring out taxes on distributions under the annoying pro rata rule. The tax-free Roth IRA wins out handily over a traditional nondeductible IRA and all its related tax-deferral reporting (Form 8606) headaches. So, forget the instant gratification of getting a tax deduction and look at the enormous long-term advantages of tax-free growth instead!

■ **Roth IRAs are overly complicated.**

If anything is overly complicated, it's the RMD rules for traditional IRAs and company plans! Sure, the Roth IRA has its share of tax rules, but if you hold the account for the minimum five years and until you turn 59½, those rules are easy. All the distributions are tax- and penalty-free forever. It's that simple! Complications arise only when you withdraw before the five-year holding period expires or before you turn 59½. Pay attention: DO NOT DO THIS! Leave the money alone, and there are no distribution rules until you die and your beneficiaries start RMDs—but even those rules are simple because distributions are income-tax–free.

■ **My money will be tied up!**

Not true! But, wait a second, didn't I tell you earlier that you cannot touch your money for five years or until you are 59½ years old? No, what I said is that the distribution rules become more complicated if you tap Roth money early. But the same is true of traditional IRAs—except it's much more expensive to get at your traditional IRA money because you have to pay the income tax on the deferred amount on top of a 10 percent penalty, whereas with a Roth IRA, what you've put in has already been taxed so that expense is already covered if you withdraw early. And you can even avoid paying a 10 percent penalty if the funds you withdraw are your original contributions and not earnings. You see, you can take out your original contributions to your Roth IRA at any time for any reason, tax *and* penalty free. Now, I ask you: How great is *that?*

No More Excuses

Don't buy into all the nebulous rationales people offer, or knee-jerk responses to any thoughts of change that people have, that may cause you to stick with your traditional IRA or company plan status quo. Many of these people are just tightwads who simply don't want to pay tax now—even with the prospect of a huge tax-free gold rush later.

Likewise, don't fall into what athletes call "paralysis by analysis" from overstudying the issue. By the time you're satisfied, the opportunity to Roth it may have passed you by. Look at Moses. He spent 40 years searching for the Promised Land and wound up picking the only spot in the whole Middle East with no oil! So, put up your hand and promise me: *no more analysis!*

There is nothing more to analyze. The Roth IRA works. The only way it might not work for you as a tax-saving strategy is if you haven't the cash to pay the tax up-front (but if you're that short of cash, then estate taxes are probably not an issue for you and neither is planning to leave the lion's share of your IRA to your beneficiaries). Another way it may not work for you is if there's a chance that you might withdraw from your Roth within five years of opening it or before you're 59½. To gain the most from a Roth, you want to keep it long-term or at least for those five years and until you hit 59½.

So, stop looking for a reason not to Roth it. You simply can't beat this strategy for building tax-free long-term wealth. It's the opportunity of a lifetime, especially if you're young—because it gives you, among whatever other assets you may possess, the greatest asset of all . . . time.

Two Flavors

Roth IRAs come in two flavors: *Roth IRA contributions* and *Roth IRA conversions*. The big-money flavor is the Roth IRA conversion—but first, here's a short primer on Roth IRA contributions.

Roth IRA Contributions

You are limited to contributing up to $3,000 annually per person (which increases to $5,000 by 2008) to a Roth IRA if your yearly income is below $95,000 (for single taxpayers) or $150,000 (for married couples filing jointly). The $3,000 annual contribution limit can be apportioned any way you want. At a minimum you should make a token contribution to start the running of the five-year holding period. For example, a 2003 Roth IRA contribution made as late as April 15, 2004, starts the five-year holding period as of January 1, 2003.

Contributions can be increased each year by $500 (with a jump to $1,000 in 2006) for taxpayers who are at least 50 years old. Contribution limits phase out for singles with incomes above $95,000 to $110,000 and for married couples filing jointly with incomes above $150,000 to $160,000. In most cases, married persons who file separate returns cannot make Roth IRA contributions.

Roth contributions are permitted without regard to age. Thus, children with summer jobs can fund a Roth IRA based on their earnings. And individuals over 70½ who are still working can continue to fund a Roth IRA as long as they've got the dollars.

Roth IRA contributions also are permitted without regard to participation in a qualified retirement plan.

Roth IRA Conversions

The Roth IRA conversion is where you can really stockpile tax-free cash, but, of course, you have to be able to pay the conversion tax first. This up-front tax payment is the biggest roadblock for most people. But it shouldn't be. If you do not pay the conversion tax now, you or your beneficiaries will pay more income tax later, because all the growth in your traditional IRA will eventually be taxed anyway, and withdrawals from that account must begin after your RBD. That is not the case with a Roth IRA.

The costliest tax blunders occur because people refuse to spend now to gain later. I understand their feelings that "a bird in the hand is worth two in the bush." But parting with some money now is the best way to leverage your assets for future growth. In effect, you're paying for seed so the crop will be free. If there is one overriding message to this book, it's this: Doing nothing because you can't part with a buck is the surest way to build up your retirement savings account for Uncle Sam.

Here's the incredible thing about a Roth IRA conversion: There is no limit, no cap, no ceiling on the amount that can be converted—if you're willing to pay the income tax. You can convert $10 million if you have it. You'll owe about $4 million in income tax (but if you've got the $10 million in the first place, this should be easy), and it would still pay to do the conversion because growth on the back end is practically limitless and all tax-free.

If your annual income isn't more than $100,000 and you don't file married-separate, you can convert a traditional IRA to a Roth IRA. Congress has given no reason why it does not want separate filers to have a Roth. I think it just doesn't trust people who file married-separate. But there is an exception to this rule. If you are married and live apart from your spouse for the entire tax year, then you can treat yourself as not being married for Roth conversion eligibility purposes (though you will still file a married-separate return, and your own income still cannot exceed $100,000).

Congress has also offered no reason for this $100,000 income eligibility limit, which applies to all taxpayers. It creates a huge marriage penalty. For example, two single people can earn up to $100,000 apiece and each will still be eligible to convert. But if they get married, their joint income is added and could exclude them from being able to convert. So, if your income is just below $100,000 and you are getting married to someone who also has income, you may want to convert (to a Roth IRA, that is) before the year you marry, or else marry someone with no job and no prospects of future income. That's the incentive our tax laws have created when it comes to qualifying for the Roth.

The $100,000 income limit is not just *any* income. By now you should know that Congress uses the Tax Code to make you work for every tax break. To make it a chore for you to determine your Roth eligibility income, it came up with a bunch of factors to consider in finding out if you qualify.

You might surmise that the annual income amount to use in determining Roth IRA conversion eligibility would be your *adjusted gross income (AGI)*. But that's just the starting point; you see, our creative tax writers decided that AGI must be modified into another subacronym: *MAGI*. No, this is not short for "Gift of the MAGI" (you wish). It stands for *modified adjusted gross income*, and it works this way:

Any income produced by converting a traditional IRA to a Roth IRA is included in your AGI, but does not increase your MAGI, and therefore does not count toward the $100,000 Roth eligibility limit.

For example, if your AGI (from Form 1040, your personal tax return) is, say, $80,000 and you want to convert $50,000 from your traditional IRA to a Roth IRA, your new AGI will be $130,000, but your MAGI will be only $80,000, which does not exceed the $100,000 conversion eligibility limit.

Here's another example: If your AGI is, say, $99,000 after you have contributed $3,000 to a deductible IRA, your MAGI will be $102,000, so you would not be eligible to convert your traditional IRA to a Roth IRA—because the IRA deduction ($3,000 in this example) cannot be used to reduce your MAGI in order to qualify for the Roth conversion.

Convert before You Reach 70½

If you are close to 70½ years old and thinking about converting to a Roth, you'd better hurry up—because once you reach the first day of your 70½ year, you are subject to RMDs from your traditional IRA, and these RMDs can throw your income level above the $100,000 limit for Roth conversion eligibility. Why? Because even though the conversion itself doesn't count, your RMD does and can disqualify you from converting. And if your traditional IRA is large enough, you may not be able to convert at all until 2005 (when the law will start treating RMDs on traditional IRAs similar to Roth conversion income, which does not affect eligibility).

Converting before you're 70½ avoids the minimum distribution problem. But once you pass January 1 of your 70½ year, you must add your first RMD to your income for Roth conversion eligibility—even if you do not actually take your first required distribution until April 1 of the following year.

Until you have satisfied your required minimum distribution, all money withdrawn in your 70½ year up to that amount will not be eligible for conversion, as it too will be treated as part of your RMD, and, remember that RMDs can never be converted to a Roth! Any amounts in excess of the RMD can be converted, but only if the income from the RMD does not throw your income over the $100,000 eligibility limit.

That's why it is important to convert before the year you reach your 70½ birthday. If you don't, you may not be able to convert again until the law changes in 2005. If you do nothing now when you're younger than 70½ and ultimately find yourself in the Roth conversion snafu I've described, all income earned in your traditional IRA from now until you can convert again in 2005 will be taxed then (if you convert in 2005), whereas if you had converted before your 70½ year, all that income would have been accumulating tax-free in the Roth.

With this strategy, you can ignore all those darn after-70½ distribution rules that attach themselves to traditional IRAs like flies on s***. In fact, many people convert to Roth IRAs just for that reason alone.

Ways to Reduce Your Income to Qualify for a Roth Conversion

If you are close to the $100,000 limit for eligibility, you may want to consider reducing your income so that you will qualify for a Roth IRA conversion. The quickest way, of course, is to quit your job. But since that's a bit extreme, try these:

- Contribute more to tax-deferred company plans such as your 401(k) or 403(b).
- Delay any year-end bonuses (this must be prearranged with your company).
- Take stock losses.
- Take ordinary losses from complete disposition of investment interests (e.g., limited partnership interests). These losses are often significant. In addition to helping you qualify for the Roth conversion, they may also substantially reduce or eliminate the tax on the conversion. Timing is everything.
- Take passive losses (e.g., on rental real estate).
- Alimony always reduces income . . . the hard way, but it works.
- Use moving expenses.
- If you're retired, withdraw your RMD and not a penny more; use other savings for living expenses that are not taxable as income.
- Use Keogh, SEP, and SIMPLE contributions (only traditional IRA contributions cannot be used to lower income for Roth eligibility).

- Convert taxable income to tax-free income (for example, get out of CDs and other taxable investments and invest in, say, tax-free municipal bonds).

ITEMS THAT WON'T REDUCE YOUR MAGI

Itemized deductions or the standard deduction, tax credits, or personal exemptions (MAGI is figured before these items) may not reduce your MAGI for converting, but if you qualify for the conversion, then these items will lower the tax cost of converting and make converting a better move. You may also find that if you are in a higher tax bracket this year, but in a lower bracket next year, you'd rather put off converting until next year, or do a partial conversion (some this year, some next). It's not an all-or-nothing choice.

Exercise Tax Audit Caution When Trying to Qualify

Small business owners with high income and expenses are *five times more likely* to be audited than most other taxpayers. So, if you are close to the $100,000 eligibility limit, don't go crazy piling up aggressive deductions (particularly in the travel-and-entertainment, home-office, or auto expense area) that may be considered questionable by the IRS if it's just to lower your MAGI. If two years later, for example, your return is selected for audit, the disallowance of these items may push your MAGI back over the $100,000 limit, thereby negating your Roth IRA conversion. You can exercise damage control by "recharacterizing" (undoing) the conversion (as I discuss later in this chapter), but the likelihood is that you will not make the cutoff date of October 15 of the following year since most audits are seldom started, let alone completed, by that date. And so, you'll be stranded with an illegal Roth IRA. What happens then? First, you will be subject to a 6 percent excise tax each year that money was in the Roth. Then, since you never had a legal Roth IRA, all the earnings you had sheltered are now taxable, plus there are interest and penalties. In addition, if you converted before you were 59½, you will be subject to the 10 percent penalty on early withdrawals from your traditional IRA.

This scenario reminds me of Frank Capra's classic film *It's a Wonderful Life,* where down-on-his-luck and suicidal George Bailey (Jimmy Stewart) is shown by a guardian angel named Clarence what life would be like if he (Bailey) had never been born. It's the same with an illegal Roth IRA. All penalties and taxes would apply as if the Roth IRA had never existed, and if, in the event of an audit, you had used any questionable deductions to qualify for the conversion, George Bailey's problems will look good to you. Remember, everything turned out happily ever after for Bailey when his friends showed up with baskets of goodies to lift his holiday spirits. But how many of your friends do you expect will show up on your doorstep with baskets of money to bail you out of an illegal Roth IRA mess?

CAUTION!

Be alert for unexpected income that can push you over the MAGI limit. Income items you might not think about in your Roth IRA planning include state tax refunds, alimony received, gains or dividends from pass-through entities (investment partnerships), royalties, rental income, and taxable IRA or pension distributions. All should be taken into account when estimating your income.

A good rule of thumb to use in choosing deductions, particularly the aggressive kind, is to consider whether you would still qualify for the Roth conversion even if all of these deductions were ultimately disallowed.

Realistically, even the "Audit from Hell" isn't likely to disallow everything. So, if you think you'll still qualify for the Roth without these deductions, then, since you are not using them to help you qualify, throw caution to the wind and take them. Disallowed items only present a problem if you've counted upon them to achieve conversion eligibility.

The following are rock solid deductions for achieving Roth conversion eligibility because of their "provability":

- Rent
- Business insurance
- Business telephone and utility bills
- Office supplies and postage
- Business dues and subscriptions
- Legal and other professional fees
- Vendors' or suppliers' invoices (if you are on the cash basis)
- Business equipment lease payments (e.g., a copier lease)
- Health insurance (a special benefit for the self-employed)
- First-year expensing (depreciation deductions increased under the new tax law)
- Advertising costs
- Business interest expense
- Pension plan deductions
- Bonuses paid to your CPA before year-end (what a great idea!)

CAUTION!

Your taxes may be slightly higher the year you convert. For example, the tax on Social Security benefits may apply solely due to the Roth conversion. The Roth conversion will also cause the following AGI-based deductions and credits to be reduced or lost completely: medical expenses, itemized deductions, HOPE scholarship tax credits, lifetime learning credits, student loan interest deductions, rental loss deductions, adoption credits, dependent exemptions, and child tax credits. Don't shy away from the Roth because of this. The tax hike and loss of benefits, if any, are for one year only—whereas your Roth lives on for decades tax-free.

A Death-Bed Roth Conversion

The up-front tax you pay to convert to a Roth IRA reduces your taxable estate, so, in effect, the government is paying for half the cost of your conversion. That's a big break, especially for older converters with large estates. Nevertheless, many older traditional IRA owners feel that the Roth conversion is not for them, because they will not have enough years to make up the out-of-pocket tax cost of conversion. The "too-old" excuse generally holds no water, however.

I had a client who was terminally ill—and one doesn't get much more "out-of-time" than that. It took some convincing, but I eventually persuaded his family to persuade him to convert his $1 million traditional IRA to a Roth IRA, which he did, paying about $400,000 in income tax for the conversion.

When he died soon after, his estate was subject to an estate tax of 50 percent. But because he had paid $400,000 in income tax on the Roth conversion, his estate had $400,000 less in it than there would have been, so, at the 50 percent rate, his estate tax was immediately reduced by $200,000 (50 percent of $400,000 = $200,000)!

If my late client had not converted, he would have died with $400,000 more in his estate and lost $200,000 more in estate tax. But instead, the government wound up paying half the cost of his Roth conversion (through lost tax revenue), and my late client's heirs inherited his $1 million Roth IRA from which they can withdraw income for the rest of their lives, tax-free.

How to Convert to a Roth IRA

You convert when you transfer (deposit) funds from your traditional IRA to your Roth IRA. If you are converting IRAs that contain nondeductible contributions, or after-tax funds rolled over from a company plan, then you must use the pro rata rule (see Chapter 3) to determine how much of the converted funds will be taxable.

Nondeductible contributions and after-tax funds are basis (already-taxed money) and can be withdrawn tax-free, but under the pro rata rule each distribution (or converted dollar in the case of a Roth conversion) is deemed part taxable and part tax-free based on the percentage of the basis (the nondeductible and after-tax contributions) to the balance in the traditional IRA.

For example, let's say you have $300,000 in your traditional IRA and you convert $30,000 of it to a Roth IRA. If there are no nondeductible contributions, then all $30,000 is taxable. But if the $300,000 IRA balance included $30,000 of nondeductible contributions and you converted $30,000, only $3,000 would be tax-free and $27,000 would be taxable.

One would think that if there is $30,000 of basis in the IRA, one could convert the $30,000 and pay no tax. But that's not the way it works. The pro rata rule requires each dollar converted to be given percentages of taxable and tax-free money. In this example, the basis is $30,000 and that is 10 percent of the $300,000 IRA balance. Under the pro rata rule, 10 percent of each distribution will be tax-free and 90 percent will be taxable. So, when you convert the $30,000, 10 percent (or $3,000) will be tax-free (a return of part of the basis) and 90 percent (or $27,000) will be taxable and included in the current year's income. All of this must be reported on Form 8606 for the year you convert.

Basically, a Roth IRA conversion is the same as a rollover because you're shifting funds from one type of account to another. As you recall from Chapter 3, rollovers are accomplished in one of two ways—a direct trustee-to-trustee transfer or a withdrawal and deposit within 60 days. For a typical rollover, the direct transfer is the preferred method of the two.

For a Roth IRA conversion, however, there is a third and better method. It's called *redesignating,* and it's easier than switching banks. For example, if you have your traditional IRA with Mutual Fund Company X, just call and say, "Make my traditional IRA a Roth IRA," and, bingo, it's done! Your account is retitled a Roth IRA and the money never has to be moved. You will still, of course, pay income tax on the conversion, but the conversion itself is achieved instantly—like magic.

The once-a-year rule that applies to rollovers (see Chapter 3) does not apply to Roth IRA conversions, even though a conversion is basically a rollover. You can convert as many times as you wish during the year. The 60-day rollover rule (see Chapters 3 and 4) does apply to Roth conversions, however, but only when you withdraw the funds yourself to redeposit in the Roth account. (There is no 60-day rule with a direct transfer or when you redesignate.)

Paying the Income Tax on Conversion

As you're well aware by now, you must pay income tax when you convert to a Roth. Ideally, that money should not come from your traditional IRA or other retirement accounts.

If you use your IRA money to pay the conversion tax, you won't be able to convert as much, and could incur a 10 percent penalty on the amount used. More importantly, you'll have less money working and growing for you tax-free in the Roth IRA!

For example, Bob wants to convert his $100,000 IRA to a Roth IRA, but the only money he has available to pay the income tax is the IRA money itself. So, he'll probably only be able to convert about $75,000 because he'll need $25,000 (depending on his tax bracket) for the tax. The $75,000 would go into the Roth and there would be no 10 percent penalty on that money—because the 10 percent penalty does not apply to amounts converted, regardless of the convert's age. However, it does apply to amounts *not converted*. In this case, let's say Bob is younger than 59½ years old; therefore, he would owe a 10 percent penalty on the $25,000 that was used to pay the tax because that money was never converted. It's considered to be a regular taxable distribution. Now Bob is paying a 10 percent penalty on top of the conversion tax in order to convert—and not getting the full $100,000 IRA into the Roth, just $75,000 of it. This is why funds other than those from your IRA should always be used to pay the income tax on a Roth conversion, if you are under 59½ years old. The extra 10 percent penalty tips the scales and makes the conversion too costly.

But if you simply don't have other money to draw on, then what do you do? Forget the idea of converting? Not at all; just convert a little less. Remember, you don't have to convert all of your traditional IRA all at one time all in one year. You can convert a smaller amount each year. This way you can structure your conversions so that you can pay the tax from non-IRA money and avoid having your Roth IRA growth cut down before it even gets started.

Here's another creative strategy using life insurance to Roth it even when you think you don't have the money to pay the tax on the conversion. Let's assume that you have a $1 million traditional IRA for which the conversion tax would be $400,000, and you would rather have your children inherit than your spouse. Here's what to do:

Buy a $1 million life insurance policy and name your spouse as beneficiary of the policy and the IRA. When you die, your spouse will receive both the $1 million of tax-free life insurance and the IRA, which your spouse can then roll over to his or her IRA. Now, if your spouse's income does not exceed $100,000, he or she can convert that $1 million traditional IRA to a Roth IRA, using money tax-free from the life insurance policy to pay the $400,000 conversion tax.

Now that he or she has a Roth IRA, your spouse is no longer subject to required IRA distributions. Your spouse never has to withdraw that money, and if he or she does, the withdrawals will be tax-free. Of course, the Roth may grow so large that it becomes subject to estate tax in your spouse's estate. If so, there is no problem.

Your spouse just uses some of the remaining life insurance money to buy another policy on his or her own life set up outside the estate and names the children as beneficiaries. When your spouse dies, the children will inherit the Roth IRA and withdrawals will be income-tax–free forever. The children will also inherit the new life insurance estate- and income-tax–free and can use some of that money to pay any estate tax due on the Roth IRA they just inherited.

WHEN IS THE CONVERSION EFFECTIVE?

The day the funds are removed from your traditional IRA to go to the Roth determines the year of conversion, even if those funds are not actually deposited in the Roth until the following year.

Roth IRA Creditor Protection

One more factor to consider in deciding whether to convert is the issue of asset (creditor) protection. As mentioned in Chapter 3, many states have extended protection from creditor claims to IRAs, as well. In some cases, however, they may not have extended the same protection to Roth IRAs.

For example, in some states, protection currently applies only to IRAs created under Code Section 408. But Roth IRAs are created under Code Section 408A. Special legislation is needed by these states to extend protection to Roth IRAs —and, in fact, most state legislatures are moving in that direction, if they haven't already.

Recharacterizations and Reconversions

What if you convert to a Roth IRA, pay income tax on the amount converted, but then your financial situation changes and you wish you had that tax money back?

Or what if you convert IRA assets worth, say, $100,000, to a Roth IRA but then, thanks to those corporate CEOs who are robbing us all blind, the value of your converted Roth IRA funds plummets to, say, $15,000? When April 15 of next year rolls around, you will still have to pay tax on the $100,000 that was converted (because the tax is owed based on the value of assets at the time they were distributed), but the Roth is now worth only $15,000, so you would scream, "No fair! I was robbed! I want a &%%$##ING do-over!!!"

Well, guess what?

"No problemo," says the IRS. "Sure, you can change your mind."

This "do-over" provision, which in tax talk is called a *recharacterization*, is what takes all the risk out of converting to a Roth IRA and is another reason—a BIG one—to convert. Wouldn't it be great if Las Vegas worked this way? Imagine placing a $100,000 bet on red and if it comes up black, you just say, "Oops, changed my mind; I think I'll take back that bet!"

Ah, but what if you take a plunge from a 20-story window after seeing your stocks hit the skids, and now you're dead. Can you still get a do-over? On that one, the answer is no—and yes. No, you'll have to stay dead, I'm afraid, but, believe it or not, yes, your heirs can recharacterize so that they aren't stuck having to pay tax on a value that no longer exists.

A recharacterization must be via direct trustee-to-trustee transfer. You cannot withdraw from the Roth and redeposit the funds (even within 60 days) into a traditional IRA.

Leaving the funds in the same financial institution and redesignating the account can also achieve a recharacterization. The bank will change the title from a Roth IRA to a traditional IRA and the conversion will be "undone." You'll receive a tax refund of any income tax paid on the conversion. If you have not yet paid the tax, then the tax liability will be removed.

"Must" Recharacterizations

If it turns out that you were ineligible to convert because either your income exceeded $100,000 or you filed married-separate (both disqualifiers for conversion eligibility) there are no two ways about it; you have to recharacterize, or you'll suffer heavy taxes and penalties.

Don't get too judgmental. It's by no means impossible or unheard of for people to make those mistakes when converting to a Roth. Anybody can. For example, many taxpayers who converted simply didn't know about the $100,000 income eligibility limit, while others who did know had no fix at the time of conversion on their MAGI for the year. That can happen easily because you must convert before you file your tax return, which means that if you convert in 2003, you may not know your exact MAGI until you file your tax return in April of 2004.

Other scenarios might include your not realizing certain income items that add to your MAGI—for example, that state tax refund you hadn't counted on, or, if you're one of those CEOs I mentioned earlier, that $3 billion in stock options you cashed in (and then forgot about) while telling people to buy your company's plummeting stock.

Whatever the slip-up, recharacterizing prevents matters from growing worse. That's why this fail-safe system of Roth IRA do-overs exists—and why my advice to you, even if you are unsure if you will qualify for the conversion because your income may be too high, is to go ahead and convert anyway. You can always recharacterize. What more of a risk-free guarantee could you want?

Plenty of Time to Recharacterize

In addition to letting you change your mind about the conversion, the IRS gives you plenty of time to do it.

For example, if you converted to a Roth at any time in 2003, you have until October 15, 2004, to recharacterize—because a recharacterization can be done up to the due date of your tax return, plus extensions. Even if you file on time by April 15 (with no extensions), you still have until October 15 of the year after the conversion (the extended due date of the tax return) to recharacterize the prior year's Roth conversion. It's like getting to bet on a horse after the race is over and you know it won.

If you filed for an extension, you must report the recharacterization on your tax return when you file it. If you already filed by April 15, 2004 (without an extension), and wish to recharacterize before October 15, 2004, you would have to file an amended tax return and report the recharacterization on Form 8606, which must be attached to the amended return (Form 1040X).

Figuring Out Your Recharacterization

A recharacterization removes your tax liability on the conversion. If you recharacterize the entire Roth IRA, you totally eliminate the tax liability that was created when you converted. But what if you are only recharacterizing a part of the Roth? Or, what if you have converted several IRAs during the year and only want to recharacterize parts of some of them? Or, what if you want to recharacterize from a Roth IRA account that includes both Roth contributions and conversions from prior years? Then it's not so simple.

If you have converted several different stocks (or other investments), some will inevitably go up, and some will go down. That's why you should keep each conversion as a separate Roth IRA account until the time for recharacterizing has expired (October 15 of the year after the conversion). This will allow you to cherry-pick and recharacterize only the losers (the underperformers).

Reconversions

A *reconversion* can only take place after a recharacterization. For example, if you converted from a traditional IRA to a Roth IRA, and then recharacterized the Roth IRA back to the traditional IRA, you can then reconvert the same funds back to a new Roth IRA. There are no limits except time limits on reconversions.

If you recharacterize a Roth IRA conversion, you cannot reconvert the same funds back to a Roth IRA in the same tax year. You must wait until the later of

1. The beginning of the tax year after the year of the conversion, or
2. Thirty days after the recharacterization.

Therefore, if you convert, say, in June 2003, and then recharacterize on December 20, 2003, you must wait until January 20, 2004, before you can reconvert the same funds. If you recharacterized on November 20, 2003, then you could reconvert on January 1, 2004. If you have different Roth IRAs for each conversion, the reconversion rules apply separately to each one.

Taking Your Money out of a Roth IRA

Withdrawals from a Roth IRA are tax-free if they are *qualified distributions*. What the heck does that mean? It means they must pass a few tests.

To be a qualified distribution, the funds must have been held in the account for more than five years AND conform to one of the following other stipulations:

■ Be taken at or after 59½ years of age.
■ Be taken upon death of the owner.

- Be taken for owner disability reasons. (The definition of *disability* is the same as that for the traditional IRA.)
- Qualify as a "special purpose distribution." (The first-time homebuyer exception would be an example of a special purpose distribution. The first-time homebuyer exception for a Roth IRA is the same as for a traditional IRA; see Chapter 4).

If you do not hold the Roth for more than five years, then even if you are 59½, dead, or disabled, or use the money for a first home, your Roth distribution could still be subject to tax.

The 10 percent early-withdrawal penalty does not apply to the amounts converted from the traditional IRA to a Roth IRA, even if you are under 59½. But if you use some of the IRA assets to pay for the conversion taxes, that amount will be subject to early-withdrawal penalty tax. The reason is that the amount withdrawn for taxes was not converted to a Roth IRA.

TWO FIVE-YEAR RULES

There are two five-year rules governing Roth IRAs. The first one determines if your Roth distribution is a qualified distribution and, therefore, free of income tax. The five-year holding period starts on the first day of the year for which the Roth IRA contribution is made, even if the actual contribution is made in the following year. You have until April 15 after the year for which you want to contribute to make the contribution. For example, if you make a 2003 Roth IRA contribution in March of 2004, the five-year holding period begins on January 1, 2003, the first day of the year for which the Roth IRA contribution was made, even though it was actually made in 2004. For Roth IRA contributions, the five-year rule does not restart for each contribution.

The second five-year rule applies only to Roth IRA conversions, and only if you are under 59½ years old. It says

that if you are younger than 59½, you must hold the converted funds for five years. Distributions of converted funds
not held for five years will be subject to the 10 percent
penalty. This five-year holding period starts over with each
new conversion.

There are no lifetime distribution rules for Roth IRA owners. You
can withdraw as much as you want any time you want, which is
one of the great beauties of this tax-free vehicle over other types of
retirement plans.

But if you can't let your money sit for that five-year minimum
and your 59½ birthday, and you start taking your money early,
you'll face two kinds of distribution rules: aggregation rules and
ordering rules.

Aggregation Rules

Under the aggregation principle, all your Roth IRA accounts, whether
conversion or contributory, are treated as one pot of money, even
if you have them in different places. So, for figuring taxation on
early withdrawals, all your accounts are simply added together.
But your withdrawals must be taken in a specific sequence.

Ordering Rules

These special rules tell you which funds must come out first by dividing the aggregated money in your Roth IRA accounts into three
distinct groups:

1. Original Roth IRA contributions
2. Roth conversions on a first-in-first-out (FIFO) basis
   a. Taxable amounts first, then
   b. Nontaxable amounts (from nondeductible IRAs)
3. Earnings on Roth IRA contributions or conversions

If you tap your account(s) early, you must start with your original Roth contributions. This money can be withdrawn tax- and penalty-free at any time for any reason. After the Roth IRA contributions are withdrawn (or if there are no Roth contributions), the next in line are the Roth conversion funds, which must be taken out on a first-in-first-out (FIFO) basis, meaning conversions from the earliest years must be withdrawn first. These withdrawals will be subject to the five-year–minimum/under-59½ 10 percent early-withdrawal penalty (but no tax because you paid it when you converted). (This rule was put into effect to close a perceived loophole that would have allowed individuals to conspire to convert from their traditional IRA and then withdraw from the Roth IRA with no penalty.)

A further complication arises at this time if you have converted nondeductible traditional IRA money to a Roth IRA—because every time you withdraw from a traditional IRA that has nondeductible contributions, you need to use that darn pro rata rule.

The group of funds off limits until last is earnings. It is what happens here that makes me so vehement about keeping your hands off your Roth for the minimum five years and until you're 59½ (or not converting in the first place if you think you'll succumb to this temptation). Earnings will be subject to both tax and 10 percent penalty (unless you qualify for any of the exceptions I described earlier: first-time homebuyer, disability, etc.). That is to say, you've lost all the benefits of the Roth!

Inheriting Roths

When a Roth IRA owner dies, the RMD rules are pretty much the same as with a traditional IRA. The only difference is that the RMDs taken by the beneficiary are tax-free—unless the deceased has not held the account for the required five years.

When a nonspouse (a child) inherits a Roth IRA, the same distribution rules that apply to a traditional IRA inherited from an owner who died before his or her required beginning date (RBD) are followed. This is because, as there is no RBD for Roth IRAs, it is a date that can never be reached, and so all Roth IRA owners are deemed to have died before it (even if they're 95 when they pass away) for distribution purposes.

A nonspouse beneficiary can never roll over or contribute new funds into an inherited IRA or Roth IRA account, whereas a spouse can inherit a traditional IRA and convert that to a Roth IRA, but only if rolling it over or electing to treat it as his or her own (see Chapter 5).

BEWARE OF THE INHERITED ROTH IRA TAX TRAP

Don't fall into the trap some Roth beneficiaries do where they say, "If the RMD on my father's Roth IRA is not taxable, then why should the IRS care if I take the distribution or not? After all, the IRS receives no tax on the distribution so why would it care if I take it?" Trust me on this. The IRS does care! It is not going to let you stockpile that tax-free account forever. That's why there are all these RMD rules . . . and the rules DO apply to inherited Roth IRAs. Even though the distribution is not taxable, it still must be taken. If you don't take it, the amount you should have taken will be subject to the 50 percent penalty. Can you imagine how awful it would be to pay a 50 percent penalty on a distribution that would have been tax-free?

If the Roth IRA owner neglected to name a beneficiary or did not name a designated beneficiary, the inherited Roth IRA must be paid out under the five-year rule, regardless of the Roth IRA owner's age when he or she died. Therefore, it is even more critical to make sure you have a designated beneficiary with a Roth IRA than it is with a traditional IRA. At least with a traditional IRA, if you die after the RBD with no designated beneficiary, the IRA can still be paid out over the IRA owner's remaining life expectancy, which is usually more than five years. There is no such safety valve for an inherited Roth IRA because there is no such thing as dying after your RBD.

To make matters worse, if there is no designated beneficiary, the estate may become the beneficiary, which—as you'll recall from Chapters 5 and 6 (you better recall!)—is the WORST of all inherited IRA or Roth IRA scenarios.

A WORD TO THE WISE

Here's one final note for nonspouse Roth IRA beneficiaries: Because you cannot roll over or treat inherited Roth IRAs as your own (as with inherited traditional IRAs, only spouse beneficiaries can do that), the deceased Roth IRA owner's name must remain on the account and titled the same way as outlined for traditional IRAs in Chapter 6.

Perfect Plan Protection Is Near

If you follow the steps outlined in the previous chapters, you will now have created what I consider to be the almost-perfect retirement account.

You will have a game plan for that Biggest Check You'll Ever Get.

You will know how to protect it (with insurance), how to stretch it (with a beneficiary form), and how to Roth it (if you qualify) to be tax-free.

In summary, you will have set up your retirement next egg to last for decades with income on distribution substantially reduced or outright eliminated.

However, your IRA still has to pass to your beneficiaries in the most cost-efficient way. For example, make sure, your beneficiaries can pay the estate taxes on your inherited account(s) with the insurance money you've provided. But wouldn't it be even better if the estate taxes on your retirement savings could be minimized as well?

That's the next, and last, step. Then you're home free.

EIGHT

Step #5: Avoid the Death Tax Trap

"I can't die. I'm booked."
—George Burns (1896–1996), comedian and "deity"

The surest way to avoid the death tax trip is to live forever. But since that is not an option, at least not at this moment in medical history, we must opt for plan B, "estate planning," which is what avoiding the death tax trap is called.

Of course, there's a plan C too, which is to do nothing at all and make paying estate tax voluntary.

Whoa! Hold on there a second! How can doing nothing make paying voluntary?

By doing nothing to avoid the death tax trap, you're choosing to pay it, right? Well, in my book that spells v-o-l-u-n-t-a-r-y.

There are a host of reasons why people sidestep the issue of estate planning. That it's too complicated, for instance. (This is a myth; it's easy.) Or, that it's too expensive because you have to hire a lawyer, CPA, insurance agent, or other financial services professional. (Is that the sound of "cheap, cheap," I hear?) Or, they think their estate isn't large enough to warrant estate planning. (Think again.) Or—and this is usually the biggest reason of all—it's just too disturbing to contemplate the prospect of one's own demise.

"If I start thinking about estate planning, I'll jinx myself, and I may die," people say. Well, guess what? There's no *may* about it. You *will* die. Someday. And it'll happen regardless of whether you jinx yourself. I've done some informal research on the subject, and three out of three people who die pass on if they have an estate plan or not. The only difference is that those who die *with* an estate plan pass more of their hard-earned wealth on to their families and disinherit Uncle Sam a lot more successfully than people who die without a plan.

This book is about action, not talk. Ask most estate planning attorneys and they will tell you that many clients just talk a lot but never really do anything. Insurance agents who know that their clients need life insurance tell me that same thing. Their clients say, "I'll think about it." What's to think about? That's just an excuse to do nothing. You must make a decision and implement that decision. Most decisions can be changed so don't wait to make the perfect decision. That will never happen. As General Ulysses S. Grant said when asked if he was sure of a decision he had just made, " No, I am not, but . . . anything is better than indecision. We must decide. If I am wrong, we shall soon find it out and can do the other thing. But not to decide wastes time and money and may ruin everything."

By now it should be clear to you that I have little patience with people who are "all talk, no action." I could fill another three books with stories about them—people who gave most of their money to the IRS not because taxes were so high, but because they did nothing to avoid paying those taxes.

Many of the steps in this book involve spending relatively small amounts of money now for a windfall later. Don't be one of those people who wind up leaving their money to the IRS due to being penny-wise and pound-foolish. Remember, if you don't pay something now, your family will pay later.

Your Estate Is Larger Than You Think

People think that the estate tax applies to anyone with an estate. In truth, it applies to anyone the government decides has too much money. How much is too much? The government decides that too. It's currently $1.5 million—otherwise known as the federal estate tax exemption or your "credit shelter amount."

Think your estate won't hit that number? Think again. Most people grossly underestimate the size of their estates. Remember the rule of 72 in Chapter 5? Even if your retirement account is nowhere near $1.5 million today, it may be by the time you die through compounding interest built up over the years. And what about your home, those joint accounts, or jointly owned property such as that summer house you own in upstate New York or that condo in Florida? They're part of your estate. Don't forget to include them. Or that property you baby boomers inherited (or may inherit) from your folks? Do the math; it belongs in your estate now, or it will.

Together these items add up, making that $1.5 million exemption not all that hard to reach. Ann almost did it in Chapter 1—on a teacher's salary!

OK, so everybody is allowed to die with $1.5 million in the kitty going to their heirs tax-free. But does that federal exemption automatically translate to the state level? Many states do not assess additional estate taxes, but some do. And even those such as New York and Florida that have no state estate tax may start levying one when the cut of estate tax money collected by the IRS they currently share in goes bye-bye. Then these states will likely pass estate tax bills of their own to plug the gaps in their budgets.

As noted in Chapter 5, the estate tax was repealed by EGTRRA 2001 (but the gift tax was not), and so, you're thinking, estate taxes may not be a headache your heirs will even have to face. That's true, if you die at the right time. As noted too in Chapter 5, the repeal goes into effect in 2010, but then the repeal "sunsets" the following year, which means that unless it is extended, it comes back from the dead full force in 2011—and the $1.5 million federal exemption, which will have climbed steadily higher each year (reaching a cap of $3.5 million in 2009) due to this same legislation, goes back to the 2002 figure of $1 million again—and to the pre-2002 tax rate of 55 percent! Therefore, under this crazy law,

Figure 10. Estate Tax Phase-Out . . . and Phase-In Again

The estate tax is repealed on January 1, 2010. It comes back on January 1, 2011, unless the repeal is extended by future legislation. Beginning in 2010, when the estate tax is repealed, the decedent's estate will be limited to an increase (step-up) in basis of $1,300,000 and $3,000,000 for property transferred to a surviving spouse. Assets to receive the step can be selected by the executor, but not all estate assets will qualify for a step-up in basis. For example, IRAs and similar property that is income in respect of a decedent (IRD, which I discuss in this chapter) is not eligible for a step-up in basis.

Year of Death	Estate-Tax Exemption	Top Estate Tax (and GST Tax*) Rate
2002	$1,000,000	50%
2003	1,000,000	49%
2004	1,500,000	48%
2005	1,500,000	47%
2006	2,000,000	46%
2007	2,000,000	45%
2008	2,000,000	45%
2009	3,500,000	45%
2010	Estate tax is repealed	–0–
2011	It's back! $1,000,000	55% (Pre-2002 top estate tax rate)

*The Generation skipping transfer (GST) tax is an additional estate tax at the highest estate tax rates on transfers of assets to grandchildren from grandparents in excess of $1 million (indexed each year for inflation), skipping the generation in between—thus, the name. If both the estate tax and the GST tax apply, the combined tax in 2002, for example, could be 100 percent. The top estate and GST tax rates in 2002 are 50 percent (pre-2002, they were 55 percent). The GST will also be repealed in 2010, but then it too comes back.

you will have to plan on dying in 2010 in order to be able to take full advantage of it! Can you just imagine what the assisted suicide or murder rate of uncooperative rich people will be that year? Here's an interesting but eerie fact: In 2010, Dr. Death himself, Jack Kevorkian, gets out of jail. Do you believe in coincidence?

Because of all the uncertainty surrounding this tax law, you should focus, as I will in this chapter, on the provisions that are likely to occur, which would be the provisions that phase in early, such as the increasing federal estate tax exemption (see Figure 10). Assume there will always be an estate tax and incorporate the exemption increase into your planning process, since you can count on it occurring, and staying in place . . . for now.

The Unlimited Marital Deduction

If each person receives a $1.5 million estate tax exemption, then it should follow that a married couple should receive two exemptions (one each) and be able to pass the first $3 million of property to their heirs estate tax-free. That sounds logical, but in reality most couples lose the first exemption and only have $1.5 million of their assets protected from estate tax.

The reason most couples don't receive the first exemption is because they leave all, or most, of their assets to each other.

Under our tax laws, you are allowed to leave as much as you wish to your spouse estate-tax–free. The sky's the limit (as long as your spouse is a U.S. citizen). That's why this provision is called the *unlimited marital deduction*. The government doesn't care that no tax is paid at the first death, even if a billion dollars is left to the surviving spouse; the IRS can just kick back and wait until the surviving spouse dies, and then take the whole kaboodle.

The unlimited marital deduction causes many couples to lose the estate exemption when the first spouse dies. It's a trap that lulls people into thinking that they're beating the taxman. True, you never pay your *own* estate tax; your beneficiaries do.

You must set up your estate properly so that each spouse receives his or her own estate tax exemption. **Leaving everything to your spouse because there is no estate tax at the first death guarantees the loss of your first estate tax exemption.**

For example, George and Martha have an estate worth $3 million. Their estate consists of a home they own jointly and some joint bank accounts plus George's IRA account worth $1.5 million. Martha is the beneficiary of George's IRA account. George dies first and all of his property goes to Martha, reducing the value of George's estate to zero. Property that goes to your spouse is not subject to estate taxes. Because George has no estate, he does not need to use his estate tax exemption, so his $1.5 million estate exemption is wasted. (You can only use the exemption when there is an estate that is left to someone other than your spouse.) The fact that George did not use it does not mean that Martha can get a $3 million estate tax exemption when she dies. Alas, the unused exemption is lost forever. Martha now owns the entire $3 million estate and then dies. The value of Martha's estate is $3 million, but she only receives a $1.5 million estate tax exemption, so she will have a taxable estate of $1.5 million, requiring $705,000 of federal estate tax to be paid within nine months of Martha's death by her beneficiary.

If instead of leaving the $1.5 million IRA to Martha, George leaves it to their son, John, he will be able to use George's $1.5 million estate-tax exemption and get the entire IRA estate-tax–free. You know the rest by now. John would be able to stretch that out for 40 years or more by taking RMDs over his life expectancy.

Let's get back to Martha. She has the other $1.5 million balance of the estate that was not left to John. When Martha dies, her estate is worth $1.5 million and she has a $1.5 million estate tax exemption her beneficiary, John, gets to use, so there will be no estate tax on her estate, either. Compare this scenario to the one where $705,000 had to be shelled out, and there's no contest! That's the difference when you do a little estate planning.

OK, so if you leave everything to your spouse, you lose your first-death estate tax exemption. But to retain the exemption, your spouse must give up part of his or her inheritance. Talk about a catch-22! Is there no way to leave everything to your spouse and retain the exemption? Yes, there is. Well, sort of—it allows you to almost have your cake and eat it too.

The solution is to set up your estate so that each of you receives your own estate tax exemption, which can be achieved by creating a *credit shelter trust*. For this to work, the surviving spouse must be willing to forgo being named the beneficiary and be content with just *controlling* the distribution of the inherited assets instead. There really is no difference; the surviving spouse still has limited access to the assets, but they belong to the credit shelter trust, not the spouse, for tax purposes.

Because the estate tax exemption keeps changing, credit shelter trusts are set up without an amount included. They usually offer wording such as "the maximum allowable amount that can pass free of federal estate tax" or some other language indicating that only property valued up to the amount of the estate tax exemption (the credit shelter amount) will go to the trust. All other property in excess of the estate tax exemption amount will go to the spouse or even to a trust for the spouse's benefit. In the tax world, this federal estate exemption is actually an estate tax credit, which currently exempts the first $1.5 million from federal estate tax. That's why the trust that is created to ensure this exemption is called the "credit shelter trust." It shelters the estate tax credit, which most people refer to a the estate tax exemption.

The credit shelter trust can be set up and funded with assets while you are alive (through a *revocable living trust,* for example) or it can be set up upon your death through a will; if it's set up upon your death, property that is in your name alone would go to the trust, up to the exemption amount, at the time of your death. Your credit shelter trust would then get funded (filled with assets or inherited assets) after your death. For example, if you died and had $4 million of assets in your name and had a credit shelter trust provision set up in your will, then only $1.5 million of your property would go into the trust (assuming that $1.5 million was the exemption amount at the time of your death) and the rest, the other $2.5 million, would go to your spouse or a trust for his or her benefit.

Most decent wills have this credit shelter trust provision. It does not always have to be used, but if you need it, it's there for your family—which is why you often see it referred to as a *family trust* as well. That's because the assets in the trust will grow estate-tax–free for your family. For example, if the $1.5 million of property goes into the credit shelter or family trust at your death, then $1.5 million is included in your estate, but now you get to use your estate tax exemption, which would have otherwise been wasted had you left everything directly to your spouse. Since the value of your estate (the amount that was left to the trust) is $1.5 million and you have a $1.5 million exemption available, you use it to eliminate all the estate tax at the first death. Now all the assets in the trust are estate-tax–free. Your spouse can have limited control over those assets and even receive any income the assets throw off, but any growth of the assets will be estate-tax–free for your children.

The assets remain in the trust until the death of your spouse. This way your spouse has control over them for the rest of his or her life. For example, if the house goes into the trust, even though the spouse does not own it, he or she has the right to live in it or sell it. If the spouse sells it, the funds go back into the trust and he or she can draw income from it. If the spouse actually needs some of the trust principal, he or she can get that too by having special invasion provisions included in the trust for things such as health, education, maintenance, and support. These broadly encompass most anything a surviving spouse would need money for. The hope is that the spouse will never need to touch this money. If, for example, he or she withdraws it from the trust just to put in a bank savings account and leave it there, and then dies, the money that was withdrawn will be included in his or her estate and could be subject to estate tax (if the balance of the estate exceeds his or her estate tax exemption). Withdrawing funds that don't need to be spent only unwinds a good estate plan. The credit shelter trust concept gives surviving spouses plenty of access to funds, but they should only take from the trust if they need the money.

If your spouse takes out only what's needed to live on and lets the trust money grow for the rest of his or her life, what remains

in the trust when your spouse dies will go to your spouse's beneficiaries (the children), who are known as *remainder beneficiaries*
because they get what "remains," estate-tax–free no matter how
much the property is worth at that time. And the trust ends. (It
doesn't have to end, but most do since the whole point of setting
up the trust is to keep the assets intact and available to the surviving spouse during his or her lifetime, and then estate-tax–free for
the kids.)

The credit shelter trust is not set up to save you estate taxes; it
is set up to give you control. You don't need the trust to make sure
that the first estate exemption is used. You can do that simply by
leaving property up to the exemption amount directly to your children, as was done in the George-and-Martha example. The $1.5
million IRA was left directly to their son John when George died,
so the exemption was used. The extra $705,000 of estate tax was
avoided without having to set up a credit shelter trust. But if
Martha wanted to control access to all the estate assets, she would
want to set up the credit shelter trust. She could inherit the assets
directly (and most spouses do), but then, at her death, all the assets
are included in her estate and she will pay—that is, her beneficiaries will pay—the extra $705,000 (or more depending on the value
of the estate). This is why you want assets that will be appreciat-
ing to do so estate-tax–free, either in the hands of your children directly or in the credit shelter trust. If the surviving spouse owns all
the assets at his or her death, then all that appreciation will suffer
an estate tax.

The key here is that if a spouse wants full control of all assets
(which is perfectly normal) before anything goes to a child, then
the credit shelter trust provides that, and also ensures that the first-
death exemption is not lost. This is how the credit shelter trust
concept gives you everything you want—estate-tax savings and
control. But the estate-tax savings can be accomplished without
the credit shelter trust if you are willing to give up control. That is
hard for many people, but if you can do it, then you don't need to
bother at all with the credit shelter trust concept. You can simply
leave assets up to the estate exemption amount directly to your

children, but they will have full control. The decision is yours. You know your children best and know whether control is necessary and for how long.

If your retirement plan is larger than the exemption amount or the bulk of your estate, I recommend that you consider splitting the account and creating a "stretch" option for postdeath required minimum distributions (see Chapter 6 for the details). This does not mean giving anything away or withdrawing from your IRA. Splitting means dividing your IRA into two or more IRAs and naming different beneficiaries on each. Splitting IRAs is a way to take full advantage of the estate tax exemption at the first death without the complications of funding a credit shelter trust with an IRA.

For example, David splits his $4 million IRA into a $2,500,000 IRA that names his wife Lynne as the primary beneficiary and a $1,500,000 IRA that names their daughter Nicole as the beneficiary. Upon David's death the $1,500,000 IRA will pass estate-tax–free to Nicole because it equals the $1.5 million estate tax exemption amount. If Lynne wanted control over the $1.5 million IRA, it could be left to a credit shelter trust instead of outright to Nicole. Either way, the estate exemption is used. And if Nicole is the designated beneficiary, she can elect to stretch required distributions over her life expectancy, which, depending upon her age at the time, could be upward of 50 years or more.

The $2.5 million IRA meanwhile will also pass estate-tax–free to Lynne because of the unlimited marital deduction. At her death, the remaining IRA balance will be included in her estate. If, for example, the whole $2.5 million remains, there will be a hefty estate tax to pay even after using her $1.5 million exemption. (But as you know from Chapter 5, life insurance can be set up outside the estate to pay the tax.)

A single person only gets one exemption, and gets it automatically by dying, so setting up a trust to avoid losing it is not an issue. However, a single person may want postdeath control over the timing and amounts of distribution to beneficiaries that setting up a trust can achieve. But in this case, the trust would be a revocable living trust, an irrevocable living trust, or a trust under the person's will, not a credit shelter trust.

You don't have to make all your decisions now if you have well–thought-out contingent beneficiaries. For example, if your spouse is unsure whether he or she will need all or part of the IRA and doesn't want to commit or stress out over it now, then name your spouse as beneficiary on the entire IRA, but name your children or a credit shelter trust for their benefit as a contingent beneficiary. This gives the spouse the option of disclaiming yet still keeping some control.

For example, Fred has a $1.5 million IRA and few other assets, so Fred's wife Betty is named on the entire IRA. After Fred dies, if it turns out that maybe there was life insurance or sufficient other assets for Betty's financial security, then Betty could disclaim all or part of the $1.5 million IRA and it would pass to the contingent beneficiaries Fred had named (probably his children). If Betty disclaimed the entire $1.5 million IRA, then the $1.5 million IRA would pass to the children estate-tax–free using the $1.5 million estate tax exemption in Fred's estate. If Betty inherited everything, that exemption would have been wasted. But here, Betty was not sure what kind of financial shape she would be in and it was nice that she did not have to commit to having Fred name the children instead of her as the primary beneficiary.

How much of a retirement plan should you leave to a nonspouse beneficiary—for example, a 40-year-old child—to gain the most tax and stretch IRA benefits? Generally speaking, as much as can pass estate-tax–free, providing there are enough other assets for the surviving spouse. If not, then consider the life insurance solution (see Chapter 5) to create whatever the spouse will need. Remember, if you leave a retirement plan to a child or a grandchild, you're using the first-death exemption (yours) that might otherwise have been lost.

If your retirement plan is at or below the current $1.5 million exemption limit and your spouse has sufficient funds to live on, it may pay to leave the plan to your kids and use the exemption against it. This way the kids start off with 100 percent of the plan.

It is not eroded by estate taxes, which could happen if they wait to get the plan at the second death from the surviving spouse, whose estate may be much larger at that point. The kids can also spread distributions over their life expectancies and parlay a $1,500,000 retirement plan into many more millions at even a modest interest rate. This is a powerful estate- and income-tax–planning tool and it's a great way to pass a retirement account on to your child (or children) estate-tax–free, up to the exemption amount.

Naming Trusts as IRA Beneficiaries

Most people don't need to name trusts as their IRA beneficiaries. It's costly (you'll need an attorney and perhaps even a tax advisor who specializes in the complex area of IRA trusts, and they don't come cheap), it's cumbersome, and *there is no tax benefit that can be gained with a trust that cannot be gained without one!* Stop right now and read the last part of that sentence again . . . and again, until you've committed it to memory.

The only reason to name a trust as the beneficiary of your IRA is for personal (nontax) reasons, such as restricting access to the build-up by beneficiaries who might be too young (e.g., a minor child), mentally incompetent, or prone to squandering it on a hot Ferrari or a cool vacation. But these are all reasons why you would leave *any* property in trust, including an IRA!

Sometimes though you may want to name a trust as your IRA beneficiary to gain IRA advantages unavailable to other assets, such as the stretch IRA. For example, if you want to make sure that your beneficiaries only take the required minimum amounts each year so that the IRA lasts for their lifetime, you can guarantee that kind of postdeath control by naming a trust as your IRA beneficiary and your wishes will be upheld.

Exercising control from beyond the grave over the ultimate disposition of your IRA in the event of a second marriage would be another reason to name a trust as beneficiary—in this case, a *qualified terminable interest property trust (QTIP)*. This is a special trust that is created to qualify for the marital deduction and also give you (the IRA owner and trust creator) control over the trust principal (the IRA) after your death.

For example, a spouse (say, your second wife) can have the income or RMDs each year to live on, but after her death, the remaining trust assets will go to your children and not hers (if there are two sets of kids). Here again, RMDs are the fly in the ointment. If she lives long enough and receives the RMDs each year, your children will be disinherited until she dies. This is a recipe for disaster (or a good TV movie).

In many second or later marriages, there is some type of tension or adverse relationship between the second spouse (let's say a stepmom) and the adult children, especially if they are older than the stepmom. If the children have to wait for the stepmom to die to receive anything, they are effectively disinherited. That was probably not the intention of Dad (the IRA owner) when he was advised to set up the QTIP trust. He was probably told that his new wife would receive income for life and his children would get the principal when she dies. Well, guess what? If she lives long enough, taking RMDs each year, there won't be any principal left for the children (or their children)! The entire IRA could end up in Stepmom's family, not Dad's, contrary to his wishes (and expectations) when he set this all up. Bottom line: If the QTIP trust is the beneficiary of the IRA, the only way the children will ever see a dime is if they have Stepmom whacked!

Seriously, QTIP trusts create unique problems, which is why I generally advise against naming them as an IRA beneficiary. My only purpose in making you aware of their existence, frankly, is so that you'll stay away from them.

You should never name a trust as the beneficiary of your IRA just because it's an IRA (even if your attorney tells you that's the reason to do it). That's wrong—because trusts as IRA beneficiaries create unique problems and tax complications even when executed perfectly.

IRA trusts cannot provide the panacea of tax and personal solutions that many IRA owners are looking for. There are trade-offs and consequences. Consider this paragraph a disclaimer and warning. **Don't name trusts as IRA beneficiaries unless you know what you are doing and it's the only solution.**

If an IRA trust is the only solution for you, it must meet the following requirements to qualify as a designated beneficiary and allow the life expectancy of the oldest trust beneficiary to be used in calculating postdeath required minimum distributions (the "stretch-it" step discussed in Chapter 6):

- The trust must be a valid trust under state law.
- The trust must be irrevocable at death.
- The beneficiaries of the trust must be identifiable.
- A copy of the trust instrument must be provided to the financial institution with the account by October 31 of the year following the year of the IRA owner's death.

If there are several trust beneficiaries, you cannot separate them the way you can by splitting inherited IRA accounts into separate shares after the death of the IRA owner (see Chapter 6). The IRS rules generally do not allow separate shares for trust beneficiaries so your beneficiaries will be stuck with the age of the oldest trust beneficiary in calculating RMDs. In a typical credit shelter trust, that would be the surviving spouse. The children would be remainder beneficiaries. They get what's left in the trust after the surviving spouse dies. The children then would be stuck with the surviving spouse's life expectancy. The stretch IRA, based on their own life expectancies, would be lost if the credit shelter trust was the IRA beneficiary (unless the spouse was not a trust beneficiary). That's one of the trade-offs.

If the trust fails to qualify as a designated beneficiary, then there is no designated beneficiary, and the trust beneficiaries will not be able to stretch postdeath required distributions even over the surviving spouse's life expectancy. In that case, the IRA will be paid out either under the five-year rule (if the IRA owner dies before his or her required beginning date) or over the remaining life expectancy of the deceased IRA owner (if the IRA owner dies after his or her RBD).

244 ■ THE RETIREMENT SAVINGS TIME BOMB

Let me be very clear about this: When I say, "IRA trusts," that's exactly what I'm referring to—a trust named as an IRA beneficiary. I do not mean regular estate planning trusts used for passing non–retirement-account assets such as a house or bank accounts to beneficiaries. Regular estate planning trusts are fine, and I recommend them. But an IRA often does not mesh well with trusts. An IRA is like the character Pigpen in the "Peanuts" comic strip. He always has a circle of dust around him; wherever he goes, the dirt goes with him. Wherever an IRA goes, the RMD rules go too, and integrating them with the trust provisions often causes conflict.

For example, RMDs must still be paid out of the IRA and into the trust. That defeats the purpose of the trust, or throws a big monkey wrench into it anyway, if the trust's purpose is to preserve trust property for an ultimate beneficiary down the line. And if an RMD is missed, the same 50 percent penalty that applies to all other IRA owners and beneficiaries who miss an RMD gets levied.

No other asset in a trust creates the problems that an IRA does because of the RMD rules. If you put a house in a trust, there are no rules that say, "The first year, the kitchen must come out; the second year, the dining room; the third year, the bathroom; the fourth year, the bedroom; and . . ." You get the point. But when an IRA is left to a trust, the RMD rules force a part of the IRA out each year. After enough years, the RMD process slowly unwinds the estate plan until eventually there is nothing left for the ultimate beneficiaries.

Because of this problem, trusts are often set up to accumulate money in order to make sure that there will be something left for the ultimate beneficiaries. Once the RMD is paid to the trust, the trust terms say how much of that RMD (if any, depending upon how liberally or rigidly you set the trust up) passes through the trust to the trust beneficiaries, and how much will stay in the trust. But accumulating RMD income in the trust leads to other problems.

Once the RMD comes out of the IRA, it is taxable the same as any IRA distribution to a beneficiary. The only difference with a trust as beneficiary is who pays the tax—the trust or the trust beneficiary? That's easy. It's the one who gets the RMD. If the RMD passes through the trust and is distributed from the trust to the trust beneficiaries, then the beneficiaries pay the income tax at their own personal income tax rates. If instead of paying out the RMD to the trust beneficiary, that amount is accumulated in the trust, then the trust pays the income tax on the RMD at trust tax rates.

Trust tax rates are the highest in the land. Accumulate just $9,351 of income and trust tax rates jump to the highest bracket. (Adding state income tax to the mix could result in a combined tax rate as high as 40 percent!) By contrast, an individual doesn't jump to the top tax bracket until he or she earns more than $300,000 of income.

The main reason IRA owners who leave their IRA to a trust want the trust to accumulate RMDs rather than pay them out to the trust beneficiaries is because they don't "trust" those beneficiaries with the money and want to control their access to it. But what's the difference if your beneficiaries blow it when the alternative is to lose as much as 40 percent to the IRS anyway? What's gone is gone.

If you leave your IRA to a trust, it is generally best to pay RMDs out to the beneficiary from the trust. A trust that does this is known as a *conduit trust* because each RMD passes through the trust on the way from the IRA to the trust beneficiary, and the rest of your money remains protected until the last RMD is paid out.

TIP!

If you need to name a trust as your IRA beneficiary and you will want to accumulate RMDs in the trust, one solution is to convert the IRA to a Roth IRA and leave that to the trust. This will remove the high–tax-rate problem that goes with trusts because there is generally no income tax on Roth IRA distributions to beneficiaries (see Chapter 7).

A WORD TO THE WISE

Another problem with a trust is that after the IRA owner dies, trust tax returns will have to be filed each year for the life of the IRA trust. This can get expensive and creates even more paperwork and possible IRS problems if the IRS decides to audit your trust tax returns. If your trust tax returns are selected for audit, you had better hope that the IRA trust was correctly drafted, particularly with respect to the IRA tax rules. Also, the IRA trust beneficiaries (your children), depending on the flexibility of the trust, are generally locked in to the trust terms for life. There may be some family resentment for leaving your IRA beneficiary(s) with this kind of legacy, even if it may have been for their own good.

For Your IRA Beneficiaries: Don't Miss This Deduction!

Back in 1918, every asset in an estate received a step-up in basis, which meant that beneficiaries paid no income tax on the value of property they inherited. Can you imagine that? (If this were the system today, no beneficiary would pay tax on an inherited retirement account.) So, in 1934, our nation's lawmakers decided certain income items should not receive a step-up in basis and defined these items as *income in respect of a decedent (IRD)*. (There were no IRAs then so they did not foresee the amount of income tax revenue that would one day be generated by their IRD concept.)

Step-up in basis works this way: If a person dies with a stock portfolio or a home, the beneficiary will receive a step-up in basis and be able to use the fair market value at the date of death as his or her cost for determining any gain of loss on a future sale of the asset. So, if a stock was bought by the decedent for $1,000 and was worth $100,000 at death, the beneficiary would receive a step-up in basis and be relieved from reporting the $99,000 gain the decedent would have been taxed on had the stock been sold by the decedent before he or she died.

But IRD items receive no such step-up in basis. Instead, the beneficiary receives what is called a *carryover basis,* which means *the same basis as the decedent.* In other words, IRD is income the decedent earned but did not yet pay tax on. So, when the beneficiary inherits and collects the income, the beneficiary will owe the income tax. (Income items that are IRD include money owed to the decedent at death, such as accounts receivable from a business, installment sale income, rental income, and even alimony owed at death . . . and, of course, retirement and annuity income.)

Recognizing that the IRD concept effectively causes double taxation (estate and income tax), our lawmakers, rather than junking the concept, chose instead the Band-Aid approach to fixing it, and created an income tax deduction for beneficiaries to offset this double taxation. It is the called the *IRD deduction* (or estate tax deduction), and it's the government's way of throwing us a bone.

The IRD deduction is like when you go to Las Vegas and lose $50,000 at the tables, so the house feels bad, buys you lunch, and maybe even treats you to a show. That's the IRD deduction. Don't count on it to correct any damage to your IRA caused by not following the steps in this book. With the IRD deduction instead of losing 90 percent of your retirement savings to the IRS, you may only lose 70 percent. That still stinks, but it beats the alternative— so make sure your beneficiaries know enough not to make matters worse by missing out on this deduction, or the taxman really could take up to 90 percent!

Calculating the IRD Deduction in Five Easy Steps

How can you tell if you as a beneficiary are a candidate for the IRD deduction? Not all beneficiaries are. First, you must check your 1099-R form. Every distribution from a retirement account (including distributions to beneficiaries) generates a 1099-R that is sent both to the recipient of the distribution and to the IRS. The only way to know if the distribution may qualify for the IRD deduction is to look on your 1099-R for what I call "the Death Code." It is the number 4. If you see a 4 in box 7 ("distribution code") on your 1099-R, that means the distribution was made to a beneficiary—in this case, you.

Now you must determine whether any federal estate tax was paid on the IRA that you inherited. To find this out, you will have to look at the decedent's estate tax return (Form 706). If there was no federal estate tax paid, then there is no IRD deduction. But if there was federal estate tax paid, then you qualify for the deduction to offset the effect of double taxation.

TIP!

Federal is the key word in the IRD deduction equation because there is no deduction for any state estate tax paid—so, on a state level, double taxation still exists. Under our new tax laws though, the amount of federal tax that goes toward the IRD deduction is increased since the credit for state death taxes was reduced by 25 percent in 2002 and by 50 percent in 2003, and will be reduced by 75 percent in 2004 and then eliminated and replaced with a tax deduction in 2005. A higher federal estate tax means a larger IRD deduction.

To calculate your IRD deduction, follow these five simple steps. (Don't worry. An example follows using real numbers to make this even clearer.)

1. Find out the amount of federal estate tax paid. That's easy. It's listed on page 1 of the decedent's IRS Form 706.

2. Create an imaginary estate tax return that assumes no IRA. This step is also easy, but you'll need an estate tax

planning software program for it. (I use "Number Cruncher" by Stephan R. Leimberg and Robert T. LeClair, which can be ordered online at www.leimberg.com or by calling 610-924-0515. No, I don't get a commission!) Plug in the value of the estate after subtracting the value of the IRA (and other IRD items, if any). This will tell you what the federal estate tax would have been if there were no IRA in the estate; once you know that, you know how much of the federal estate tax on the actual return filed after the decedent's death was directly due to the IRA and other IRD items.

3. Subtract the imaginary federal estate tax as if there were no IRA (figured in step 2) from the federal estate tax actually paid to the U.S. Treasury (in step 1). That result is the amount of the IRD deduction.

4. Divide the federal estate tax on the IRA (from step 3) by the amount of the IRA included in the estate. This will give you the percentage of the deduction you (the beneficiary) will be able to claim at each withdrawal from the inherited IRA.

5. Multiply the amount of the IRA distribution you took during the year by the percentage in step 4 to get the amount of your IRD deduction. The deduction can only be taken as you report income from the inherited IRA withdrawals. You cannot claim this deduction in a year that you did not withdraw from the inherited IRA.

Here's an example:

Harry, the IRA owner, dies in 2002. His taxable estate (after all estate deductions) is $3,000,000, which includes an IRA valued at $1,200,000. His daughter Sally is his beneficiary, and she withdraws $100,000 from the IRA in the first year after Harry's death. Now she must figure out how much of that $100,000 taxable withdrawal can be offset by the IRD deduction.

1. Reading Harry's estate tax return, she sees that he paid $793,500 in federal estate tax, which qualifies her for the IRD deduction.

2. Using estate tax planning software, she figures out what the federal estate tax would have been if the $3,000,000 estate hadn't included the $1,200,000 IRA: $3,000,000 − $1,200,000 = $1,800,000. The federal estate tax on an estate of $1,800,000 in 2002 was $281,100.

3. By subtracting the $281,100 from the $793,500 (figured in step 1), she knows that the federal estate tax on the IRA is $512,400, which is also the amount of her IRD deduction.

4. If Sally were to withdraw the entire $1,200,000 IRA in one year, then she would receive the entire $512,400 IRD deduction in that year and pay tax on a rough net amount of $687,600 ($1,200,000 IRA − $512,400 = $687,600). But with the distribution rules as they are, it is unlikely that she would do this (though you never know; Sally's new boyfriend may need cash for his hot new surfboard collection); instead, she will probably take advantage of stretching the IRA payouts over many years. And so, she needs to know the percentage of the total $512,400 IRD deduction she can take each year as she withdraws from her IRA. She gets that percentage by dividing the $512,400 by $1,200,000 (the total value of the IRA included in the estate). Here, the percentage comes out to 42.7 ($512,400/$1,200,000 = 42.7 percent).

5. Since Sally withdrew $100,000 from the inherited IRA, then she is entitled to an IRD deduction of $42,700 ($100,000 × 42.7 percent = $42,700). She claims the deduction on her personal tax return as a miscellaneous itemized deduction (Form 1040, Schedule A). To figure the IRD deduction for future years, Sally would use the same 42.7 percent and apply it to each future year's distribution amount until the original $512,400 IRD deduction is used up. (Incidentally,

pass this on to your accountant. The IRD deduction is not subject to the 2 percent AGI limit and not subject to the alternative minimum tax [AMT]. But it is subject to the overall 3 percent limit applying to itemized deductions for certain high-income taxpayers, which therefore might result in the IRD deduction's not being a total offset.)

If there are several IRA beneficiaries, then they share the IRD deduction, based on the percentage each beneficiary inherits.

I may have been a little too harsh when I called the IRD deduction a "bone." It's more than that because it's usually large. The deduction our fictional beneficiary Sally got was 42.7 percent. Most generally hover around that 40 percent mark, which is a *huge* number; it certainly makes for a deduction that one should never miss out on. And yet most beneficiaries do miss out.

If you're an IRA beneficiary, you're probably thinking at this point, "Yikes! I never knew to claim the IRD deduction on the account I inherited. I've probably lost thousands by now! I wonder if it's too late to stop the bleeding?"

The answer is NO. You can go back and amend three years of tax returns and claim the deduction for each year. You'll even receive interest on your tax refund. Don't forget to also amend your state tax return and get any refunds due if you paid state income tax on the distributions from your inherited IRA.

Now that you've tripled your tax savings, you can host an IRD deduction party to tell your friends! (Be sure to invite your accountant.)

Creating the Perfect IRA Estate Plan

The perfect one-size-fits-all estate plan does not exist. But I can show you the next best thing: the perfect retirement account estate plan for avoiding the death tax trap for you and your family.

Based on what you've learned in this chapter, you now know that everyone with a large retirement account wants three things. (By "large" I mean one that, combined with other assets in the estate, exceeds the current federal estate tax exemption of $1.5 million.)

WHAT EVERY LARGE IRA OWNER WANTS

1. The estate tax exemption
2. The "stretch IRA" option
3. Control for financial security

From the list, pick any two items.

No, you can't have all three. That's because estate planning for retirement accounts means making trade-offs. You have to prioritize. This forces you to decide what's most important to you. The result will be the perfect retirement account estate plan for *you*. (Of course, if your estate is not large enough to be subject to an estate tax, then there may not be any trade-offs since there will be no estate tax.)

Here's how this works:

Let's say that at first glance you decide what you want most is not to lose the first-death (yours) $1.5 million estate tax exemption and to control the distribution of assets so that none pass to your children while your spouse is still alive. Then here's your plan: *Leave your IRA to a credit shelter trust.* This provides both the first-death estate tax exemption and the control you wish. And what have you traded off? The stretch IRA option is no longer available to your children because the IRA will pass through the trust, and when that happens, the postdeath life expectancy used to calculate required distributions is that of the oldest trust beneficiary, your spouse.

OK, after realizing what you've traded away, you lower your head in embarrassment because the "stretch" is one of my key recommendations and you say, "Wait, I'm changing my mind. I want the 'stretch' and I still want control."

Here's your plan now: *Leave your IRA directly to your spouse.*

Your spouse will inherit the IRA and have full control. Your spouse will name the children as beneficiaries, and when he or she dies, the children will be able to stretch the IRA over their own life expectancies. What have you given up? You will have wasted the first-death estate tax exemption because the entire IRA went to your spouse.

"What have I done?" you exclaim, slapping your head in shock. "I've blown my exemption. That could wind up costing my family hundreds of thousands of dollars in unnecessary estate tax! I can't do that!!"

So, you change your mind again, and say, "This is my final choice. I want the exemption, and I want the 'stretch.'"

Now, here's the plan: *Leave your IRA directly to your children (up to the exemption amount).* This way, the exemption will not be wasted and your children are guaranteed the "stretch" over their lifetimes. But you will have given up control. That may be fine with you if there are enough other assets in the estate to keep it going. If not, then you can buy life insurance to cover the shortfall!

This last approach is the one I recommend because it addresses both the personal and the tax issues and is the best strategy taxwise for making the most out of your IRA.

Don't Just Sit There, Put Your Estate Plan to Work

You now have all the basics you need to pass your IRA to your children or grandchildren at the lowest possible estate tax. All you have to do is actually create the plan and put it to work. But here is where most people stop, procrastinate, and never get around to it because of all the excuses they give that I rattled off at the beginning of this chapter.

As an advisor, I can attest to the fact that getting my clients to actually implement their estate plans is one of my biggest challenges. So, when this happens, I hit them with the following true story:

An elderly couple came to my office after seeing me at a seminar on estate planning. They were 78 and 79 years old, respectively, and not in the best of health. They had a $6 million estate and had done no estate planning. I first told them, "Give some money to your kids." That was a mistake. As soon as I said it, the old man turned into what I can only describe as a geriatric version of the Incredible Hulk. He somehow corralled all the strength in his infirm little body and shouted angrily, "Give it to my kids? They'll just piss it away!"

I sat quietly for a second, giving him a chance to calm down. Then I looked him in the eye, and said, "Here's the way it is. You either give it to your kids, you spend it, or you give it to the government. *You pick the pisser!*"

And that's really what estate planning comes down to. I told you it was easy.

PART THREE

WHEN THINGS DON'T GO AS PLANNED

NINE

What to Do When S*** Happens

"Experience is a good school. But the fees are high."
—Heinrich Heine (1797–1856), German poet

Wouldn't it be great if everything always worked out just the way it was supposed to? In a perfect world, it does. But as we all know, ours is an imperfect world where, unfortunately, s*** happens—frequently.

Therefore I have saved this chapter for last. You might call it an unofficial sixth step to my five-step action plan for protecting your retirement savings. It deals with the mother(s) of all IRA problems—the unforeseen as well as those issues and situations for which there seem to be no clear-cut rules.

For example, "What if I lose my job and need to take a series of early distributions to keep afloat? Will I have to pay the 10 percent penalty over an extended period of time?"

Or, "What if I screw up and miss a required distribution? Is there no last-minute reprieve from the IRS to the 50 percent penalty?"

Those situations and others are what this chapter is for—emergency use only. Hopefully, you'll never need to know any of what follows. But if s*** happens, as it often does, luckily, this chapter provides a heads-up.

"Oh, S***! I Need It *Now!*"

The combination of people retiring early (by choice or involuntarily) and money building up in retirement accounts is causing more plan owners to look for ways to tap into their plans before they reach the magic age of 59½. Withdrawing early usually means paying a 10 percent penalty, but not always. As you found out in Chapter 4, there are exceptions.

The exception that is becoming most popular is known as *annuitizing*. It's also called *SEPPs (taking a series of substantially equal periodic payments)*. But that acronym can be confused with SEPs (simplified employee pensions), which is something completely different. So, refer to the process as "annuitizing" or, to be even more hip, as "72(t)," the section of the Internal Revenue Code where the exception is found. Try it out at parties with accountants and actuaries. What a hit you'll be!

72(t) Basics

The general purpose of annuitizing is that you can tap your IRA before age 59½ without a 10 percent penalty. This can be done by committing to a plan of withdrawals according to the rules set out in Section 72(t)(2)(A)(iv) of the Internal Revenue Code. You can begin a 72(t) payment schedule at any age. There is no required starting age. However, if you want to annuitize a company retirement plan, you first must have terminated your employment with that company. This rule does not apply to IRAs. The 72(t) payments from an IRA qualify at any age even if you are still working.

The payments must continue for five years or until you reach 59½, whichever period is longer. During the payment period, the withdrawals cannot be "modified," meaning the method you elect for calculating the payments cannot be changed. Once you commit to 72(t)s from an IRA, you must continue with your chosen payment schedule from that IRA until you reach the end of the five-year period or age 59½. If you do not stick with your chosen method of payments, you will no longer qualify for the exemption from the 10 percent penalty. Actually, it's even worse: The penalty will be reinstated retroactively.

Say, for example, you (the IRA owner) were 42 years old when you began your 72(t)s. You must continue your chosen withdrawal plan for 17½ years until you reach age 59½. Assume you are now 57 and you have been sticking to the plan for the past 15 years; you've withdrawn $10,000 per year ($150,000) during that time. You have only 2½ more years to go. But your IRA has grown substantially and next year, at age 58, you decide to withdraw $50,000 instead of the usual $10,000. You figure, "What the hell, the IRS won't care; it'll be getting more tax dollars from me, faster."

Wrong! The IRS will consider that extra withdrawal a modification of the payment schedule and you will blow your penalty exemption. Because the 10 percent penalty is triggered retroactively, that means you will owe the penalty on the $150,000 of previous withdrawals plus the $50,000 withdrawal from the current year. You'll owe $20,000 in penalties ($200,000 of withdrawals × 10 percent = $20,000). The penalty plus interest is all due in the year of the modification—i.e., the year you fell off the 72(t) wagon. Furthermore, you would owe interest on that amount figured back to each year's 10 percent penalty. The entire amount would be due on the tax return for the year that you changed the schedule and withdrew the $50,000. In addition, the tax on the $50,000 would be due in that year. It's a veritable domino effect of penalties! This is why it is so important not to stop the payments and not to increase or decrease them during the 72(t) payment period.

Here's another side of the coin: If during the 72(t) payment term it turns out that your financial situation changed and you do not need as much as you thought you would, you cannot contribute the money you do not need back to your IRA. That's because payments that are part of "a series of substantially equal periodic payments" (now you know why it's easier to call them 72[t] payments) are not eligible to be rolled over. This also means then that these payments cannot be converted to a Roth IRA, because only eligible rollover distributions can be converted to a Roth. (The IRA account balance itself can be converted to a Roth during the 72[t] term, but the 72[t] distributions cannot.) If you wish to convert to a Roth IRA during your 72(t) term, you will remain exempt from the 10 percent penalty as long as the 72(t) payments continue (unchanged) from the Roth IRA. If you are annuitizing a traditional IRA and want to convert it to a Roth IRA during the payment term, you should convert the entire IRA, not just a portion of it. This way, you won't have to maintain two 72(t) payments schedules—one for the Roth and one for the balance remaining (the part not converted) in the traditional IRA.

Before you convert a traditional IRA that you are annuitizing to a Roth IRA, make sure that you are still eligible. Although the actual conversion will not count toward the $100,000 Roth conversion eligibility limit, the 72(t) distributions do. They can throw your income over the $100,000 limit, disqualifying you from being able to convert.

If you are eligible to convert, Roth IRAs can be annuitized in the same manner and under the same rules as traditional IRAs. But the only situation where you would find yourself annuitizing your Roth IRA would be if you needed to withdraw from it within the first five years of the conversion. Otherwise, all withdrawals of converted Roth funds are tax-free, and if they are tax-free, they cannot be subject to the 10 percent penalty (because that only applies to taxable distributions and to withdrawals of converted funds if they have not been held for five years). Therefore, if you needed to withdraw from your Roth IRA before age 59½, you would first simply withdraw your contributions tax- and penalty-free (see Chapter 7).

If you have withdrawn all your contributions, and you still need more money, you could then set up a 72(t) schedule for the Roth IRA earnings. But that seems a little ridiculous unless the earnings are huge and you need to tap into those earnings—in which case, you probably should not have converted in the first place. But if you already have, you are probably better off simply taking what you need from the Roth IRA, paying the tax and penalty on the earnings, and not bothering to maintain a 72(t) schedule for Roth IRA earnings, which are likely minimal at this point and would result in equally minimal 72(t) payments. Even though the 72(t) payments on the Roth earnings will be penalty-free, they will still be subject to income tax, since you have not yet reached age 59½.

Death and Disability Exceptions

If the payment schedule is interrupted during the 72(t) term due to death or disability, the 10 percent penalty does not apply. For the disability exception to apply, however, the disability must be serious and qualify under IRS guidelines (as defined in Chapter 4). If the IRA owner is disabled, then any distribution, even a lump-sum distribution of the entire IRA during the 72(t) payment term, will be exempt from the 10 percent penalty. Under the disability exception, the 72(t) payment schedule can be either stopped or accelerated penalty-free.

72(t) Planning Opportunities Using Multiple IRAs

Taking 72(t)s from one IRA has no effect on your other IRAs. If you have several IRAs and only annuitize one of them, then you are only committed to the 72(t) payment schedule for that particular IRA. Since each IRA is treated separately, there are both planning opportunities to take advantage of and tax traps to beware of.

If you have one IRA and are considering annuitizing to generate monthly or annual income, first calculate how much you will need. If you will need more income than your IRA will pay out using the 72(t) payment schedule, then there is nothing else you can do but annuitize that entire IRA. But if you need less cash than your IRA will pay out, you should consider splitting your IRA into two or more separate IRAs, enabling you to annuitize one IRA and leave the other IRAs alone. If it turns out later on that you require more income, your other IRAs are still available for 72(t) withdrawals. You can have an unlimited number of payment schedules ongoing at the same time or at different times, providing you with the most flexibility.

Even though you must commit to a payment schedule, by splitting IRAs you can be a little more conservative and take only what you need currently from one IRA. If your cash needs increase, you can always start a new 72(t) plan with IRA #2. Before you begin annuitizing IRA #2, you might consider splitting that IRA, leaving you with still another IRA (IRA #3). You should always try to keep some IRA money free from a 72(t) commitment. This way, if your financial situation changes and you no longer need that much income, you still have an IRA that remains intact. If it turns out that you need more income, you will still have an IRA to deploy with a new 72(t) schedule or you can simply withdraw from that IRA for a one-time expense and pay the penalty without having to tap an IRA that is already being annuitized, which would cause a retroactive 10 percent penalty.

72(t) Payment Options

Neither the tax code nor the regulations explain how annual 72(t) withdrawals should be calculated. The code only states that the series of payments must be "part of a series of substantially equal periodic payments (not less frequently than annually) made for the life (or life expectancy) of the employee or the joint lives (or joint life expectancies) of such employee and his designated beneficiary." (Internal Revenue Code Section 72[t][2][A][iv])

Like our Constitution, these words are ripe for interpretation; they can mean many things, depending upon the interpreter. IRS Revenue Ruling 2002-62 and Notice 89-25 (see Figure 11) provide the only official guidance that all IRA owners can rely on as to what is an acceptable 72(t) payment plan for withdrawing before age 59½ penalty-free.

Figure 11. IRS Guidelines for Taking 72(t) Payments

This is the official IRS explanation of what constitutes "a series of substantially equal periodic payments." IRS Notice 89-25 reproduced below describes the three acceptable methods for taking 72(t) payments. However, Revenue Ruling 2002-62 allows a one-time switch from either the amortization or annuity factor methods to the minimum distribution method, providing some relief for those whose retirement account balances have declined and would have been forced by the 72(t) amortization or annuity factor methods to take payments that were disproportionately large, given the size of their account balance. For more details on Revenue Ruling 2002-62, see the section "72(t) Payments and IRA Losses" on page 284.

IRS Notice 89-25
IRS Guidance for Taking 72(t) Payments

Q-12: In the case of an IRA or individual account plan, what constitutes a series of substantially equal periodic payments for purposes of section 72(t)(2)(A)(iv) ?

A-12: Section 72(t)(1) imposes an additional tax of 10 percent on the portion of early distributions from qualified retirement plans (including IRAs) includible in gross income. However, section 72(t)(2)(A)(iv) provides that this tax shall not apply to distributions which are part of a series of substantially equal periodic payments (not less frequently than annually) made for the life (or life expectancy) of the employee or the joint lives (or joint life expectancies) of the employee and beneficiary. Section 72(t)(4) provides that, if the series of periodic payments is subsequently modified within five years of the date of the first payment, or, if later, age 59½, the exception to the 10 percent tax under section 72(t)(2)(A)(iv) does not apply, and the taxpayer's tax for the year of modification shall be increased by an amount, determined under regulations, which (but for the 72[t][2][A][iv] exception) would have been imposed, plus interest.

Figure 11. IRS Guidelines for Taking 72(t) Payments (*cont.*)

Payments will be considered to be substantially equal periodic payments within the meaning of section 72(t)(2)(A)(iv) if they are made according to one of the methods set forth below.

Payments shall be treated as satisfying section 72(t)(2)(A)(iv) if the annual payment is determined using a method that would be acceptable for purposes of calculating the minimum distribution required under section 401(a)(9). For this purpose, the payment may be determined based on the life expectancy of the employee or the joint life and last survivor expectancy of the employee and beneficiary.

Payments will also be treated as substantially equal periodic payments within the meaning of section 72(t)(2)(A)(iv) if the amount to be distributed annually is determined by amortizing the taxpayer's account balance over a number of years equal to the life expectancy of the account owner or the joint life and last survivor expectancy of the account owner and beneficiary (with life expectancies determined in accordance with proposed section 1.401(a)(9)-1 of the regulations) at an interest rate that does not exceed a reasonable interest rate on the date payments commence. For example, a 50-year-old individual with a life expectancy of 33.1, having an account balance of $100,000, and assuming an interest rate of 8 percent, could satisfy section 72(t)(2)(A)(iv) by distributing $8,679 annually, derived by amortizing $100,000 over 33.1 years at 8 percent interest.

Finally, payments will be treated as substantially equal periodic payments if the amount to be distributed annually is determined by dividing the taxpayer's account balance by an annuity factor (the present value of an annuity of $1 per year beginning at the taxpayer's age attained in the first distribution year and continuing for the life of the taxpayer) with such annuity factor derived using a reasonable mortality table and using a interest rate that does not exceed a reasonable interest rate on the date payments commence. If

---

Figure 11. IRS Guidelines for Taking 72(t) Payments (*cont.*)

substantially equal monthly payments are being determined the taxpayer's account balance would be divided by an annuity factor equal
to the present value of an annuity of $1 per month beginning at the
taxpayer's age attained in the first distribution year and continuing
for the life of the taxpayer. For example, if the annuity factor for a $1
per year annuity for an individual who is 50 years old is 11.109 (assuming an interest rate of 8 percent and using the UP-1984 Mortality
Table), an individual with a $100,000 account balance would receive
an annual distribution of $9,002 ($100,000/11.109 = $9,002).

All 72(t) payment methods are based on the IRA owner's single
life expectancy (or on the joint life expectancy of you, the IRA
owner, and your IRA beneficiary). If you are looking to create
higher annual withdrawals, you would use only a single life expectancy. This does not mean that you should not name a beneficiary on your IRA (you should); it just means that for 72(t)
payment purposes, you will use a single life expectancy calculation. When you are annuitizing your IRA before 59½, you cannot
change the life expectancy once you elect it, so electing single life
at this point affords the highest possible payments to meet your income needs.

By electing single life for calculating 72(t)s, you'll get more
mileage out of your IRA than you would with a joint life expectancy, allowing you to annuitize less of your IRA. This is the
fundamental strategy for gaining the most benefit out of annuitizing your IRA—because you want to be able to produce the largest
possible 72(t) payment from the smallest amount of IRA money.
This will preserve more of your IRA for future 72(t) payments if
needed. Once you have accomplished this goal of gaining the most
from the least, you can then split your IRA into two or more IRAs
and annuitize only the one you need income from.

Three Methods—Which Should You Choose?

Revenue Ruling 2002-62 (released by IRS on October 3, 2002) and IRS Notice 89-25 describe three allowable methods for calculating 72(t) payments:

1. Minimum distribution method
2. Amortization method
3. Annuity factor method

The *minimum distribution method* is calculated in the same manner as required minimum distributions (RMDs) when you reach your required beginning date (RBD) (see Chapter 4). This method, however, will generally produce the lowest annual 72(t) payment. Increases in the IRA balance each year will increase the annual payments using the minimum distribution method. But unless the IRA balance appreciates substantially each year, the minimum distribution method will still produce lower payments than the other two methods. The IRA balance could also decline and under the minimum distribution method that would reduce your 72(t) payments.

This is why the *amortization method* or the *annuity factor method* is recommended if you are looking for consistently higher annual withdrawals. Both the amortization and annuity factor methods allow you to beef up annual 72(t) payments by applying an interest rate to the payment schedule. The higher the interest rate, the larger your payments will be. You can't go crazy here though. IRS Notice 89-25 states that the interest rate must "not exceed a reasonable interest rate on the date payments commence."

But what is a reasonable interest rate? In the latest release by IRS Revenue Ruling 2002-62, IRS has defined a reasonable interest rate as "any interest rate that is not more than 120 percent of the federal mid-term rate . . . for either of the two months immediately preceding the month in which the distribution begins."

The requirement under all methods that the payments be made at least annually does not mean that you must use a calendar year. You can choose any year (a fiscal or calendar year) you wish, but once you make your choice you must stick with that year. For example, if your year for taking 72(t) payments begins on September 21, 2003, you must take your required payments for that year by September 20, 2004. You must continue using a September 20 fiscal year for the duration of your 72(t) payment term.

A WORD TO THE WISE

Although the only official authority on acceptable 72(t) distribution methods are Revenue Ruling 2002-62 and IRS Notice 89-25, this does not mean that these methods are the only acceptable ones. According to numerous IRS rulings, as long as the payments are "part of a series of substantially equal periodic payments," any method that achieves that would be fine. If you do not use one of the three methods officially "blessed" by the IRS in Notice 89-25, however, you should request your own IRS ruling. It would be foolish to risk a penalty by not having your method "blessed" too.

72(t)s from Your Company Retirement Plan

The annuitizing exception is also available to withdrawals from company plans, but only if you are no longer working for that company. You can begin at any age as long as the 72(t) payments from your company plan begin after your separation from service.

If you qualify to annuitize from your company plan, your distributions are exempt from the 20 percent mandatory withholding tax requirements that apply to most other distributions from qualified plans.

If you begin annuitizing from your company plan, you can still

Chart 1. Comparing 72(t) Payment Methods at a Glance

Minimum Distribution Method

Features	Advantages	Disadvantages	Best Used When
■ Uses the same method as calculating required distributions by your RBD. ■ 72(t) payment amount is figured each year; payments can increase or decrease each year. ■ Can use single or joint life expectancy. (Single life produces higher annual payments.)	■ Easy calculation. No computer program required. Simply use the IRS life expectancy tables. ■ No inflation risk. Annual payments increase as IRA account balance increases. ■ 72(t) payments reflect annual investment returns. ■ No risk that IRS won't allow this method since there are no variables (such as an interest rate) that could create payments considered too high by IRS.	■ Produces the lowest initial 72(t) payments. Unless the IRA account grows dramatically, the annual payments will be lower than with the other two methods. ■ Uncertainty of annual 72(t) payment amounts since payments change each year based on the account balance. ■ A decline in the IRA balance will reduce future 72(t) payments.	■ You want to take advantage of the growth in the IRA account and be able to create larger 72(t) payments in future years. ■ You expect your income needs and IRA account balance to increase. ■ You want simplicity.

Chart 1. Comparing 72(t) Payment Methods at a Glance (continued)

Amortization Method

Features	Advantages	Disadvantages	Best Used When
■ Amortizes the IRA, similar to a home mortgage. ■ Payments do not have to be refigured each year. The 72(t) payment can be calculated once for the first year, and the annual payment amount can remain the same for all years during the term. ■ Payments are based on the IRS life expectancy tables and a reasonable interest rate.	■ Produces higher payments than the minimum distribution method. ■ Larger payments can be computed by using a higher (reasonable) interest rate. ■ Certainty of payment amounts. The payments remain fixed throughout the 72(t) term. A decrease in the IRA balance will not cause the 72(t) payments to decrease (unless the IRA balance is being redetermined each year*).	■ Complicated calculation. Computer program or calculator would be needed. ■ Inflation risk. An increase in the IRA balance will not result in higher 72(t) payments. The payments remain fixed throughout the 72(t) term. Payments will not reflect annual investment returns.* ■ IRS could disallow the 72(t) exception if it deems the interest rate to be unreasonable and the resulting payments too high.	■ You want larger 72(t) payments but do not want the complications of using the various actuarial tables needed for the annuity factor method. ■ This method generally produces larger payments than the minimum distribution method, but smaller payments than the annuity factor method. Most people use this method in favor of the annuity factor method because of its simplicity compared to the annuity factor method, but using a computer program would equalize the complexity and make this a nonissue.

Chart 1. Comparing 72(t) Payment Methods at a Glance (*continued*)

Annuity Factor Method

Features	Advantages	Disadvantages	Best Used When
■ Payments are based on the 2003 annuity table in Revenue Ruling 2002-62. ■ Payments are calculated using a reasonable interest rate.	■ This method generally produces the largest annual 72(t) payment. It allows you to gain the largest possible 72(t) payment from the smallest amount of IRA funds. This allows you the most efficient use of your retirement account. ■ Larger payments can be computed by using a higher (reasonable) interest rate.	■ The most complicated method to use. The annuity factor tables are not as readily available as the life expectancy factors from IRS Publication 590. However, there are computer programs available that contain the 2003 annuity table used for the annuity factor method.	■ You want the largest possible 72(t) payments. ■ You have software to do the calculations.

Chart 1. Comparing 72(t) Payment Methods at a Glance (continued)

Annuity Factor Method (continued)

Advantages	Disadvantages	Best Used When
■ Certainty of payment amounts. The payments remain fixed throughout the 72(t) term. A decrease in the IRA balance will not cause the 72(t) payments to decrease (unless the IRA balance is being redetermined each year*).	■ Inflation risk. An increase in the IRA balance will not result in higher 72(t) payments. The payments remain fixed throughout the 72(t) term. 72(t) payments will not reflect annual investment returns.* ■ IRS could disallow the 72(t) exception if it deems the interest rate to be unreasonable and the resulting payments too high.	■ You have access to the 2003 annuity mortality table, which generally will produce the largest 72(t) payments. You can obtain that table from the Conference of Consulting Actuaries (847-419-9090; $15). However, it's best to use the software ("Pension Distributions Calculator"; $149, by Brentmark Software; 800-879-6665 or order online at www.brentmark.com). Brentmark's software includes the 2003 annuity table. An excellent resource for 72(t) payments, tables, and calculators is the website http://72t.net hosted by Gordon F. Weis, a 72(t) specialist. Imagine dedicating your life to 72(t). That's Gordon F. Weis.

*Combination (hybrid) methods:

In several private letter rulings using the annuity and amortization methods, the IRS has allowed the life expectancy, interest rate, and retirement account balance to be redetermined annually, creating a "hybrid" type method combining the best features of the minimum distribution method with the amortization and annuity factor methods. These "hybrid" methods generally result in higher payments than if either of the methods were used on its own. However, if the account balance declines, the 72(t) payments may be reduced. Revenue Ruling 2002-62 casts doubt on whether hybrid methods will be permitted. Do not use a hybrid method without requesting a private letter ruling from the IRS.

roll the plan money over to an IRA during the payment term as long as the 72(t) payment schedule that originated with your plan continues as is (without modification) from your IRA. The IRS allowed this in two private letter rulings (PLRs 9103046 and 9221052). The IRS did not allow the reverse, however. In another private letter ruling (PLR 9818055) the IRS would not allow an IRA owner who was taking 72(t) payments from her IRA to roll the IRA back to a company plan without triggering the 10 percent penalty retroactively. Here, the IRS said that this would be a modification because the 72(t) schedule was terminated after the transfer back to the employer plan. But that was before EGTRRA 2001, which now allows all taxable IRA funds (not only conduit IRAs, which are explained in "Talking the Talk" at the start of this book) to be rolled over to company retirement plans. So, the IRS could change its mind on this.

Is 72(t) Right for You?

There are four common situations where annuitizing a retirement account before reaching 59½ may be a good move: early retirement, estate planning, divorce, and financial hardship.

Early Retirement

This is the most common situation. There are more and more early retirees (or, unfortunately, forced retirees) who do not want to, or may not be able to, go back to work just yet. Many of them do not know what they want to do. They often leave their company with a large retirement account, but have little else to live on while they are on hiatus. If this sounds like you, then a 72(t) schedule fits the bill. Since you do not have other money besides your retirement savings, you'll need to tap your retirement account. If you are under 59½, a 72(t) schedule can help to provide you with a stream of income to live on without incurring the 10 percent penalty. If you are age 55 or over in the year you retire, you can tap your company retirement plan penalty-free. If you do not qualify for the age-55 exception, then you should roll over the retirement account to an IRA. If you are no longer working for your company, you could begin the 72(t) schedule from your company plan, but that is usually not practical, as you have more flexibility in your IRA. After you roll it over, your IRA can then be split into two or more IRAs. One IRA will be annuitized and the other(s) will remain intact. The amount of the split is dependent on the amount of annual income that you'll need during the 72(t) term.

Estate Planning

If you are married and your IRA is your largest single asset, then annuitizing may make sense. For example, if you had a $3 million IRA, but you had little other property and your spouse had little or no property in his or her name, annuitizing can help fund your spouse's credit shelter amount (the federal estate tax exemption of $1.5 million in 2004). Because your spouse has no property of his or her own, if your spouse dies before you do, his or her estate exemption will be wasted. Annuitizing your IRA can help to provide the funds needed to build up assets in your spouse's name. This way, if your spouse dies first, some or all of your spouse's credit shelter amount can be used. If it is not used, it is lost! The larger the IRA, the better this works because you'll need some pretty big 72(t) payments to provide enough money after taxes to reach the $1.5 million exemption. Even on a large IRA, though, if you are young (in your 30s or 40s), your long life expectancy will result in smaller annual payments. But the younger you are, the more years you'll have to build up your spouse's estate.

Another estate planning objective is liquidity. This means having money (other than IRA money) to pay estate taxes. Buying life insurance is the most cost-effective way to provide this kind of money. But if all your funds are tied up in your IRA, where will the money come from to pay the insurance premiums? 72(t) payments may be the answer. This is a powerful strategy because you are highly leveraging this with life insurance. The life insurance should be set up outside your estate to keep the proceeds estate-tax–free, but you already know that from Chapter 5.

If your IRA is large and represents most of your estate, you can annuitize it and use the money to make gifts and remove some of your IRA from your estate without having to wait until age 59½, when the 10 percent penalty will no longer apply.

The trade-off with each of the estate planning strategies I've cited is that you will be giving up the long-term benefits of the tax deferral.

Divorce

"She cried, and the judge wiped her tears with my checkbook," commented much-married millionaire Tommy Manville (1894–1967) on the subject of divorce. Since an IRA these days often represents the largest single asset in an estate, it is no surprise that it's being thrust into the divorce arena more frequently. If there is a need for cash to fund a property settlement or to pay ongoing maintenance (alimony), the IRA may be the only place to find money to make these payments. If you are under 59½, then a 72(t) payment schedule may be the answer. The only problem is, again, that the payments under even the best 72(t) method may not be enough to cover the actual expense, especially for young IRA owners.

An IRA can be transferred tax- and penalty-free to a former spouse pursuant to a divorce or separate maintenance decree by making a direct trustee-to-trustee transfer of the IRA assets to the former spouse's IRA. But that means a partial or entire loss of the IRA by the IRA owner. By using the 72(t) exception instead, the IRA owner keeps his or her IRA and can tap it penalty-free (not tax-free though as in the transfer to the former spouse) and use the 72(t) payments to make ongoing support or alimony payments without giving the IRA to the former spouse.

If the IRA owner is bound by the divorce agreement to transfer a part of the IRA he or she is currently taking 72(t) payments from to the former spouse, then the IRS will allow the 72(t) payments to be reduced based on the amount of the IRA he or she has left.

For example, if you are taking 72(t) payments from your IRA and the divorce agreement says you are to give 55 percent of that IRA to your ex-spouse, you can reduce your 72(t) payment schedule so it is based on having only 45 percent of your IRA left. This will not be considered a modification and your ex-spouse will not have to continue taking 72(t) payments on the 55 percent of your IRA balance that she receives. Several IRS PLRs have allowed this treatment.

Another divorce scenario that might call for 72(t) payments is when most of one spouse's non-IRA property is transferred to the former spouse. In return for transferring the non-IRA property, the spouse keeps his or her large IRA. Since this may now be his or her only source of funds to live on, a 72(t) payment schedule could be set up to provide current income.

Financial Hardship

Before you begin a 72(t) schedule to raise money to resolve financial problems, first see if one of the other exceptions to the 10 percent penalty applies. For example, a common problem is medical bills. There is already an exception for medical expenses that exceed 7.5 percent of your adjusted gross income. You do not have to itemize on your taxes to qualify for this exception. You are also exempt from the 10 percent penalty if you need to withdraw from your IRA to pay for higher education, you qualify as a first-time homeowner, or you need to pay health insurance premiums while you are unemployed. There is no exception from the 10 percent penalty for a "financial hardship" that is not specifically covered under one of the other exceptions. The 72(t) schedule then should only be used as a last resort if no other funds are available and no other exceptions apply.

Who Should Be Using 72(t)?
Many early retirees look at 72(t) as an easy way to get to their retirement cash without paying the 10 percent toll. Before you take the 72(t) plunge, ask yourself the following questions:

Can You Afford to Deplete Your Retirement Savings Now?

With all the exceptions it offers, Congress has actually made it too easy to tap retirement funds early. The "R" in IRA is for retirement. Although your IRA or other retirement account has built up nicely over the years, the build-up is *not* for spending now. So, any decision to dip into your nest egg early should be carefully and seriously evaluated. Annuitizing your IRA early should be a last resort, and used only for necessities, not for a vacation, big-screen TV, or other purchase that you could do without and still survive. (Well, maybe not the big-screen TV!)

If you tap now, what will be left for you when you retire? It's very hard to just withdraw a little. That's like being on a diet and cheating a little. You know how it goes. You (and I) figure that since you have already had the fried chicken, you may as well have the french fries and then you may as well have dessert. Pretty soon you're combing the local convenience stores for new Ben & Jerry ice cream flavors that you haven't tried this week—and then you're too tired to go to the gym.

Tapping your retirement account early is just as tempting. Even though under Section 72(t), you will only be withdrawing a small amount penalty-free, the fact that you are already breaking into it (just like going off your diet a little) may lead you to start withdrawing more and paying the penalty, rationalizing along the way that there's still plenty of money left in the account and why shouldn't you enjoy it now? But soon it becomes a costly piggy bank for all kinds of things. That temptation may lead you to eventually wipe out your retirement savings before you have even reached age 59½.

How Much Do You Have in Your Retirement Account?

The more you have in an IRA or other retirement account, the higher your 72(t) payments will be and even after you complete the 72(t) term you will have plenty left for retirement. There are many people, especially professionals and executives, who have large retirement accounts and few other assets to live on. For this group and others with a healthy retirement account, the 72(t) option works well.

The question is how little do you have in your IRA? That is usually the problem. If there is not much to annuitize, then your 72(t) payments will be too small to make a difference, unless you don't really need much.

Are You Too Young or Too Old?

Did you ever think that being 45 years old would be too young for anything? Well, it's probably too young for 72(t). If you begin annuitizing too early, you'll be stuck with a long-term payment schedule. The payments will be small and not likely to be enough to meet your needs. That's because you have two factors working against you.

First is your life expectancy. The younger you are, the longer your life expectancy is for 72(t) calculation purposes and the smaller your annual payments will be. No, you cannot file for a living-on-the-edge exception to lower your life expectancy and withdraw larger amounts under 72(t).

The second problem with starting a 72(t) schedule too early is that the younger you are, the less money you are likely to have accumulated in your IRA. If you are in your 40s and need some cash, the last thing you should be considering is a long-term plan to deplete your retirement savings. You might be better off with a home equity loan. Or, if you need the funds for a one-time expense and have no other place to withdraw from except your IRA, then you could withdraw what you need for that one time and pay the 10 percent penalty. This way, you take the hit and don't have to bother with maintaining a 72(t) schedule.

For those of you between 55 and 59½ years old, you will have to maintain the 72(t) for five years. If you can wait it out without withdrawing from your IRA until you reach 59½, you are probably better off doing so because then you can take out as much as you like with no penalty. You don't have to stick to any schedule at all. In fact, between 59½ and 70½, you will not have an IRA penalty. The 10 percent penalty only applies before age 59½.

If you are close to 59½, it may even pay to forget the 72(t) schedule, withdraw what you need from your IRA, and pay the 10 percent penalty on the amount you withdraw.

For example, let's say you are 58 and need $50,000 for a one-time expense, but have no source to tap other than your IRA. Unfortunately, your IRA balance is not large enough to produce a $50,000 annual payment under any of the various 72(t) payment methods. You can withdraw the $50,000 from your IRA, pay the tax and a $5,000 penalty, and be done with it. The following year, you'll turn 59½ years old and after that you can withdraw any amount you like penalty-free and you are not stuck with a payment schedule (one that does not produce enough annually anyway).

If you borrowed from a bank or, worse, used your credit card, the interest cost over even a few years would far exceed the $5,000 IRS penalty. You could also borrow on your home (take out a home equity loan), pay the loan over five years, and take 72(t) IRA distributions over that time to pay back the loan. Here, the tax-deductible interest will offset the taxable income created by the 72(t) distributions and, in turn, reduce the income tax on those distributions.

Are You Ready for a Commitment?

I'm not talking about marriage here, but something that lasts longer than many marriages: a 72(t) payment schedule. At a minimum, you will be locked into a five-year schedule. Depending on your age, that schedule can extend over many more years. For example, a 40-year-old has to continue the 72(t) schedule for almost 20 years. That's a major commitment. Are you ready to commit for that long? Even on the short side, for those age 55 or over, it's still a five-year plan. The younger you are, the longer your schedule will be and the more you should give the 72(t) option some serious thought before saying, "I do."

What Other (Non-IRA) Sources of Funds Are Available?

IRA withdrawals are expensive even without the 10 percent penalty. You must pay ordinary income tax on your IRA or retirement plan distributions. There are no capital gains rates or any other preferential tax treatment on IRA withdrawals. Even 10-year lump-sum averaging only applies to withdrawals from a qualified plan, and you must have been born before 1936 to take advantage of that anyway (see Chapter 3). That would mean you were over 59½ years old and therefore would not need to worry about the 10 percent penalty and 72(t) payments.

A sale of stock that was held more than one year is only taxed at 20 percent. Withdrawing money from a savings account is not taxable at all. Borrowing is also tax-free, but carries an interest cost, although that cost may be offset if the interest is tax-deductible as either home mortgage interest or investment interest expense, whereas the interest on a loan from your 401(k) plan is personal nondeductible interest. I may sound like a broken record, but this is important: Don't use your IRA money first. Use it only as a last resort. Retirement money is not only the most expensive money to use; it is also the hardest money to replace since it accumulates over many years of disciplined saving. You'll also be losing out on the benefit of the long-term tax-deferred build-up.

Have You *Really* Retired?

Have you actually retired before reaching 59½? If so, you had better have a ton of cash put away because you will need it. You may spend more years in retirement than you did working—so, before you consider annuitizing your IRA, factor in the possibility of your taking another job out of either necessity or sheer boredom.

If you are pretty sure about early retirement and most of your wealth is tied up in an IRA or qualified retirement plan, then annuitizing your IRA would be a good idea for two reasons. First, it's the only money have; second, you are using the money for its intended purpose: your retirement (albeit a bit early). If you can afford it, good for you (I'm jealous)! Once you complete your 72(t) term, you'll keep withdrawing at any pace you like.

If there is at least a possibility of your going back to work, you may be better off not beginning a long-term 72(t) schedule. See if you can use other non-IRA funds until you are sure that early retirement at 35 years old is right for you. Where do you sign up for that anyway?

Do You Have a Company Plan?

If you have a retirement plan from a company you've left at age 55 or older (but still younger than 59½), you can withdraw from your company plan with no 10 percent penalty. It does not matter why you are no longer working. Whether you quit, got fired, retired, or were downsized, as long as you were what the tax law calls "separated from service" at age 55 or older, you can withdraw from your company plan with no 10 percent penalty.

The age-55 exception is only available on withdrawals from company plans (401[k]s, qualified plans, etc.) and not from IRAs. If this applies to you (for example, if you are 56 years old and have left your company after you turned 55), then you do not need to annuitize your IRA. Do not roll your plan money over to your IRA until you reach 59½. Until then, you can withdraw as much as you wish penalty-free from your company plan. You'll still pay income tax, of course, but no 10 percent penalty.

"Oh, S***! My IRA Has Fallen and It Can't Get Up!"

What if the stock market heads south and the value of your IRA or 401(k) is in freefall? Are you entitled to any tax benefits on losses? Unfortunately, there is little help available from Uncle Sam in this regard because it's all a question of *basis*.

As you learned earlier in this book, when you invest money that you have already paid tax on, you create basis. Basis is reduced by any tax deductions you receive. For example, if you contribute

---

Chart 2. Snapshot of the 72(t) Rules

The 72(t) payments:

- Must continue for at least five years or until age 59½, whichever period is longer.
- Must be distributed at least annually (calendar year).
- Must be substantially equal; the payment formula cannot be changed; the payments cannot be stopped during the payment term, unless you become disabled or die. (Except that the IRS allows a one-time switch to the RMD method.)
- Can be computed using either a single or joint life, but once you select single or joint life, you must stick with that choice throughout the 72(t) term.
- Will be larger using a single life expectancy as opposed to a joint life expectancy.
- Cannot begin from a company plan until after you leave your company.
- Can begin at any age from an IRA.
- Are only applicable to the IRA being annuitized. IRAs can be split. One IRA can be annuitized while others can remain intact for future use.

$3,000 to a tax-deductible IRA, you do not have basis, because the tax deduction reduced your basis to zero. If on the other hand you contribute to a nondeductible IRA (or Roth IRA, which is nondeductible by definition), you have created basis. If you do not recover your basis, you may have a deductible loss. Losses can only be recognized once ALL funds have been withdrawn from ALL your IRAs.

For example, if you contributed $3,000 to a nondeductible IRA and it earned $100 and was now worth $3,100, you would still owe tax on the $100 when the entire IRA was withdrawn. You would not owe tax on the $3,000 because that is your basis. It was paid for with after-tax dollars. Upon withdrawal, your selling price is $3,100 and your basis is $3,000, leaving you with a $100 gain (taxable amount) upon distribution. But if the $3,000 was only worth $1,400 when you withdrew it, you would have a loss of $1,600 (the $1,400 selling price less your basis of $3,000 = – $1,600 loss) and be able to claim a deduction to the extent of your unrecovered basis.

You cannot withdraw only some of the IRA and take a proportionate loss. The IRS takes the position that the true loss is not known until every dollar of the IRA is withdrawn. Only then can a loss be calculated and deducted. If you have several IRA accounts, this means you must withdraw the entire balance in each IRA in order to claim a loss. (If you have several Roth IRAs, the same procedure must be followed. You must withdraw the entire balance from each of them to claim a loss.)

IRA Losses May Be Limited

If you are able to deduct your loss because you have withdrawn all your IRA funds, it may not be as large a deduction as you might think because it is only available as an itemized deduction. Not everyone can itemize, but even if you can, the deduction is further limited since it must be taken as a *miscellaneous* itemized deduction subject to the 2 percent limit on your adjusted gross income.

If you make it across that threshold, you're still not guaranteed a deduction because of the overall 3 percent reduction on itemized deductions. And if you get past that obstacle, you could still lose the deduction altogether if you become subject to the alternative minimum tax (AMT), which disallows most miscellaneous itemized deductions. But let's say you're lucky and make it through. Then you may be rewarded with a tax deduction for some part of your IRA losses—but only if there were *nondeductible contributions* made to your IRA.

For example, let's say you have $20,000 of nondeductible contributions in an IRA (you only have one). You contributed $2,000 per year for 10 years. The IRA is now worth $12,000. Your basis is $20,000. If you withdraw the entire $12,000, you'll have an $8,000 loss which you will claim as a miscellaneous itemized deduction, subject to the 2 percent AGI limit. It's the same as if you sold a stock for $12,000 and your basis (cost) was $20,000. The only difference is that a stock loss is usually a capital loss and is not subject to the itemized deduction limitations. A stock loss that cannot be used in one tax year may be carried over to another tax year. That is not the case with IRAs. If you cannot deduct the loss in the year of the IRA distribution, you cannot claim it in any future year. The loss is wasted. Also, a stock loss can be claimed even if only part of the stock is sold. With IRAs, you must sell (distribute from the IRA) the entire IRA account before a loss can be claimed.

If, in addition to the $20,000 nondeductible IRA contributions above, you also had an IRA rollover account that included $500,000 of funds transferred from your 401(k), you could not take the loss until this IRA was also distributed in its entirety. Even if the accounts were maintained separately, they still must be aggregated in order to qualify for any loss on the IRA. It is unlikely that you would empty the IRA rollover account in order to possibly deduct a loss of $20,000 (at most). You cannot deduct a loss greater than your basis, so you would never have a loss of greater than the amount of your nondeductible contributions.

Once you bring the $500,000 rollover into the mix, any loss will be wiped out by the taxable distribution from the rollover IRA. The basis in both IRAs is still $20,000 because the rollover IRA has no basis since none of that money has been taxed yet. The total withdrawal would be $512,000 (the $500,000 rollover IRA plus the $12,000 nondeductible IRA). Since the basis is $20,000, there would still be a taxable distribution of $492,000 (the $512,000 distribution less the $20,000 basis = $492,000). You would receive the $8,000 loss in full, but it would cost you the tax on $492,000 to get it. That's a lousy deal.

So, before taking IRA losses, consider tax factors such as amounts in other IRAs that would have to be distributed in order to claim the loss. You should also compute the amount of the deduction available for any IRA loss incurred, after required reductions from tax law limitations such as the 2 percent AGI limits, the 3 percent overall reduction, and the effect of the AMT, all of which could erase the tax deduction for your IRA losses.

72(t) Payments and IRA Losses

If you are withdrawing a series of substantially equal periodic payments—also known as *72(t) payments* as you know by now—to avoid the 10 percent early-withdrawal penalty, a market decline may create tax problems for you. If the value of the IRA you are withdrawing your 72(t) payments from has declined substantially, there may not be enough funds in the IRA to satisfy your required 72(t) payment—or, your payment may be eating up a much larger portion of your IRA than you had planned. And if you do not satisfy your required 72(t) payment, you will have modified the payment schedule, thus triggering the 10 percent penalty retroactively.

But take heart. Happily, all is not lost. The IRS has come through with some relief for you, however limited. Revenue Ruling 2002-62 allows you a one-time-only switchover from either the amortization or annuity factor method you are currently using to determine your 72(t) payments to the minimum distribution method. Under this method, 72(t) payments for future years are based on your updated retirement account balance. If your balance increases, your payments increase. If it declines, your 72(t) payments decline—but you don't trigger the dreaded 10 percent retroactive penalty.

Company Stock

If you are in a 401(k) or other company retirement plan, and it contains highly appreciated company stock, you can withdraw the stock instead of rolling it over and only pay tax on the original cost to the plan. So, if the cost of the stock in your plan was $10 and now it is worth $50, your stock has appreciated by $40. This appreciation is called *net unrealized appreciation (NUA)* and is explained in detail in Chapter 3. But here's the *Reader's Digest* version: NUA is not taxed until the stock is actually sold, and even then it is only taxed at capital gains rates, regardless of how long the stock was held in the plan. But what happens if the stock declines in value? Is there such a thing as *net unrealized depreciation (NUD)?* By golly, Jethro, yes there is! Here's a real-life example of NUA at work, then NUD:

Assume that the cost of the stock in your plan was $10 and the value at the time you distribute the shares from the plan to your taxable broker account (not a rollover) is $50. The NUA is $40. When you transfer the shares out of the plan, you'll pay tax on only the $10 cost. The NUA is not taxed until the shares are sold. The $40 NUA will be taxed at capital gains rates when the shares are sold.

Now let's say instead that you sell the shares 10 months after they were transferred from the plan to you, at which time they are worth $55. The $40 of NUA is taxed at capital gains rates and the $5 of further appreciation is taxed at ordinary income tax rates. If the stock had been held for more than one year from the date of the distribution from the plan, then the $5 would be taxed at capital gains rates.

OK, same facts as before, except now the stock has dropped in value from $55 to $30 when you sell your shares. Are you locked into paying tax on the $40 NUA? No. That value does not exist anymore. To determine the amount that will be taxed when the stock is sold for $30, you begin with your basis in the stock, which is the original $10 cost you already paid tax on. You'll now pay tax on $20. If the shares dropped to $4 when you sold, you would have a long-term capital loss of $6 (the $10 basis less the $4 selling price).

Alternate Valuation and IRAs

This is one way to get the government to really share your pain when the market drops. If you're killed by a plunging decline in the value of your estate—and I mean literally—then your heirs

286 ■ THE RETIREMENT SAVINGS TIME BOMB

may benefit from any subsequent declines. This benefit is called *alternate valuation*, and your estate may get to pay estate tax on a lower value (generally measured six months after you're gone) because of it.

Alternate valuation can only be used to reduce estate tax—and only if elected on all estate assets. It cannot be elected, say, only on your IRA.

Hardship Withdrawals

Contrary to myth (often a stand-in word for *wishful thinking*), there is no exemption from the 10 percent early-withdrawal penalty for financial hardship due to a plunging stock market (see Chapter 4 for all legit exemptions). If you tap your IRA before you're 59½ and no exception applies, you pay the penalty. The End.

There is, however, a financial hardship provision in many 401(k) plans. But it only permits participants to withdraw earlier than the plan otherwise allows. The withdrawal itself is still taxable and still subject to the 10 percent early-withdrawal penalty (assuming no other exceptions apply).

TIP!

If your IRA has bottomed out as a result of a plunging stock market, consider converting to a Roth IRA if you qualify (see Chapter 7). For example, if you have an IRA that has lost 40 percent of its value, you will only pay tax on its current value by converting now. That's like a 40-percent–off sale! And when the market rebounds and grows over the long haul, which has historically been the case, all of that increase in value will go untaxed in the Roth!

"Oh, S***! I Forgot to Take My RMD!"

Can you get out of the 50 percent penalty, or are you completely screwed? The answer is yes! (Yes, you can get out of it. Scared you at first, didn't I?)

It is not unknown for the IRS to waive this penalty for those who make an honest mistake—and even the IRS can consider forgetting an RMD to be an honest mistake (unless you've read this book—in which case, make sure the IRS doesn't find out). Just don't just let things slide and do nothing when you realize you missed an RMD, hoping the IRS won't catch you. People often ask me, "How will the IRS find out?" And my answer, usually accompanied by a shrug, is "Beats me; ask the guy in the cell next to you!"

An amended return isn't required if you miss an RMD because the past cannot be changed on this. For example, if it is now 2004 and you just discovered that you forgot to withdraw your required amount for 2003, it is not possible to withdraw in 2003 anymore because that year has ended. Any withdrawal now will be deemed a 2004 withdrawal or a withdrawal in whatever year you actually withdraw the money.

Report the back distributions you missed (you'll owe tax on them) on your tax return (Form 1040). Attach Form 5329 ("Additional Taxes on Qualified Plans [Including IRAs] and Other Tax-Favored Accounts") to your tax return. Also attach an explanation of why you did not take the RMD. The best explanation, as in most things, is the truth. If you were not aware of RMDs, say it. If you hired a tax preparer and he or she did not advise you of a required distribution, then say that. These are acceptable reasons for which the IRS has waived the 50 percent penalty. But remember, the IRS may not be so liberal once the RMD reporting that financial institutions must do (see Chapter 4) is in full swing.

Many times it isn't a case of not taking the distribution itself, but of not taking enough (the required minimum) because you and/or your advisor miscalculated. That can happen quite easily, especially to beneficiaries, who may not be aware of their distribution requirements. A miscalculation is the most common mistake and the IRS would waive the 50 percent penalty for that reason also—because it feels you at least made a good-faith attempt to withdraw your RMD.

Taking your RMD out of another person's IRA triggers the penalty as well, and is another mistake people often make because they misunderstand the rule that says you can withdraw your RMD from any one of your IRAs. One taxpayer (and he's not alone) believed this meant his or his wife's IRA and so he took both of their RMDs from his wife's IRA. That is not what the rule means. You cannot take your RMD from another person's IRA, even if that person is your spouse. In this case the IRS waived the 50 percent penalty but disallowed any credit towards his RMD amount for the RMD he'd wrongly taken from his wife's account. The IRS still required him to take the back RMD he missed taking from his own. So, he ended up having to withdraw more and pay more tax, but at least the damage wasn't compounded by a 50 percent penalty.

The IRS policy prefers that you pay the 50 percent penalty first, and then request a waiver. If it agrees to your request, it will then refund your money. This approach is a bit harsh—and one-sided—in my opinion because you're out the money for the duration, while it's earning interest for the IRS, not you. Also, there's a realistic chance that your waiver request (and the penalty enclosed with it) may get lost in the bureaucracy because the tax return processing and penalty forgiveness sections are in two different areas.

What's my advice? Don't miss an RMD. But in the event that you do, the best course of action is to disclose that you missed it (on Form 5329), but show no penalty to be paid and instead put, "See attached explanation." Then attach a written statement explaining why you messed up and asking (begging, actually) for the penalty to be waived. *You must ask.* The IRS will not automatically waive the penalty, just because you disclosed it before you were caught.

"Oh, S***! I Inherited Under the Old Rules. Can I Still Stretch My IRA?"

All hope is not lost. In the April 2002-issued Final Regulations (the new rules) many IRA beneficiaries who inherited under the old rules (from the 1987 Proposed Regulations) are given a second chance to keep inherited IRAs growing longer. If this is you (meaning if you inherited before 2002), you may be permitted to switch to the new rules and extend the life of your inherited IRA.

Under the old rules, you might have been forced to empty that inherited IRA sooner. Therefore, you should look at these new rules and see if the distribution schedule can be lengthened. Some of you may be able to increase the life of your inherited IRA by more than 10 times!

Beneficiaries affected:

- Beneficiaries withdrawing based on their own or someone else's life expectancy.

Beneficiaries Withdrawing Based on Their Own or Someone Else's Life Expectancy

Beneficiaries who withdraw based on anybody's life expectancy are subject to two concepts that are new to the Final Regulations: *"Redetermination of the designated beneficiary"* and *"Reconstruction of the life expectancy."* These concepts may sound ominous, like medical procedures, but, in fact, they are necessary to calculate required distributions for most beneficiaries who inherited under the old rules.

In essence, the processes involved are forensic in that you have to go back and see what happened at the IRA owner's death and up to September 30 of the year thereafter. This doesn't mean having to dig up the body, but you may have to resurrect old IRA documents. And if you are the beneficiary involved, some of the strange results of the redetermination and reconstruction processes may surprise and even shock you.

Redetermination of the Designated Beneficiary

This process applies to all beneficiaries who inherited before 2002, regardless of how far back—yes, even as long ago as before e-mail! The only beneficiaries to whom it doesn't apply are those who have already withdrawn the entire IRA balance or who should have by now. It requires seeing who the designated beneficiary would have been under these new rules. This means going back in time to September 30 of the year following the year of the IRA owner's death—the convoluted schedule for determining designated beneficiaries, as you learned in Chapter 6.

In most cases, the designated beneficiary will stay the same and the payout schedule will improve slightly, but there are situations where the identity of the beneficiary may change and the payout schedule could change dramatically as a result, adding decades to the life of the inherited IRA. However, the payout schedule could also end up being shortened—with the result that some beneficiaries may end up having to withdraw more under the new rules.

Reconstruction of the Life Expectancy

The second phase for beneficiaries switching to the new rules is to reconstruct their life expectancy. This is based on the results of the redetermination process. Once you redetermine the designated beneficiary, you will know the life expectancy that needs to be reconstructed.

Reconstructing simply means going back to either the year of death or the year after and looking up the age from the Single Life Expectancy Table. You then bring that life expectancy factor up to date by subtracting one year for each year that has passed since the beneficiary's RMDs began. Even if the identity of the designated beneficiary does not change, you must still reconstruct the life expectancy.

Even though the new rules say that beginning in 2003 all beneficiaries who inherited before 2003 must reconstruct, the provision has no real teeth. For example, if you did not reconstruct your life expectancy and stuck with the old table, you would be withdrawing more than you are required to, and you can always do that. Any real change will show up if the beneficiary changes as a result of the redetermination process. In that case, the reconstruction of life expectancy might also cause a substantial change in the distribution schedule. You do not have to go back and "correct" the distributions for prior years when the distribution period is reconstructed.

The redetermination process cannot create a designated beneficiary when there was none to begin with. In most cases, redetermining the designated beneficiary will lengthen the distribution schedule allowing beneficiaries to hold on to their inherited IRAs longer. That is the overall intent of the new rules, but there are a few situations where the distribution schedule could be adversely affected and cause a quicker payout of the inherited IRA. A beneficiary who finds himself or herself with a shorter payout after the redetermination process is stuck with that, unless the IRS issues a ruling or other guidance.

Events that will change the designated beneficiary include a change of beneficiary after the RBD, splitting inherited IRAs after the IRA owner's death, and disclaiming an IRA.

A Change of Beneficiary After the RBD

For example, in 1992, his first distribution year, Nathan (the IRA owner), age 70, had named his spouse Joanne, age 67, as his beneficiary and elected to take RMDs using the old joint life expectancy method. In 1993 (after his RBD), he changed the beneficiary to his grandson, Amos, who was 8 years old in 1992. Nathan dies in 1994. In 1992, distributions were based on a joint life expectancy (from the old Joint Life Expectancy Table) of 22.0 years. Grand-

son Amos began required distributions in 1995, the year after
death, based on the remaining joint life expectancy of 19 years (22
years less 3 years [1995 – 1992] = 19 years). Under the old rules,
for 2003, Amos would have 11 years remaining on the payout (22
years less 11 years [2003 – 1992] = 11 years). Under the old rules,
the designated beneficiary was Joanne (because she was the named
beneficiary on the RBD), and Nathan's changing the beneficiary to
Amos after the RBD had no effect on that. But now, under the new
rules, the designated beneficiary must be redetermined. So, grandson
Amos looks back to September 30, 1995 (September 30 is a crucial
date under the new rules because that's when designated beneficiaries are determined), to see who the designated beneficiary would
have been had these new rules applied back then. In this case, the
designated beneficiary changes from Joanne, the IRA owner's
spouse, to Amos, the grandson, because Amos was the named beneficiary on September 30, 1995. Amos can now go back and reconstruct his life expectancy. He was 11 years old in 1995, the year
after Nathan's death. He looks up the life expectancy factor for an
11-year-old from the new Single Life Expectancy Table. That factor is 71.8 years. He then reduces the 71.8 factor by one for each
year that has passed since 1995. For his 2003 required distribution, he will use a life expectancy factor of 63.8 years (the 71.8
years less 8 years since 1995 = 63.8 years). This factor will continue to be reduced by one each year to calculate the RMD for future distribution years. In this example the new rules caused a
change in the designated beneficiary. Also, the remaining distribution schedule was increased dramatically from 11 years to 63.8
years. Can you imagine the difference in tax-deferred compounding in this situation on even a modest IRA?

Splitting Inherited IRAs After the IRA Owner's Death

This is yet another situation where the identity of the designated
beneficiary can change after the redetermination process. Under
the old rules, if you had named your three children on your IRA at
your required beginning date, after your death the designated ben-

eficiary would have been the oldest child even if the children split the IRA equally right after your death. Under the redetermination provision, if the children split the account before September 30 of the year following the year of death, they could each use their own age for calculating their required distributions, rather than being stuck with the age of the oldest.

Disclaiming an IRA

If a contingent beneficiary were named, then, as a result of the disclaimer, the contingent beneficiary would become the designated beneficiary after the designated beneficiary was redetermined. But if no contingent beneficiary was named, it's too late to fix the problem. As you'll recall from Chapter 6, you cannot go back and name a contingent beneficiary. The IRA owner had to do that while he or she was alive.

"Oh, S***! I Missed the Deadline for Recharacterizing My Roth!"

If you converted to a Roth IRA in an earlier year (say, 1999), you had until October 15, 2000, to recharacterize back to your traditional IRA (see Chapter 7). But if you missed the deadline, what happens now? There are no further extensions. If you did not have to recharacterize, but would have liked to because you changed your mind or decided that you did not really want to pay the conversion tax, you really have no problem other than you are stuck with your Roth. In the long run, it may be the best move you ever made.

If you had to recharacterize, however, since it turned out that you could not convert for 1999 because either your 1999 income exceeded $100,000 or you filed married-separate, you have a problem. Now you have money in a Roth IRA that is not allowed to be there. You are immediately subject to an excess contribution penalty of 6 percent for each year the funds remain in the Roth

IRA. You cannot put the money back in a traditional IRA, because now it is 2003 and that had to be done by October 15, 2000. You already paid the income tax when you converted, so no more tax will be owed on that money, but you will pay a 10 percent penalty if you happen to be younger than 59½ (if no exceptions apply). That's pretty much the end of your retirement savings, and all you did was try to convert to a Roth IRA.

Right now you might be thinking that you wish you never heard of Senator Roth and his new IRA. After all, if there were no Roth IRA, all your money would still be safely growing tax-deferred in your good old traditional IRA, with no tax problems. Is there no way out of this mess?

Yes.

Of course, all the regular tax rules say no, but there is always (or at least sometimes) a higher authority to appeal to, so do not touch or remove the funds from your Roth IRA. If you withdraw the money, you will have no chance of relief, because then it can never be recharacterized back to your traditional IRA and you'll be subject to all the excessive tax and penalties I've described above with no way out. If you leave the funds in the Roth and are granted an additional extension of time to recharacterize, you will be able to take advantage of that and be relieved of the entire problem. So for now, touch nothing.

IRS Pardons Illegal Roth Converters

Illegal Roth converters are not exactly criminals. They're nice people whose only malfeasance was converting to a Roth IRA when they did not qualify. In effect, they were guilty of paying too much tax! What could the penalty for that be?

Let's find out.

In 1998 a married couple filing jointly each converted their traditional IRAs to Roth IRAs. Their 1998 income turned out to be well over the $100,000 limit. It was actually closer to $200,000, and they were not eligible to convert. Under IRS Announcement

99-104 (November 1, 1999), all taxpayers had up to December 31, 1999, to recharacterize (undo) any 1998 Roth conversion and transfer the converted funds plus any earnings on those funds back to a traditional IRA. These taxpayers were not aware that they failed to qualify for the Roth conversion and did not recharacterize by the December 31, 1999, deadline. In addition, the CPA who prepared their tax return (not me!) failed to realize that the converted Roths should have been recharacterized.

In early 2000 the CPA discovered the error, but according to the tax law it was too late for the couple to recharacterize. The IRS had already granted an extension of time to recharacterize 1998 Roth conversions until December 31, 1999. This is when I made my appearance in the drama. The CPA contacted me to see if anything could be done for his client.

It was June 2000 when, on behalf of the couple, I requested a private letter ruling (PLR) from the IRS National Office asking that the date to recharacterize be extended to December 31, 2000. The IRS ruling was "Yes."

Several issues here were key to this favorable ruling. The first was that the couple never removed the money from the Roth IRA. If they had withdrawn the money and not transferred it back to a traditional IRA (which they were not yet allowed to do), then they would have been stuck with a taxable IRA distribution and no Roth IRA. They still have no Roth IRA, but at least now they are able to transfer it back to their traditional IRAs and maintain their original retirement accounts.

The other key to this ruling was that it was requested before the IRS discovered the error. In other words, the couple voluntarily came forward before they were caught. This was important enough for the IRS to have mentioned it three times in the ruling!

The relief was granted under Section 301.9100 of the Internal Revenue Code. That section lists certain tax elections for which the IRS can grant an automatic extension of time. By considering the Roth recharacterization a tax election, the IRS opened the door for granting relief to confused taxpayers or anyone relying in good faith on the advice of a professional. This section won't get you out of everything, but it's good to know that it exists, which is why I filed for an extension of the recharacterization date under this section.

Literally speaking, this PLR (like all PLRs) applies only to the taxpayers requesting the ruling. Nevertheless, if their situation mirrors yours, you can be reasonably certain that the same ruling would apply in your case if you obtained it. Numerous PLRs have allowed late Roth recharacterizations. Only a few have been denied.

"Oh, S***! I Did a Bad, Bad Thing!"

With IRA stock market investments taking such a beating in recent years, many IRA holders are asking about alternative investments for their besieged IRAs. There are alternatives, but you have to be careful. If not handled the right way, these transactions could be deemed "prohibited" by the IRS. What happens then? Tax law grants the IRS the power to make your IRA go the way of the dinosaur and cease to exist. The entire balance in your IRA will be stripped of its tax-deferred status. The account will be treated as if you withdrew all the money from it; the withdrawal will be subject to income tax and could further be subject to the 10 percent penalty if you're under 59½ as of the deemed date of your total withdrawal (which is deemed to be the first of the year). You can keep whatever is left after taxes, but your IRA tax shelter is lost forever.

Prohibited Transactions

IRS Publication 590 defines a *prohibited transaction* as "any improper use of your account . . . by you or any disqualified person." A *disqualified person* is defined as a fiduciary, you, a member of your family, or any other entity such as a corporation, partnership, trust, or estate that is 50 percent or more controlled by you or your family members. For an IRA plan, you, the IRA owner, are a fiduciary even though you are not the plan custodian. This is because you have discretion and control over the IRA investments. In other words, you can't blame it on the bank. If you misuse your IRA, it's your fault.

More simply stated, prohibited transactions, for IRAs, are those that would put the government at risk of never getting the tax on it, because you got cute and bought the alternative investment with IRA money not reported as a taxable distribution. To be clear, prohibited transactions only occur when funds *within* your IRA are used improperly. You can always withdraw from your IRA, pay the tax (and penalty if you are under 59½ and no exceptions apply), and spend the money any way you wish, because now the government got its tax and the money you are spending is no longer IRA money.

The Internal Revenue Code specifically prohibits these transactions:

▪ **Buying, selling, or leasing any property to or from your IRA.** This is considered "self-dealing," and your IRA plan cannot engage in these transactions with you, even if the price is reasonable and fair. This would include setting up your own corporation and having it funded by your IRA plan, which buys the stock of your new company. Also, as a fiduciary, you have an obligation to invest prudently. Investing in your own business may seem more prudent to you than investing in the stock market, but that is not the way the IRS looks a it. The IRS feels you'll lose all your IRA money, if not withdraw it all for salary and other personal use (and the IRS is probably right.) You also cannot get a family member to act in your place. By *family member,* the IRS means your spouse, ancestors (your parents and grandparents), lineal descendants (your children and grandchildren), or a spouse of a lineal descendant. For example, you cannot have your IRA trustee (the financial institution holding your IRA funds) buy a building owned by your spouse and arrange to lease it back to your spouse.

- **Borrowing from or lending money to your IRA.** You cannot borrow from your IRA or use or pledge it as collateral for a loan, even if the interest rate and other loan terms are fair. Any amount pledged as security for a loan will be treated as a taxable distribution. You cannot personally guarantee a loan given to your IRA to buy property. That would be deemed the same as you loaning the money to your IRA. You can, however, borrow from the bank, for example, to make an IRA contribution. That's OK, but you cannot personally borrow your IRA money and your IRA cannot borrow from you.

- **Receiving compensation for managing your own IRA.** Your IRA cannot pay you for managing it. Looking at some of the investment returns people with IRAs have received, they should pay back their IRAs for the losses they caused them. But that's prohibited too.

- **Buying property for personal use with IRA funds.** You cannot use your IRA money to buy property that you (or your family) use personally—for example, a home that you use as your personal residence. This is a prohibited transaction, even if you claim (as one wise guy did) that the home was to be a retirement home and since IRA money is retirement money, then using it to buy a retirement home should be OK. It isn't, and he lost.

- **Purchasing collectibles.** You cannot invest your IRA funds in collectibles such as works of art, rugs, antiques, metals, gems, stamps, coins, and even baseball cards (not even worthless Bill Buckner cards!). IRS Code Section 408(m) also includes alcoholic beverages as collectibles. My guess is this means either a Dom Perignon '59, or a 20-year-old can of Bud. Too bad. The amount of IRA money used to buy collectibles will be treated as a taxable distribution. There is an exception however for gold, silver, platinum coins minted by the Department of the Treasury, and state-issued coins.

- **Buying life insurance.** You cannot use your IRA to buy a life insurance policy. ("I knew that!" said Chapter 5.)

Real Estate in Your IRA

But what if you don't trust the traditional stock-market–based investments any more what with all these corporate executives looting their companies? You feel like you're investing for *their* retirement, not *yours*. Isn't there something that you can use your IRA funds to invest in to achieve better control without violating the prohibited transaction rules? Like real estate, for instance?

By Jove, you answered your own question. You can buy real estate, but that depends on what type of real estate. If you or your family intend to use the real estate personally (for example, to live on it), then the answer is no, because that qualifies as self-dealing. You can purchase investment real estate with your IRA funds, even though I would not advise it. However, if you want to diversify and have some of your IRA invested in real estate, the best way to do that is to invest in a real estate mutual fund. It is like any other fund investment and is generally free of the problems detailed below. Other than that, buying real estate with IRA funds is fraught with problems. In fact, the only reason I am even addressing it is because so many people are looking to change their IRA investments from stocks and funds to real estate because they feel there is better appreciation potential, and also because any gains or appreciation in the value of the real estate would remain tax-deferred in the IRA (tax-free with a Roth). That may be true, but even if you want to go ahead and invest your IRA funds in real estate, it won't be easy.

There are two ways to do it, and both of them present problems (only because IRA investments are subject to rules not applicable to other investments). The easiest way would be to invest in a limited partnership (LP) that invests in real estate—commercial or residential (that you do not control or use personally)—or a real estate investment trust (REIT) that you also do not control or use personally.

The other way is to have your IRA buy the property and manage it, which I would never recommend because you have to be so careful not to violate the self-dealing rules. At least with the professionally managed programs (LPs and REITs), that problem is generally eliminated because you are not exercising any management control or influence.

But either option is fraught with problems now that you are aware of the prohibited transaction rules. For example, one of the rules is that you cannot loan money to your IRA to buy property or guarantee a loan by your IRA. This means then that in order to buy real estate (say, a building or some land) in your IRA, you must pay cash, unless the bank gives you a loan based only on the value of the property without requiring your personal guarantee to repay the loan. That is not likely to happen today . . . legally anyway. Therefore you generally must pay all cash to buy real estate with your IRA money. You've got to have a ton of cash in your IRA to buy any decent property today. You'll also need a financial institution willing to take that investment in your IRA. It has to be a sound investment; otherwise, you and the financial institution have violated your fiduciary obligation to make prudent investments with your IRA money. Most institutions will back away from this, unless you are a high roller and have lots of other money on deposit with them. Then they might bend their own rules for you. But if that were the case, then you probably could afford to buy the property outside of your IRA and you wouldn't need to bother using your IRA money.

In a traditional IRA, any gains would eventually be taxed upon withdrawal at ordinary income tax rates. If you purchased the property with non-IRA money and held it for more than one year, your gain would be taxed more favorably as a capital gain. Also, most non-IRA property receives a step-up in basis at your death. Your heirs will not pay any income tax on appreciation during your life. But if they inherited an IRA with real estate, that appreciation does not receive a step-up in basis and will eventually be subject to income tax at ordinary rates (see Chapter 8).

There are other problems with real estate in an IRA. What if you need to put more money into the property? Some properties turn into real money pits. You'd better have enough of a reserve in your IRA to pay the annual property taxes and fund additional and sometimes substantial cash requirements for any maintenance and unexpected expenses or improvements. You cannot just add more money to your IRA. The only money that can be contributed to your IRA is the regular annual contributions and rollovers from other IRAs or company plans. If you need more money than you have available in your IRA to fund any repairs or improvements, it will be tough finding a bank to lend funds to your IRA without a personal guarantee from you. And such a personal guarantee is the same as loaning to your IRA, which is a prohibited transaction.

What I've gone into so far are the financing problems. But there are other trouble spots—RMDs, for example. What do RMDs have to do with real estate in your IRA? Plenty. Even a Roth IRA will eventually have RMDs when a nonspouse beneficiary inherits. How will you be able to calculate RMDs? What's the value of your IRA? Who knows? With real estate, it's anybody's guess. But if you guess wrong and withdraw less than your RMD, it's a 50 percent penalty.

To find the value of your real estate within your IRA, you'll need an independent appraisal—and it had better be a good one, from a reputable real estate appraiser, not your brother-in-law or your local real estate agent, because it must hold up to the IRS's own rigid appraisal, if challenged. You'll need this appraisal done not only every year once you begin RMDs, but sometimes twice a year—once to determine the year-end balance and once when you actually take the property out of your IRA (unless you have enough in other IRA cash to withdraw). And as the withdrawal must be a little bit at a time based on life expectancy, how will you do that? How do you distribute a part of the real estate every year?

Well, if you are 70 years old and your RMD factor is 27.4 years, then you'll have to deed 1/27.4 of the property that year to yourself from your IRA as a distribution, and do the same based on the new factor for every RMD in the future, unless you have enough cash to make the distribution. But eventually you'll run out of cash and will have nothing left in the IRA but the real estate. Then you'll have to begin distributing pieces of it or sell it in the IRA and raise the cash for the distributions. But what if that turns out to be the wrong time to sell? This is another unknown that could be a problem.

Even if there are no RMDs (for example, if you are not yet 70½, or if the property is owned by your Roth IRA where distributions are not required), you will still need an annual appraisal because IRS requires your financial institution (your IRA custodian) to provide an annual value to you and the IRS on Form 5498, "IRA Contribution Information."

Although the idea of tax-deferred appreciation of real estate in your IRA may seem enticing, real estate investments work best outside of your IRA—first, because of the leverage. Most successful real estate investors make their money by leveraging their properties with mortgages, not by paying all cash up-front and tying up all their available money. That kind of leverage is rarely available in an IRA because of the loan restrictions under the prohibited transaction rules. I'm not saying that you cannot get a mortgage on property purchased with your IRA funds. You can, but who would give you one without a personal guarantee by you or a family member, and that is when the mortgage becomes a prohibited transaction, causing your IRA to cease and become immediately taxable. So, the lack of leverage is another big strike against buying real estate with your IRA money.

Another strike against it is the gains and losses. For most real estate investors, the benefits are in the tax deductions, such as depreciation and other property-related write-offs. You cannot claim any of these when you own the property in your IRA (but you also do not have to report the rental income earned in the IRA).

Finally, real estate is traditionally a long-term investment and not as liquid as investing in stocks and bonds. There is never a guarantee that your real estate will perform better than the stock market over the long term. You should assess the amount of long-term risk you are willing to take with real estate. You'll likely need this cash for retirement and may be forced to sell the property at the wrong time. That could happen with stocks too, but it is easier to sell off small amounts of stock as needed rather than having to sell an entire building, for example.

Real estate is illiquid; it eats money and is, therefore, not the most prudent investment for a retirement account that is intended, after all, to provide you with income for the rest of your life. So, take my advice here and avoid the temptation. It may look good on paper, but consider the problems and additional expenses it can create . . . not to mention the potential loss of your IRA if you cross the line and the IRS considers your investment a prohibited transaction.

And there you have it. Everything you need to know to make the most of your retirement savings and to keep it from being devoured by the IRS.

Well, *almost* everything.

Turn the page for some additional resources that will come in mighty handy. I know. I use them myself!

RESOURCES

A t the time Woodrow Wilson wrote those words, he had no idea how wisely they would apply to today's complicated universe of IRAs and other retirement savings accounts. The proof of that is in the following sources.

Learn More about Protecting Your IRA from the IRS

Whether you are a do-it-yourselfer or a professional advisor looking to improve service to your clients, you will find the following resources by the nation's leading experts in retirement distribution planning extremely valuable. These are not the only resources for accurate IRA information, but they are the ones I use. So, I can recommend them without reservation.

Life and Death Planning for Retirement Benefits, 5th edition, by Natalie B. Choate, Esq.; $89.95, Ataxplan Publications. To order, call 1-800-247-6553 or order online at www.ataxplan.com.

Consumer's Guide to the Retirement Distribution Rules by Seymour Goldberg and Ed Slott; $19.95 for immediate download or $24.95 for a printed version. To order, call 1-800-879-6665 or order online at www.guidetorules.com.

Taxation of Individual Retirement Accounts by David J. Cartano, JD; $190, Panel Publishers, a division of Aspen Publishers, Inc. To order, call 1-800-638-8437 or order online at www.aspenpub. com.

Barry Picker's Guide to Retirement Distribution Planning by Barry C. Picker, CPA/PFS, CFP; $24.95. To order, call 800-809-0015 or order online at www.BPickerCPA.com.

Ed Slott's IRA Advisor, published monthly by Ed Slott, CPA; $89.95 per year. To order, call 1-800-663-1340 or order online at www.irahelp.com.

The IRA Handbook by William J. Wagner, JD, LLM, CLU; $29.95, The National Underwriter Co. To order, call 1-800-543-0874.

Planning for Retirement Distributions: Tax, Financial and Personal Aspects, 3rd edition, by Victor M. Finmann, Esq.; $135, Aspen Publishers, Inc. To order, call 1-800-234-1660 or order online at www.rdacademy.com.

The New IRAs and How to Make Them Work for You by Neil Downing; $18.95, Dearborn Trade Publishing. Order online at www.dearborntrade.com.

IRAs, 401(k)s & Other Retirement Plans: Taking Your Money Out by Twila Slesnick, PhD, Enrolled Agent, and John C. Suttle, Esq., CPA; $25, Nolo Press. To order, call 1-800-992-6656 or order online at www.nolo.com.

Individual Retirement Account Answer Book by Steven G. Lockwood, JD, LLM, Donald R. Levy, JD, MBA, and Martin Fleisher, JD; $170, Aspen Publishers, Inc. To order, call 1-800-234-1660 or order online at www.aspenpub.com.

Pension Answer Book by Stephen J. Krass, Esq.; $180, Aspen Publishers, Inc. To order, call 1-800-234-1660 or order online www.aspenpub.com.

The Complete Book of Trusts by Martin M. Shenkman, CPA, MBA, JD; $24.95, John Wiley & Sons, Inc. Order online at www.wiley.com.

Estate Planning After the 2001 Tax Act by Martin M. Shenkman, CPA, MBA, JD; $60, Bloomberg Press. Order online at www.bloomberg.com/books.

Roth IRA Answer Book by Gary S. Lesser, JD, Susan D. Diehl, Robert S. Keebler, CPA, MST, and Gregory Kolojeski, Esq.; $160, Aspen Publishers, Inc. To order, call 1-800-234-1660 or order online at www.aspenpub.com.

Roth to Riches: The Ordinary to Roth IRA Handbook by John D. Bledsoe; $19.95, Legacy Press, Inc. To order, call 1-800-878-7844.

Retirement Bible by Lynn O'Shaughnessy; $34.99, Hungry Minds, Inc. Order online at www.hungryminds.com.

Tax Hotline, published monthly by Martin Edelston; $59 per year. To order, call 1-800-288-1051 or order online at www.bottomlinesecrets.com.

Professional Publications
and Tax Services I Use (and Their Web Sites)

Estate Planning (www.riahome.com/riajournals)
Trusts & Estates (www.trustsandestates.com)
Goldberg Reports by Seymour Goldberg, Esq., CPA (www.goldbergreports.com)
Financial Planning Magazine (www.financial-planning.com)
CCH Retirement Benefits Tax Guide by Thomas F. Rutherford, JD (www.cch.com)
CCH Individual Retirement Plans Guide (www.cch.com)
BNA Tax Management Library (www.bnatax.com)
Tax Base by Tax Analysts (www.taxbase.com)
Aspen Publishers, Inc. (www.aspenpub.com)

IRA Information Web Sites I Use

These sites contain not only a tremendous concentration of retirement distribution information, but additional resources, articles, seminar information, discussion forums, and breaking tax news. From these sites, you can link to IRA resources anywhere.

Ed Slott's IRA Advisor (www.irahelp.com)
Seymour Goldberg, Esq., CPA (www.goldbergira.com)
Natalie Choate, Esq. (www.ataxplan.com)
Barry C. Picker, CPA/PFS, CFP (www.BPickerCPA.com)
Gordon Weis (an excellent resource on 72[t] issues) (http://72t.net)
Victor M. Finmann, Esq., president, Retirement Distribution Academy (www.rdacademy.com)
James Lange, Esq. (www.rothira-advisor.com)
Gideon Rothschild, JD, CPA (an excellent resource for information on creditor protection of retirement assets) (www.Mosessinger.com)

Leimberg Information Services, Inc. (www.leimbergservices.com).
Stephan R. Leimberg, Esq., with his company, Leimberg Information Services, Inc. (LISI), is one of the truly great professional resources I use every day . . . well, every day that I am near a computer. When I'm not near a computer, I'm always wondering what I'm missing. Steve has managed to bring together the most brilliant professional advisors and scholars and include their thoughts in LISI's daily briefings. If you want the most up-to-date tax information, court cases, IRS rulings, financial statistics, and professional opinions, I cannot recommend Steve Leimberg's information service strongly enough. Here are just a few of LISI's newsletter offerings:

- *Employee Benefits and Retirement Planning Newsletter* written by attorneys Natalie Choate, Noel C. Ice, Alvin D. Lurie, John McFadden, Robert S. Keebler, Bruce D. Steiner, and Ed Slott. Barry Picker serves as technical editor.
- *Estate Planning Newsletter* by attorneys Ronald D. Aucutt, Jonathan Blattmachr, Robert F. Collins, Daniel E. Evans, Owen G. Fiore, Alan S. Gassman, L. Paul Hood, Jerry Kasner, Michel Nelson, Richard W. Nenno, Charles L. Ratner, Howard M. Zaritsky, Steven J. Oshins, Robert Colvin, and Stephan Leimberg.
- *Business Entities Newsletter* by Professors Lisa Starczewski and James Edward Maule.
- *Asset Protection Planning Newsletter* by Alexander A. Bove Jr., Gideon Rothschild, Jay D. Adkisson, and Jonathan Gopman.
- *Charitable Planning Newsletter* by Johnine Hays, Larry Katzenstein, and Jerry J. McCoy.
- *Bob LeClair's Financial Planning Newsletter.*
- *LawThreads®* edited by Andrew J. DeMaio.

Software Resources I Depend On

Brentmark Software Inc. (www.Brentmark.com). I use Brentmark's software products almost exclusively. I find that they have an easy-to-use program for all the IRA and estate planning calculations I need. That includes minimum distributions, 72(t) payments, and a wide variety of estate tax calculations and projections that can be used for estate planning. The estate planning program ("Number Cruncher" by Stephan R. Leimberg and Robert T. LeClair at www.leimberg.com), for example, gives you the amount of estate tax for any size of estate in an instant. I find myself using it to check the tax calculations on estate tax returns (since it's used by the IRS) and to show clients what their estate tax might be. Other software programs they offer that are pertinent to this book include

- "The Pension & Roth IRA Analyzer"
- "Pension Distributions Planner"
- "Pension Distributions Calculator"
- "Minimum Distributions Calculator"

Net Worth Strategies. This company offers a program called "MRD-Determinator" developed by IRA genius Guerdon Ely. It can do all the RMD calculations and 72(t) distributions. The program's cost is $395. You can write to the company at 960 SW Disk Drive, Suite B, Bend, OR 97702, contact it by phone at 1-541-383-3899, or go straight to the company's web site for the program at www.MRD-Determinator.com.

IRS JOINT LIFE EXPECTANCY TABLES

(Joint Life and Last Survivor Expectancy)
(For Use by Owners Whose Spouses Are
More Than 10 Years Younger)

Ages	0	1	2	3	4	5	6	7	8	9
0	90.0	89.5	89.0	88.6	88.2	87.8	87.4	87.1	86.8	86.5
1	89.5	89.0	88.5	88.1	87.6	87.2	86.8	86.5	86.1	85.8
2	89.0	88.5	88.0	87.5	87.1	86.6	86.2	85.8	85.5	85.1
3	88.6	88.1	87.5	87.0	86.5	86.1	85.6	85.2	84.8	84.5
4	88.2	87.6	87.1	86.5	86.0	85.5	85.1	84.6	84.2	83.8
5	87.8	87.2	86.6	86.1	85.5	85.0	84.5	84.1	83.6	83.2
6	87.4	86.8	86.2	85.6	85.1	84.5	84.0	83.5	83.1	82.6
7	87.1	86.5	85.8	85.2	84.6	84.1	83.5	83.0	82.5	82.1
8	86.8	86.1	85.5	84.8	84.2	83.6	83.1	82.5	82.0	81.6
9	86.5	85.8	85.1	84.5	83.8	83.2	82.6	82.1	81.6	81.0
10	86.2	85.5	84.8	84.1	83.5	82.8	82.2	81.6	81.1	80.6
11	85.9	85.2	84.5	83.8	83.1	82.5	81.8	81.2	80.7	80.1
12	85.7	84.9	84.2	83.5	82.8	82.1	81.5	80.8	80.2	79.7
13	85.4	84.7	84.0	83.2	82.5	81.8	81.1	80.5	79.9	79.2
14	85.2	84.5	83.7	83.0	82.2	81.5	80.8	80.1	79.5	78.9
15	85.0	84.3	83.5	82.7	82.0	81.2	80.5	79.8	79.1	78.5
16	84.9	84.1	83.3	82.5	81.7	81.0	80.2	79.5	78.8	78.1
17	84.7	83.9	83.1	82.3	81.5	80.7	80.0	79.2	78.5	77.8
18	84.5	83.7	82.9	82.1	81.3	80.5	79.7	79.0	78.2	77.5

(Joint Life and Last Survivor Expectancy) (*continued*)

Ages	0	1	2	3	4	5	6	7	8	9
19	84.4	83.6	82.7	81.9	81.1	80.3	79.5	78.7	78.0	77.3
20	84.3	83.4	82.6	81.8	80.9	80.1	79.3	78.5	77.7	77.0
21	84.1	83.3	82.4	81.6	80.8	79.9	79.1	78.3	77.5	76.8
22	84.0	83.2	82.3	81.5	80.6	79.8	78.9	78.1	77.3	76.5
23	83.9	83.1	82.2	81.3	80.5	79.6	78.8	77.9	77.1	76.3
24	83.8	83.0	82.1	81.2	80.3	79.5	78.6	77.8	76.9	76.1
25	83.7	82.9	82.0	81.1	80.2	79.3	78.5	77.6	76.8	75.9
26	83.6	82.8	81.9	81.0	80.1	79.2	78.3	77.5	76.6	75.8
27	83.6	82.7	81.8	80.9	80.0	79.1	78.2	77.4	76.5	75.6
28	83.5	82.6	81.7	80.8	79.9	79.0	78.1	77.2	76.4	75.5
29	83.4	82.6	81.6	80.7	79.8	78.9	78.0	77.1	76.2	75.4
30	83.4	82.5	81.6	80.7	79.7	78.8	77.9	77.0	76.1	75.2
31	83.3	82.4	81.5	80.6	79.7	78.8	77.8	76.9	76.0	75.1
32	83.3	82.4	81.5	80.5	79.6	78.7	77.8	76.8	75.9	75.0
33	83.2	82.3	81.4	80.5	79.5	78.6	77.7	76.8	75.9	74.9
34	83.2	82.3	81.3	80.4	79.5	78.5	77.6	76.7	75.8	74.9
35	83.1	82.2	81.3	80.4	79.4	78.5	77.6	76.6	75.7	74.8
36	83.1	82.2	81.3	80.3	79.4	78.4	77.5	76.6	75.6	74.7
37	83.0	82.2	81.2	80.3	79.3	78.4	77.4	76.5	75.6	74.6
38	83.0	82.1	81.2	80.2	79.3	78.3	77.4	76.4	75.5	74.6
39	83.0	82.1	81.1	80.2	79.2	78.3	77.3	76.4	75.5	74.5
40	82.9	82.1	81.1	80.2	79.2	78.3	77.3	76.4	75.4	74.5
41	82.9	82.0	81.1	80.1	79.2	78.2	77.3	76.3	75.4	74.4
42	82.9	82.0	81.1	80.1	79.1	78.2	77.2	76.3	75.3	74.4
43	82.9	82.0	81.0	80.1	79.1	78.2	77.2	76.2	75.3	74.3
44	82.8	81.9	81.0	80.0	79.1	78.1	77.2	76.2	75.2	74.3
45	82.8	81.9	81.0	80.0	79.1	78.1	77.1	76.2	75.2	74.3
46	82.8	81.9	81.0	80.0	79.0	78.1	77.1	76.1	75.2	74.2
47	82.8	81.9	80.9	80.0	79.0	78.0	77.1	76.1	75.2	74.2
48	82.8	81.9	80.9	80.0	79.0	78.0	77.1	76.1	75.1	74.2
49	82.7	81.8	80.9	79.9	79.0	78.0	77.0	76.1	75.1	74.1
50	82.7	81.8	80.9	79.9	79.0	78.0	77.0	76.0	75.1	74.1
51	82.7	81.8	80.9	79.9	78.9	78.0	77.0	76.0	75.1	74.1

APPENDIX I ■ 313

(Joint Life and Last Survivor Expectancy) (*continued*)

Ages	0	1	2	3	4	5	6	7	8	9
52	82.7	81.8	80.9	79.9	78.9	78.0	77.0	76.0	75.0	74.1
53	82.7	81.8	80.8	79.9	78.9	77.9	77.0	76.0	75.0	74.0
54	82.7	81.8	80.8	79.9	78.9	77.9	76.9	76.0	75.0	74.0
55	82.6	81.8	80.8	79.8	78.9	77.9	76.9	76.0	75.0	74.0
56	82.6	81.7	80.8	79.8	78.9	77.9	76.9	75.9	75.0	74.0
57	82.6	81.7	80.8	79.8	78.9	77.9	76.9	75.9	75.0	74.0
58	82.6	81.7	80.8	79.8	78.8	77.9	76.9	75.9	74.9	74.0
59	82.6	81.7	80.8	79.8	78.8	77.9	76.9	75.9	74.9	74.0
60	82.6	81.7	80.8	79.8	78.8	77.8	76.9	75.9	74.9	73.9
61	82.6	81.7	80.8	79.8	78.8	77.8	76.9	75.9	74.9	73.9
62	82.6	81.7	80.7	79.8	78.8	77.8	76.9	75.9	74.9	73.9
63	82.6	81.7	80.7	79.8	78.8	77.8	76.8	75.9	74.9	73.9
64	82.5	81.7	80.7	79.8	78.8	77.8	76.8	75.9	74.9	73.9
65	82.5	81.7	80.7	79.8	78.8	77.8	76.8	75.8	74.9	73.9
66	82.5	81.7	80.7	79.7	78.8	77.8	76.8	75.8	74.9	73.9
67	82.5	81.7	80.7	79.7	78.8	77.8	76.8	75.8	74.9	73.9
68	82.5	81.6	80.7	79.7	78.8	77.8	76.8	75.8	74.8	73.9
69	82.5	81.6	80.7	79.7	78.8	77.8	76.8	75.8	74.8	73.9
70	82.5	81.6	80.7	79.7	78.8	77.8	76.8	75.8	74.8	73.9
71	82.5	81.6	80.7	79.7	78.7	77.8	76.8	75.8	74.8	73.8
72	82.5	81.6	80.7	79.7	78.7	77.8	76.8	75.8	74.8	73.8
73	82.5	81.6	80.7	79.7	78.7	77.8	76.8	75.8	74.8	73.8
74	82.5	81.6	80.7	79.7	78.7	77.8	76.8	75.8	74.8	73.8
75	82.5	81.6	80.7	79.7	78.7	77.8	76.8	75.8	74.8	73.8
76	82.5	81.6	80.7	79.7	78.7	77.8	76.8	75.8	74.8	73.8
77	82.5	81.6	80.7	79.7	78.7	77.7	76.8	75.8	74.8	73.8
78	82.5	81.6	80.7	79.7	78.7	77.7	76.8	75.8	74.8	73.8
79	82.5	81.6	80.7	79.7	78.7	77.7	76.8	75.8	74.8	73.8
80	82.5	81.6	80.7	79.7	78.7	77.7	76.8	75.8	74.8	73.8
81	82.4	81.6	80.7	79.7	78.7	77.7	76.8	75.8	74.8	73.8
82	82.4	81.6	80.7	79.7	78.7	77.7	76.8	75.8	74.8	73.8
83	82.4	81.6	80.7	79.7	78.7	77.7	76.8	75.8	74.8	73.8

(Joint Life and Last Survivor Expectancy) (*continued*)

Ages	0	1	2	3	4	5	6	7	8	9
84	82.4	81.6	80.7	79.7	78.7	77.7	76.8	75.8	74.8	73.8
85	82.4	81.6	80.6	79.7	78.7	77.7	76.8	75.8	74.8	73.8
86	82.4	81.6	80.6	79.7	78.7	77.7	76.7	75.8	74.8	73.8
87	82.4	81.6	80.6	79.7	78.7	77.7	76.7	75.8	74.8	73.8
88	82.4	81.6	80.6	79.7	78.7	77.7	76.7	75.8	74.8	73.8
89	82.4	81.6	80.6	79.7	78.7	77.7	76.7	75.8	74.8	73.8
90	82.4	81.6	80.6	79.7	78.7	77.7	76.7	75.8	74.8	73.8
91	82.4	81.6	80.6	79.7	78.7	77.7	76.7	75.8	74.8	73.8
92	82.4	81.6	80.6	79.7	78.7	77.7	76.7	75.8	74.8	73.8
93	82.4	81.6	80.6	79.7	78.7	77.7	76.7	75.8	74.8	73.8
94	82.4	81.6	80.6	79.7	78.7	77.7	76.7	75.8	74.8	73.8
95	82.4	81.6	80.6	79.7	78.7	77.7	76.7	75.8	74.8	73.8
96	82.4	81.6	80.6	79.7	78.7	77.7	76.7	75.8	74.8	73.8
97	82.4	81.6	80.6	79.7	78.7	77.7	76.7	75.8	74.8	73.8
98	82.4	81.6	80.6	79.7	78.7	77.7	76.7	75.8	74.8	73.8
99	82.4	81.6	80.6	79.7	78.7	77.7	76.7	75.8	74.8	73.8
100	82.4	81.6	80.6	79.7	78.7	77.7	76.7	75.8	74.8	73.8
101	82.4	81.6	80.6	79.7	78.7	77.7	76.7	75.8	74.8	73.8
102	82.4	81.6	80.6	79.7	78.7	77.7	76.7	75.8	74.8	73.8
103	82.4	81.6	80.6	79.7	78.7	77.7	76.7	75.8	74.8	73.8
104	82.4	81.6	80.6	79.7	78.7	77.7	76.7	75.8	74.8	73.8
105	82.4	81.6	80.6	79.7	78.7	77.7	76.7	75.8	74.8	73.8
106	82.4	81.6	80.6	79.7	78.7	77.7	76.7	75.8	74.8	73.8
107	82.4	81.6	80.6	79.7	78.7	77.7	76.7	75.8	74.8	73.8
108	82.4	81.6	80.6	79.7	78.7	77.7	76.7	75.8	74.8	73.8
109	82.4	81.6	80.6	79.7	78.7	77.7	76.7	75.8	74.8	73.8
110	82.4	81.6	80.6	79.7	78.7	77.7	76.7	75.8	74.8	73.8
111	82.4	81.6	80.6	79.7	78.7	77.7	76.7	75.8	74.8	73.8
112	82.4	81.6	80.6	79.7	78.7	77.7	76.7	75.8	74.8	73.8
113	82.4	81.6	80.6	79.7	78.7	77.7	76.7	75.8	74.8	73.8
114	82.4	81.6	80.6	79.7	78.7	77.7	76.7	75.8	74.8	73.8
115+	82.4	81.6	80.6	79.7	78.7	77.7	76.7	75.8	74.8	73.8

(Joint Life and Last Survivor Expectancy) (*continued*)

(Joint Life and Last Survivor Expectancy) (For Use by Owners Whose Spouses Are More Than 10 Years Younger)

Ages	10	11	12	13	14	15	16	17	18	19
10	80.0	79.6	79.1	78.7	78.2	77.9	77.5	77.2	76.8	76.5
11	79.6	79.0	78.6	78.1	77.7	77.3	76.9	76.5	76.2	75.8
12	79.1	78.6	78.1	77.6	77.1	76.7	76.3	75.9	75.5	75.2
13	78.7	78.1	77.6	77.1	76.6	76.1	75.7	75.3	74.9	74.5
14	78.2	77.7	77.1	76.6	76.1	75.6	75.1	74.7	74.3	73.9
15	77.9	77.3	76.7	76.1	75.6	75.1	74.6	74.1	73.7	73.3
16	77.5	76.9	76.3	75.7	75.1	74.6	74.1	73.6	73.1	72.7
17	77.2	76.5	75.9	75.3	74.7	74.1	73.6	73.1	72.6	72.1
18	76.8	76.2	75.5	74.9	74.3	73.7	73.1	72.6	72.1	71.6
19	76.5	75.8	75.2	74.5	73.9	73.3	72.7	72.1	71.6	71.1
20	76.3	75.5	74.8	74.2	73.5	72.9	72.3	71.7	71.1	70.6
21	76.0	75.3	74.5	73.8	73.2	72.5	71.9	71.3	70.7	70.1
22	75.8	75.0	74.3	73.5	72.9	72.2	71.5	70.9	70.3	69.7
23	75.5	74.8	74.0	73.3	72.6	71.9	71.2	70.5	69.9	69.3
24	75.3	74.5	73.8	73.0	72.3	71.6	70.9	70.2	69.5	68.9
25	75.1	74.3	73.5	72.8	72.0	71.3	70.6	69.9	69.2	68.5
26	75.0	74.1	73.3	72.5	71.8	71.0	70.3	69.6	68.9	68.2
27	74.8	74.0	73.1	72.3	71.6	70.8	70.0	69.3	68.6	67.9
28	74.6	73.8	73.0	72.2	71.3	70.6	69.8	69.0	68.3	67.6
29	74.5	73.6	72.8	72.0	71.2	70.4	69.6	68.8	68.0	67.3
30	74.4	73.5	72.7	71.8	71.0	70.2	69.4	68.6	67.8	67.1
31	74.3	73.4	72.5	71.7	70.8	70.0	69.2	68.4	67.6	66.8
32	74.1	73.3	72.4	71.5	70.7	69.8	69.0	68.2	67.4	66.6
33	74.0	73.2	72.3	71.4	70.5	69.7	68.8	68.0	67.2	66.4
34	73.9	73.0	72.2	71.3	70.4	69.5	68.7	67.8	67.0	66.2
35	73.9	73.0	72.1	71.2	70.3	69.4	68.5	67.7	66.8	66.0
36	73.8	72.9	72.0	71.1	70.2	69.3	68.4	67.6	66.7	65.9
37	73.7	72.8	71.9	71.0	70.1	69.2	68.3	67.4	66.6	65.7

(Joint Life and Last Survivor Expectancy) (*continued*)

Ages	10	11	12	13	14	15	16	17	18	19
38	73.6	72.7	71.8	70.9	70.0	69.1	68.2	67.3	66.4	65.6
39	73.6	72.7	71.7	70.8	69.9	69.0	68.1	67.2	66.3	65.4
40	73.5	72.6	71.7	70.7	69.8	68.9	68.0	67.1	66.2	65.3
41	73.5	72.5	71.6	70.7	69.7	68.8	67.9	67.0	66.1	65.2
42	73.4	72.5	71.5	70.6	69.7	68.8	67.8	66.9	66.0	65.1
43	73.4	72.4	71.5	70.6	69.6	68.7	67.8	66.8	65.9	65.0
44	73.3	72.4	71.4	70.5	69.6	68.6	67.7	66.8	65.9	64.9
45	73.3	72.3	71.4	70.5	69.5	68.6	67.6	66.7	65.8	64.9
46	73.3	72.3	71.4	70.4	69.5	68.5	67.6	66.6	65.7	64.8
47	73.2	72.3	71.3	70.4	69.4	68.5	67.5	66.6	65.7	64.7
48	73.2	72.2	71.3	70.3	69.4	68.4	67.5	66.5	65.6	64.7
49	73.2	72.2	71.2	70.3	69.3	68.4	67.4	66.5	65.6	64.6
50	73.1	72.2	71.2	70.3	69.3	68.4	67.4	66.5	65.5	64.6
51	73.1	72.2	71.2	70.2	69.3	68.3	67.4	66.4	65.5	64.5
52	73.1	72.1	71.2	70.2	69.2	68.3	67.3	66.4	65.4	64.5
53	73.1	72.1	71.1	70.2	69.2	68.3	67.3	66.3	65.4	64.4
54	73.1	72.1	71.1	70.2	69.2	68.2	67.3	66.3	65.4	64.4
55	73.0	72.1	71.1	70.1	69.2	68.2	67.2	66.3	65.3	64.4
56	73.0	72.1	71.1	70.1	69.1	68.2	67.2	66.3	65.3	64.3
57	73.0	72.0	71.1	70.1	69.1	68.2	67.2	66.2	65.3	64.3
58	73.0	72.0	71.0	70.1	69.1	68.1	67.2	66.2	65.2	64.3
59	73.0	72.0	71.0	70.1	69.1	68.1	67.2	66.2	65.2	64.3
60	73.0	72.0	71.0	70.0	69.1	68.1	67.1	66.2	65.2	64.2
61	73.0	72.0	71.0	70.0	69.1	68.1	67.1	66.2	65.2	64.2
62	72.9	72.0	71.0	70.0	69.0	68.1	67.1	66.1	65.2	64.2
63	72.9	72.0	71.0	70.0	69.0	68.1	67.1	66.1	65.2	64.2
64	72.9	71.9	71.0	70.0	69.0	68.0	67.1	66.1	65.1	64.2
65	72.9	71.9	71.0	70.0	69.0	68.0	67.1	66.1	65.1	64.2
66	72.9	71.9	70.9	70.0	69.0	68.0	67.1	66.1	65.1	64.1
67	72.9	71.9	70.9	70.0	69.0	68.0	67.0	66.1	65.1	64.1
68	72.9	71.9	70.9	70.0	69.0	68.0	67.0	66.1	65.1	64.1
69	72.9	71.9	70.9	69.9	69.0	68.0	67.0	66.1	65.1	64.1
70	72.9	71.9	70.9	69.9	69.0	68.0	67.0	66.0	65.1	64.1

(Joint Life and Last Survivor Expectancy) (*continued*)

Ages	10	11	12	13	14	15	16	17	18	19
71	72.9	71.9	70.9	69.9	69.0	68.0	67.0	66.0	65.1	64.1
72	72.9	71.9	70.9	69.9	69.0	68.0	67.0	66.0	65.1	64.1
73	72.9	71.9	70.9	69.9	68.9	68.0	67.0	66.0	65.0	64.1
74	72.9	71.9	70.9	69.9	68.9	68.0	67.0	66.0	65.0	64.1
75	72.8	71.9	70.9	69.9	68.9	68.0	67.0	66.0	65.0	64.1
76	72.8	71.9	70.9	69.9	68.9	68.0	67.0	66.0	65.0	64.1
77	72.8	71.9	70.9	69.9	68.9	68.0	67.0	66.0	65.0	64.1
78	72.8	71.9	70.9	69.9	68.9	67.9	67.0	66.0	65.0	64.0
79	72.8	71.9	70.9	69.9	68.9	67.9	67.0	66.0	65.0	64.0
80	72.8	71.9	70.9	69.9	68.9	67.9	67.0	66.0	65.0	64.0
81	72.8	71.8	70.9	69.9	68.9	67.9	67.0	66.0	65.0	64.0
82	72.8	71.8	70.9	69.9	68.9	67.9	67.0	66.0	65.0	64.0
83	72.8	71.8	70.9	69.9	68.9	67.9	67.0	66.0	65.0	64.0
84	72.8	71.8	70.9	69.9	68.9	67.9	67.0	66.0	65.0	64.0
85	72.8	71.8	70.9	69.9	68.9	67.9	66.9	66.0	65.0	64.0
86	72.8	71.8	70.9	69.9	68.9	67.9	66.9	66.0	65.0	64.0
87	72.8	71.8	70.9	69.9	68.9	67.9	66.9	66.0	65.0	64.0
88	72.8	71.8	70.9	69.9	68.9	67.9	66.9	66.0	65.0	64.0
89	72.8	71.8	70.9	69.9	68.9	67.9	66.9	66.0	65.0	64.0
90	72.8	71.8	70.9	69.9	68.9	67.9	66.9	66.0	65.0	64.0
91	72.8	71.8	70.9	69.9	68.9	67.9	66.9	66.0	65.0	64.0
92	72.8	71.8	70.9	69.9	68.9	67.9	66.9	66.0	65.0	64.0
93	72.8	71.8	70.9	69.9	68.9	67.9	66.9	66.0	65.0	64.0
94	72.8	71.8	70.8	69.9	68.9	67.9	66.9	66.0	65.0	64.0
95	72.8	71.8	70.8	69.9	68.9	67.9	66.9	66.0	65.0	64.0
96	72.8	71.8	70.8	69.9	68.9	67.9	66.9	66.0	65.0	64.0
97	72.8	71.8	70.8	69.9	68.9	67.9	66.9	66.0	65.0	64.0
98	72.8	71.8	70.8	69.9	68.9	67.9	66.9	66.0	65.0	64.0
99	72.8	71.8	70.8	69.9	68.9	67.9	66.9	66.0	65.0	64.0
100	72.8	71.8	70.8	69.9	68.9	67.9	66.9	66.0	65.0	64.0
101	72.8	71.8	70.8	69.9	68.9	67.9	66.9	66.0	65.0	64.0
102	72.8	71.8	70.8	69.9	68.9	67.9	66.9	66.0	65.0	64.0
103	72.8	71.8	70.8	69.9	68.9	67.9	66.9	66.0	65.0	64.0

(Joint Life and Last Survivor Expectancy) (*continued*)

Ages	10	11	12	13	14	15	16	17	18	19
104	72.8	71.8	70.8	69.9	68.9	67.9	66.9	66.0	65.0	64.0
105	72.8	71.8	70.8	69.9	68.9	67.9	66.9	66.0	65.0	64.0
106	72.8	71.8	70.8	69.9	68.9	67.9	66.9	66.0	65.0	64.0
107	72.8	71.8	70.8	69.9	68.9	67.9	66.9	66.0	65.0	64.0
108	72.8	71.8	70.8	69.9	68.9	67.9	66.9	66.0	65.0	64.0
109	72.8	71.8	70.8	69.9	68.9	67.9	66.9	66.0	65.0	64.0
110	72.8	71.8	70.8	69.9	68.9	67.9	66.9	66.0	65.0	64.0
111	72.8	71.8	70.8	69.9	68.9	67.9	66.9	66.0	65.0	64.0
112	72.8	71.8	70.8	69.9	68.9	67.9	66.9	66.0	65.0	64.0
113	72.8	71.8	70.8	69.9	68.9	67.9	66.9	66.0	65.0	64.0
114	72.8	71.8	70.8	69.9	68.9	67.9	66.9	66.0	65.0	64.0
115+	72.8	71.8	70.8	69.9	68.9	67.9	66.9	66.0	65.0	64.0

(Joint Life and Last Survivor Expectancy)
(For Use by Owners Whose Spouses Are
More Than 10 Years Younger)

Ages	20	21	22	23	24	25	26	27	28	29
20	70.1	69.6	69.1	68.7	68.3	67.9	67.5	67.2	66.9	66.6
21	69.6	69.1	68.6	68.2	67.7	67.3	66.9	66.6	66.2	65.9
22	69.1	68.6	68.1	67.6	67.2	66.7	66.3	65.9	65.6	65.2
23	68.7	68.2	67.6	67.1	66.6	66.2	65.7	65.3	64.9	64.6
24	68.3	67.7	67.2	66.6	66.1	65.6	65.2	64.7	64.3	63.9
25	67.9	67.3	66.7	66.2	65.6	65.1	64.6	64.2	63.7	63.3
26	67.5	66.9	66.3	65.7	65.2	64.6	64.1	63.6	63.2	62.8
27	67.2	66.6	65.9	65.3	64.7	64.2	63.6	63.1	62.7	62.2
28	66.9	66.2	65.6	64.9	64.3	63.7	63.2	62.7	62.1	61.7
29	66.6	65.9	65.2	64.6	63.9	63.3	62.8	62.2	61.7	61.2
30	66.3	65.6	64.9	64.2	63.6	62.9	62.3	61.8	61.2	60.7
31	66.1	65.3	64.6	63.9	63.2	62.6	62.0	61.4	60.8	60.2
32	65.8	65.1	64.3	63.6	62.9	62.2	61.6	61.0	60.4	59.8
33	65.6	64.8	64.1	63.3	62.6	61.9	61.3	60.6	60.0	59.4
34	65.4	64.6	63.8	63.1	62.3	61.6	60.9	60.3	59.6	59.0

(Joint Life and Last Survivor Expectancy) (*continued*)

Ages	20	21	22	23	24	25	26	27	28	29
35	65.2	64.4	63.6	62.8	62.1	61.4	60.6	59.9	59.3	58.6
36	65.0	64.2	63.4	62.6	61.9	61.1	60.4	59.6	59.0	58.3
37	64.9	64.0	63.2	62.4	61.6	60.9	60.1	59.4	58.7	58.0
38	64.7	63.9	63.0	62.2	61.4	60.6	59.9	59.1	58.4	57.7
39	64.6	63.7	62.9	62.1	61.2	60.4	59.6	58.9	58.1	57.4
40	64.4	63.6	62.7	61.9	61.1	60.2	59.4	58.7	57.9	57.1
41	64.3	63.5	62.6	61.7	60.9	60.1	59.3	58.5	57.7	56.9
42	64.2	63.3	62.5	61.6	60.8	59.9	59.1	58.3	57.5	56.7
43	64.1	63.2	62.4	61.5	60.6	59.8	58.9	58.1	57.3	56.5
44	64.0	63.1	62.2	61.4	60.5	59.6	58.8	57.9	57.1	56.3
45	64.0	63.0	62.2	61.3	60.4	59.5	58.6	57.8	56.9	56.1
46	63.9	63.0	62.1	61.2	60.3	59.4	58.5	57.7	56.8	56.0
47	63.8	62.9	62.0	61.1	60.2	59.3	58.4	57.5	56.7	55.8
48	63.7	62.8	61.9	61.0	60.1	59.2	58.3	57.4	56.5	55.7
49	63.7	62.8	61.8	60.9	60.0	59.1	58.2	57.3	56.4	55.6
50	63.6	62.7	61.8	60.8	59.9	59.0	58.1	57.2	56.3	55.4
51	63.6	62.6	61.7	60.8	59.9	58.9	58.0	57.1	56.2	55.3
52	63.5	62.6	61.7	60.7	59.8	58.9	58.0	57.1	56.1	55.2
53	63.5	62.5	61.6	60.7	59.7	58.8	57.9	57.0	56.1	55.2
54	63.5	62.5	61.6	60.6	59.7	58.8	57.8	56.9	56.0	55.1
55	63.4	62.5	61.5	60.6	59.6	58.7	57.8	56.8	55.9	55.0
56	63.4	62.4	61.5	60.5	59.6	58.7	57.7	56.8	55.9	54.9
57	63.4	62.4	61.5	60.5	59.6	58.6	57.7	56.7	55.8	54.9
58	63.3	62.4	61.4	60.5	59.5	58.6	57.6	56.7	55.8	54.8
59	63.3	62.3	61.4	60.4	59.5	58.5	57.6	56.7	55.7	54.8
60	63.3	62.3	61.4	60.4	59.5	58.5	57.6	56.6	55.7	54.7
61	63.3	62.3	61.3	60.4	59.4	58.5	57.5	56.6	55.6	54.7
62	63.2	62.3	61.3	60.4	59.4	58.4	57.5	56.5	55.6	54.7
63	63.2	62.3	61.3	60.3	59.4	58.4	57.5	56.5	55.6	54.6
64	63.2	62.2	61.3	60.3	59.4	58.4	57.4	56.5	55.5	54.6
65	63.2	62.2	61.3	60.3	59.3	58.4	57.4	56.5	55.5	54.6
66	63.2	62.2	61.2	60.3	59.3	58.4	57.4	56.4	55.5	54.5
67	63.2	62.2	61.2	60.3	59.3	58.3	57.4	56.4	55.5	54.5

(Joint Life and Last Survivor Expectancy) (*continued*)

Ages	20	21	22	23	24	25	26	27	28	29
68	63.1	62.2	61.2	60.2	59.3	58.3	57.4	56.4	55.4	54.5
69	63.1	62.2	61.2	60.2	59.3	58.3	57.3	56.4	55.4	54.5
70	63.1	62.2	61.2	60.2	59.3	58.3	57.3	56.4	55.4	54.4
71	63.1	62.1	61.2	60.2	59.2	58.3	57.3	56.4	55.4	54.4
72	63.1	62.1	61.2	60.2	59.2	58.3	57.3	56.3	55.4	54.4
73	63.1	62.1	61.2	60.2	59.2	58.3	57.3	56.3	55.4	54.4
74	63.1	62.1	61.2	60.2	59.2	58.2	57.3	56.3	55.4	54.4
75	63.1	62.1	61.1	60.2	59.2	58.2	57.3	56.3	55.3	54.4
76	63.1	62.1	61.1	60.2	59.2	58.2	57.3	56.3	55.3	54.4
77	63.1	62.1	61.1	60.2	59.2	58.2	57.3	56.3	55.3	54.4
78	63.1	62.1	61.1	60.2	59.2	58.2	57.3	56.3	55.3	54.4
79	63.1	62.1	61.1	60.2	59.2	58.2	57.2	56.3	55.3	54.3
80	63.1	62.1	61.1	60.1	59.2	58.2	57.2	56.3	55.3	54.3
81	63.1	62.1	61.1	60.1	59.2	58.2	57.2	56.3	55.3	54.3
82	63.1	62.1	61.1	60.1	59.2	58.2	57.2	56.3	55.3	54.3
83	63.1	62.1	61.1	60.1	59.2	58.2	57.2	56.3	55.3	54.3
84	63.0	62.1	61.1	60.1	59.2	58.2	57.2	56.3	55.3	54.3
85	63.0	62.1	61.1	60.1	59.2	58.2	57.2	56.3	55.3	54.3
86	63.0	62.1	61.1	60.1	59.2	58.2	57.2	56.2	55.3	54.3
87	63.0	62.1	61.1	60.1	59.2	58.2	57.2	56.2	55.3	54.3
88	63.0	62.1	61.1	60.1	59.2	58.2	57.2	56.2	55.3	54.3
89	63.0	62.1	61.1	60.1	59.1	58.2	57.2	56.2	55.3	54.3
90	63.0	62.1	61.1	60.1	59.1	58.2	57.2	56.2	55.3	54.3
91	63.0	62.1	61.1	60.1	59.1	58.2	57.2	56.2	55.3	54.3
92	63.0	62.1	61.1	60.1	59.1	58.2	57.2	56.2	55.3	54.3
93	63.0	62.1	61.1	60.1	59.1	58.2	57.2	56.2	55.3	54.3
94	63.0	62.1	61.1	60.1	59.1	58.2	57.2	56.2	55.3	54.3
95	63.0	62.1	61.1	60.1	59.1	58.2	57.2	56.2	55.3	54.3
96	63.0	62.1	61.1	60.1	59.1	58.2	57.2	56.2	55.3	54.3
97	63.0	62.1	61.1	60.1	59.1	58.2	57.2	56.2	55.3	54.3
98	63.0	62.1	61.1	60.1	59.1	58.2	57.2	56.2	55.3	54.3
99	63.0	62.1	61.1	60.1	59.1	58.2	57.2	56.2	55.3	54.3
100	63.0	62.1	61.1	60.1	59.1	58.2	57.2	56.2	55.3	54.3

(Joint Life and Last Survivor Expectancy) (*continued*)

Ages	20	21	22	23	24	25	26	27	28	29
101	63.0	62.1	61.1	60.1	59.1	58.2	57.2	56.2	55.3	54.3
102	63.0	62.1	61.1	60.1	59.1	58.2	57.2	56.2	55.3	54.3
103	63.0	62.1	61.1	60.1	59.1	58.2	57.2	56.2	55.3	54.3
104	63.0	62.1	61.1	60.1	59.1	58.2	57.2	56.2	55.3	54.3
105	63.0	62.1	61.1	60.1	59.1	58.2	57.2	56.2	55.3	54.3
106	63.0	62.1	61.1	60.1	59.1	58.2	57.2	56.2	55.3	54.3
107	63.0	62.1	61.1	60.1	59.1	58.2	57.2	56.2	55.3	54.3
108	63.0	62.1	61.1	60.1	59.1	58.2	57.2	56.2	55.3	54.3
109	63.0	62.1	61.1	60.1	59.1	58.2	57.2	56.2	55.3	54.3
110	63.0	62.1	61.1	60.1	59.1	58.2	57.2	56.2	55.3	54.3
111	63.0	62.1	61.1	60.1	59.1	58.2	57.2	56.2	55.3	54.3
112	63.0	62.1	61.1	60.1	59.1	58.2	57.2	56.2	55.3	54.3
113	63.0	62.1	61.1	60.1	59.1	58.2	57.2	56.2	55.3	54.3
114	63.0	62.1	61.1	60.1	59.1	58.2	57.2	56.2	55.3	54.3
115+	63.0	62.1	61.1	60.1	59.1	58.2	57.2	56.2	55.3	54.3

(Joint Life and Last Survivor Expectancy)
(For Use by Owners Whose Spouses Are
More Than 10 Years Younger)

Ages	30	31	32	33	34	35	36	37	38	39
30	60.2	59.7	59.2	58.8	58.4	58.0	57.6	57.3	57.0	56.7
31	59.7	59.2	58.7	58.2	57.8	57.4	57.0	56.6	56.3	56.0
32	59.2	58.7	58.2	57.7	57.2	56.8	56.4	56.0	55.6	55.3
33	58.8	58.2	57.7	57.2	56.7	56.2	55.8	55.4	55.0	54.7
34	58.4	57.8	57.2	56.7	56.2	55.7	55.3	54.8	54.4	54.0
35	58.0	57.4	56.8	56.2	55.7	55.2	54.7	54.3	53.8	53.4
36	57.6	57.0	56.4	55.8	55.3	54.7	54.2	53.7	53.3	52.8
37	57.3	56.6	56.0	55.4	54.8	54.3	53.7	53.2	52.7	52.3
38	57.0	56.3	55.6	55.0	54.4	53.8	53.3	52.7	52.2	51.7
39	56.7	56.0	55.3	54.7	54.0	53.4	52.8	52.3	51.7	51.2
40	56.4	55.7	55.0	54.3	53.7	53.0	52.4	51.8	51.3	50.8
41	56.1	55.4	54.7	54.0	53.3	52.7	52.0	51.4	50.9	50.3

(Joint Life and Last Survivor Expectancy) (*continued*)

Ages	30	31	32	33	34	35	36	37	38	39
42	55.9	55.2	54.4	53.7	53.0	52.3	51.7	51.1	50.4	49.9
43	55.7	54.9	54.2	53.4	52.7	52.0	51.3	50.7	50.1	49.5
44	55.5	54.7	53.9	53.2	52.4	51.7	51.0	50.4	49.7	49.1
45	55.3	54.5	53.7	52.9	52.2	51.5	50.7	50.0	49.4	48.7
46	55.1	54.3	53.5	52.7	52.0	51.2	50.5	49.8	49.1	48.4
47	55.0	54.1	53.3	52.5	51.7	51.0	50.2	49.5	48.8	48.1
48	54.8	54.0	53.2	52.3	51.5	50.8	50.0	49.2	48.5	47.8
49	54.7	53.8	53.0	52.2	51.4	50.6	49.8	49.0	48.2	47.5
50	54.6	53.7	52.9	52.0	51.2	50.4	49.6	48.8	48.0	47.3
51	54.5	53.6	52.7	51.9	51.0	50.2	49.4	48.6	47.8	47.0
52	54.4	53.5	52.6	51.7	50.9	50.0	49.2	48.4	47.6	46.8
53	54.3	53.4	52.5	51.6	50.8	49.9	49.1	48.2	47.4	46.6
54	54.2	53.3	52.4	51.5	50.6	49.8	48.9	48.1	47.2	46.4
55	54.1	53.2	52.3	51.4	50.5	49.7	48.8	47.9	47.1	46.3
56	54.0	53.1	52.2	51.3	50.4	49.5	48.7	47.8	47.0	46.1
57	54.0	53.0	52.1	51.2	50.3	49.4	48.6	47.7	46.8	46.0
58	53.9	53.0	52.1	51.2	50.3	49.4	48.5	47.6	46.7	45.8
59	53.8	52.9	52.0	51.1	50.2	49.3	48.4	47.5	46.6	45.7
60	53.8	52.9	51.9	51.0	50.1	49.2	48.3	47.4	46.5	45.6
61	53.8	52.8	51.9	51.0	50.0	49.1	48.2	47.3	46.4	45.5
62	53.7	52.8	51.8	50.9	50.0	49.1	48.1	47.2	46.3	45.4
63	53.7	52.7	51.8	50.9	49.9	49.0	48.1	47.2	46.3	45.3
64	53.6	52.7	51.8	50.8	49.9	48.9	48.0	47.1	46.2	45.3
65	53.6	52.7	51.7	50.8	49.8	48.9	48.0	47.0	46.1	45.2
66	53.6	52.6	51.7	50.7	49.8	48.9	47.9	47.0	46.1	45.1
67	53.6	52.6	51.7	50.7	49.8	48.8	47.9	46.9	46.0	45.1
68	53.5	52.6	51.6	50.7	49.7	48.8	47.8	46.9	46.0	45.0
69	53.5	52.6	51.6	50.6	49.7	48.7	47.8	46.9	45.9	45.0
70	53.5	52.5	51.6	50.6	49.7	48.7	47.8	46.8	45.9	44.9
71	53.5	52.5	51.6	50.6	49.6	48.7	47.7	46.8	45.9	44.9
72	53.5	52.5	51.5	50.6	49.6	48.7	47.7	46.8	45.8	44.9
73	53.4	52.5	51.5	50.6	49.6	48.6	47.7	46.7	45.8	44.8
74	53.4	52.5	51.5	50.5	49.6	48.6	47.7	46.7	45.8	44.8

(Joint Life and Last Survivor Expectancy) (*continued*)

Ages	30	31	32	33	34	35	36	37	38	39
75	53.4	52.5	51.5	50.5	49.6	48.6	47.7	46.7	45.7	44.8
76	53.4	52.4	51.5	50.5	49.6	48.6	47.6	46.7	45.7	44.8
77	53.4	52.4	51.5	50.5	49.5	48.6	47.6	46.7	45.7	44.8
78	53.4	52.4	51.5	50.5	49.5	48.6	47.6	46.6	45.7	44.7
79	53.4	52.4	51.5	50.5	49.5	48.6	47.6	46.6	45.7	44.7
80	53.4	52.4	51.4	50.5	49.5	48.5	47.6	46.6	45.7	44.7
81	53.4	52.4	51.4	50.5	49.5	48.5	47.6	46.6	45.7	44.7
82	53.4	52.4	51.4	50.5	49.5	48.5	47.6	46.6	45.6	44.7
83	53.4	52.4	51.4	50.5	49.5	48.5	47.6	46.6	45.6	44.7
84	53.4	52.4	51.4	50.5	49.5	48.5	47.6	46.6	45.6	44.7
85	53.3	52.4	51.4	50.4	49.5	48.5	47.5	46.6	45.6	44.7
86	53.3	52.4	51.4	50.4	49.5	48.5	47.5	46.6	45.6	44.6
87	53.3	52.4	51.4	50.4	49.5	48.5	47.5	46.6	45.6	44.6
88	53.3	52.4	51.4	50.4	49.5	48.5	47.5	46.6	45.6	44.6
89	53.3	52.4	51.4	50.4	49.5	48.5	47.5	46.6	45.6	44.6
90	53.3	52.4	51.4	50.4	49.5	48.5	47.5	46.6	45.6	44.6
91	53.3	52.4	51.4	50.4	49.5	48.5	47.5	46.6	45.6	44.6
92	53.3	52.4	51.4	50.4	49.5	48.5	47.5	46.6	45.6	44.6
93	53.3	52.4	51.4	50.4	49.5	48.5	47.5	46.6	45.6	44.6
94	53.3	52.4	51.4	50.4	49.5	48.5	47.5	46.6	45.6	44.6
95	53.3	52.4	51.4	50.4	49.5	48.5	47.5	46.5	45.6	44.6
96	53.3	52.4	51.4	50.4	49.5	48.5	47.5	46.5	45.6	44.6
97	53.3	52.4	51.4	50.4	49.5	48.5	47.5	46.5	45.6	44.6
98	53.3	52.4	51.4	50.4	49.5	48.5	47.5	46.5	45.6	44.6
99	53.3	52.4	51.4	50.4	49.5	48.5	47.5	46.5	45.6	44.6
100	53.3	52.4	51.4	50.4	49.5	48.5	47.5	46.5	45.6	44.6
101	53.3	52.4	51.4	50.4	49.5	48.5	47.5	46.5	45.6	44.6
102	53.3	52.4	51.4	50.4	49.5	48.5	47.5	46.5	45.6	44.6
103	53.3	52.4	51.4	50.4	49.5	48.5	47.5	46.5	45.6	44.6
104	53.3	52.4	51.4	50.4	49.5	48.5	47.5	46.5	45.6	44.6
105	53.3	52.4	51.4	50.4	49.4	48.5	47.5	46.5	45.6	44.6
106	53.3	52.4	51.4	50.4	49.4	48.5	47.5	46.5	45.6	44.6
107	53.3	52.4	51.4	50.4	49.4	48.5	47.5	46.5	45.6	44.6

(Joint Life and Last Survivor Expectancy) (*continued*)

Ages	30	31	32	33	34	35	36	37	38	39
108	53.3	52.4	51.4	50.4	49.4	48.5	47.5	46.5	45.6	44.6
109	53.3	52.4	51.4	50.4	49.4	48.5	47.5	46.5	45.6	44.6
110	53.3	52.4	51.4	50.4	49.4	48.5	47.5	46.5	45.6	44.6
111	53.3	52.4	51.4	50.4	49.4	48.5	47.5	46.5	45.6	44.6
112	53.3	52.4	51.4	50.4	49.4	48.5	47.5	46.5	45.6	44.6
113	53.3	52.4	51.4	50.4	49.4	48.5	47.5	46.5	45.6	44.6
114	53.3	52.4	51.4	50.4	49.4	48.5	47.5	46.5	45.6	44.6
115+	53.3	52.4	51.4	50.4	49.4	48.5	47.5	46.5	45.6	44.6

(Joint Life and Last Survivor Expectancy)
(For Use by Owners Whose Spouses Are
More Than 10 Years Younger)

Ages	40	41	42	43	44	45	46	47	48	49
40	50.2	49.8	49.3	48.9	48.5	48.1	47.7	47.4	47.1	46.8
41	49.8	49.3	48.8	48.3	47.9	47.5	47.1	46.7	46.4	46.1
42	49.3	48.8	48.3	47.8	47.3	46.9	46.5	46.1	45.8	45.4
43	48.9	48.3	47.8	47.3	46.8	46.3	45.9	45.5	45.1	44.8
44	48.5	47.9	47.3	46.8	46.3	45.8	45.4	44.9	44.5	44.2
45	48.1	47.5	46.9	46.3	45.8	45.3	44.8	44.4	44.0	43.6
46	47.7	47.1	46.5	45.9	45.4	44.8	44.3	43.9	43.4	43.0
47	47.4	46.7	46.1	45.5	44.9	44.4	43.9	43.4	42.9	42.4
48	47.1	46.4	45.8	45.1	44.5	44.0	43.4	42.9	42.4	41.9
49	46.8	46.1	45.4	44.8	44.2	43.6	43.0	42.4	41.9	41.4
50	46.5	45.8	45.1	44.4	43.8	43.2	42.6	42.0	41.5	40.9
51	46.3	45.5	44.8	44.1	43.5	42.8	42.2	41.6	41.0	40.5
52	46.0	45.3	44.6	43.8	43.2	42.5	41.8	41.2	40.6	40.1
53	45.8	45.1	44.3	43.6	42.9	42.2	41.5	40.9	40.3	39.7
54	45.6	44.8	44.1	43.3	42.6	41.9	41.2	40.5	39.9	39.3
55	45.5	44.7	43.9	43.1	42.4	41.6	40.9	40.2	39.6	38.9
56	45.3	44.5	43.7	42.9	42.1	41.4	40.7	40.0	39.3	38.6
57	45.1	44.3	43.5	42.7	41.9	41.2	40.4	39.7	39.0	38.3
58	45.0	44.2	43.3	42.5	41.7	40.9	40.2	39.4	38.7	38.0

(Joint Life and Last Survivor Expectancy) (*continued*)

Ages	40	41	42	43	44	45	46	47	48	49
59	44.9	44.0	43.2	42.4	41.5	40.7	40.0	39.2	38.5	37.8
60	44.7	43.9	43.0	42.2	41.4	40.6	39.8	39.0	38.2	37.5
61	44.6	43.8	42.9	42.1	41.2	40.4	39.6	38.8	38.0	37.3
62	44.5	43.7	42.8	41.9	41.1	40.3	39.4	38.6	37.8	37.1
63	44.5	43.6	42.7	41.8	41.0	40.1	39.3	38.5	37.7	36.9
64	44.4	43.5	42.6	41.7	40.8	40.0	39.2	38.3	37.5	36.7
65	44.3	43.4	42.5	41.6	40.7	39.9	39.0	38.2	37.4	36.6
66	44.2	43.3	42.4	41.5	40.6	39.8	38.9	38.1	37.2	36.4
67	44.2	43.3	42.3	41.4	40.6	39.7	38.8	38.0	37.1	36.3
68	44.1	43.2	42.3	41.4	40.5	39.6	38.7	37.9	37.0	36.2
69	44.1	43.1	42.2	41.3	40.4	39.5	38.6	37.8	36.9	36.0
70	44.0	43.1	42.2	41.3	40.3	39.4	38.6	37.7	36.8	35.9
71	44.0	43.0	42.1	41.2	40.3	39.4	38.5	37.6	36.7	35.9
72	43.9	43.0	42.1	41.1	40.2	39.3	38.4	37.5	36.6	35.8
73	43.9	43.0	42.0	41.1	40.2	39.3	38.4	37.5	36.6	35.7
74	43.9	42.9	42.0	41.1	40.1	39.2	38.3	37.4	36.5	35.6
75	43.8	42.9	42.0	41.0	40.1	39.2	38.3	37.4	36.5	35.6
76	43.8	42.9	41.9	41.0	40.1	39.1	38.2	37.3	36.4	35.5
77	43.8	42.9	41.9	41.0	40.0	39.1	38.2	37.3	36.4	35.5
78	43.8	42.8	41.9	40.9	40.0	39.1	38.2	37.2	36.3	35.4
79	43.8	42.8	41.9	40.9	40.0	39.1	38.1	37.2	36.3	35.4
80	43.7	42.8	41.8	40.9	40.0	39.0	38.1	37.2	36.3	35.4
81	43.7	42.8	41.8	40.9	39.9	39.0	38.1	37.2	36.2	35.3
82	43.7	42.8	41.8	40.9	39.9	39.0	38.1	37.1	36.2	35.3
83	43.7	42.8	41.8	40.9	39.9	39.0	38.0	37.1	36.2	35.3
84	43.7	42.7	41.8	40.8	39.9	39.0	38.0	37.1	36.2	35.3
85	43.7	42.7	41.8	40.8	39.9	38.9	38.0	37.1	36.2	35.2
86	43.7	42.7	41.8	40.8	39.9	38.9	38.0	37.1	36.1	35.2
87	43.7	42.7	41.8	40.8	39.9	38.9	38.0	37.0	36.1	35.2
88	43.7	42.7	41.8	40.8	39.9	38.9	38.0	37.0	36.1	35.2
89	43.7	42.7	41.7	40.8	39.8	38.9	38.0	37.0	36.1	35.2
90	43.7	42.7	41.7	40.8	39.8	38.9	38.0	37.0	36.1	35.2
91	43.7	42.7	41.7	40.8	39.8	38.9	37.9	37.0	36.1	35.2

(Joint Life and Last Survivor Expectancy) (*continued*)

Ages	40	41	42	43	44	45	46	47	48	49
92	43.7	42.7	41.7	40.8	39.8	38.9	37.9	37.0	36.1	35.1
93	43.7	42.7	41.7	40.8	39.8	38.9	37.9	37.0	36.1	35.1
94	43.7	42.7	41.7	40.8	39.8	38.9	37.9	37.0	36.1	35.1
95	43.6	42.7	41.7	40.8	39.8	38.9	37.9	37.0	36.1	35.1
96	43.6	42.7	41.7	40.8	39.8	38.9	37.9	37.0	36.1	35.1
97	43.6	42.7	41.7	40.8	39.8	38.9	37.9	37.0	36.1	35.1
98	43.6	42.7	41.7	40.8	39.8	38.9	37.9	37.0	36.0	35.1
99	43.6	42.7	41.7	40.8	39.8	38.9	37.9	37.0	36.0	35.1
100	43.6	42.7	41.7	40.8	39.8	38.9	37.9	37.0	36.0	35.1
101	43.6	42.7	41.7	40.8	39.8	38.9	37.9	37.0	36.0	35.1
102	43.6	42.7	41.7	40.8	39.8	38.9	37.9	37.0	36.0	35.1
103	43.6	42.7	41.7	40.8	39.8	38.9	37.9	37.0	36.0	35.1
104	43.6	42.7	41.7	40.8	39.8	38.8	37.9	37.0	36.0	35.1
105	43.6	42.7	41.7	40.8	39.8	38.8	37.9	37.0	36.0	35.1
106	43.6	42.7	41.7	40.8	39.8	38.8	37.9	37.0	36.0	35.1
107	43.6	42.7	41.7	40.8	39.8	38.8	37.9	37.0	36.0	35.1
108	43.6	42.7	41.7	40.8	39.8	38.8	37.9	37.0	36.0	35.1
109	43.6	42.7	41.7	40.7	39.8	38.8	37.9	37.0	36.0	35.1
110	43.6	42.7	41.7	40.7	39.8	38.8	37.9	37.0	36.0	35.1
111	43.6	42.7	41.7	40.7	39.8	38.8	37.9	37.0	36.0	35.1
112	43.6	42.7	41.7	40.7	39.8	38.8	37.9	37.0	36.0	35.1
113	43.6	42.7	41.7	40.7	39.8	38.8	37.9	37.0	36.0	35.1
114	43.6	42.7	41.7	40.7	39.8	38.8	37.9	37.0	36.0	35.1
115+	43.6	42.7	41.7	40.7	39.8	38.8	37.9	37.0	36.0	35.1

(Joint Life and Last Survivor Expectancy)
(For Use by Owners Whose Spouses Are
More Than 10 Years Younger)

Ages	50	51	52	53	54	55	56	57	58	59
50	40.4	40.0	39.5	39.1	38.7	38.3	38.0	37.6	37.3	37.1
51	40.0	39.5	39.0	38.5	38.1	37.7	37.4	37.0	36.7	36.4
52	39.5	39.0	38.5	38.0	37.6	37.2	36.8	36.4	36.0	35.7

(Joint Life and Last Survivor Expectancy) (*continued*)

Ages	50	51	52	53	54	55	56	57	58	59
53	39.1	38.5	38.0	37.5	37.1	36.6	36.2	35.8	35.4	35.1
54	38.7	38.1	37.6	37.1	36.6	36.1	35.7	35.2	34.8	34.5
55	38.3	37.7	37.2	36.6	36.1	35.6	35.1	34.7	34.3	33.9
56	38.0	37.4	36.8	36.2	35.7	35.1	34.7	34.2	33.7	33.3
57	37.6	37.0	36.4	35.8	35.2	34.7	34.2	33.7	33.2	32.8
58	37.3	36.7	36.0	35.4	34.8	34.3	33.7	33.2	32.8	32.3
59	37.1	36.4	35.7	35.1	34.5	33.9	33.3	32.8	32.3	31.8
60	36.8	36.1	35.4	34.8	34.1	33.5	32.9	32.4	31.9	31.3
61	36.6	35.8	35.1	34.5	33.8	33.2	32.6	32.0	31.4	30.9
62	36.3	35.6	34.9	34.2	33.5	32.9	32.2	31.6	31.1	30.5
63	36.1	35.4	34.6	33.9	33.2	32.6	31.9	31.3	30.7	30.1
64	35.9	35.2	34.4	33.7	33.0	32.3	31.6	31.0	30.4	29.8
65	35.8	35.0	34.2	33.5	32.7	32.0	31.4	30.7	30.0	29.4
66	35.6	34.8	34.0	33.3	32.5	31.8	31.1	30.4	29.8	29.1
67	35.5	34.7	33.9	33.1	32.3	31.6	30.9	30.2	29.5	28.8
68	35.3	34.5	33.7	32.9	32.1	31.4	30.7	29.9	29.2	28.6
69	35.2	34.4	33.6	32.8	32.0	31.2	30.5	29.7	29.0	28.3
70	35.1	34.3	33.4	32.6	31.8	31.1	30.3	29.5	28.8	28.1
71	35.0	34.2	33.3	32.5	31.7	30.9	30.1	29.4	28.6	27.9
72	34.9	34.1	33.2	32.4	31.6	30.8	30.0	29.2	28.4	27.7
73	34.8	34.0	33.1	32.3	31.5	30.6	29.8	29.1	28.3	27.5
74	34.8	33.9	33.0	32.2	31.4	30.5	29.7	28.9	28.1	27.4
75	34.7	33.8	33.0	32.1	31.3	30.4	29.6	28.8	28.0	27.2
76	34.6	33.8	32.9	32.0	31.2	30.3	29.5	28.7	27.9	27.1
77	34.6	33.7	32.8	32.0	31.1	30.3	29.4	28.6	27.8	27.0
78	34.5	33.6	32.8	31.9	31.0	30.2	29.3	28.5	27.7	26.9
79	34.5	33.6	32.7	31.8	31.0	30.1	29.3	28.4	27.6	26.8
80	34.5	33.6	32.7	31.8	30.9	30.1	29.2	28.4	27.5	26.7
81	34.4	33.5	32.6	31.8	30.9	30.0	29.2	28.3	27.5	26.6
82	34.4	33.5	32.6	31.7	30.8	30.0	29.1	28.3	27.4	26.6
83	34.4	33.5	32.6	31.7	30.8	29.9	29.1	28.2	27.4	26.5
84	34.3	33.4	32.5	31.7	30.8	29.9	29.0	28.2	27.3	26.5
85	34.3	33.4	32.5	31.6	30.7	29.9	29.0	28.1	27.3	26.4

(Joint Life and Last Survivor Expectancy) (*continued*)

Ages	50	51	52	53	54	55	56	57	58	59
86	34.3	33.4	32.5	31.6	30.7	29.8	29.0	28.1	27.2	26.4
87	34.3	33.4	32.5	31.6	30.7	29.8	28.9	28.1	27.2	26.4
88	34.3	33.4	32.5	31.6	30.7	29.8	28.9	28.0	27.2	26.3
89	34.3	33.3	32.4	31.5	30.7	29.8	28.9	28.0	27.2	26.3
90	34.2	33.3	32.4	31.5	30.6	29.8	28.9	28.0	27.1	26.3
91	34.2	33.3	32.4	31.5	30.6	29.7	28.9	28.0	27.1	26.3
92	34.2	33.3	32.4	31.5	30.6	29.7	28.8	28.0	27.1	26.2
93	34.2	33.3	32.4	31.5	30.6	29.7	28.8	28.0	27.1	26.2
94	34.2	33.3	32.4	31.5	30.6	29.7	28.8	27.9	27.1	26.2
95	34.2	33.3	32.4	31.5	30.6	29.7	28.8	27.9	27.1	26.2
96	34.2	33.3	32.4	31.5	30.6	29.7	28.8	27.9	27.0	26.2
97	34.2	33.3	32.4	31.5	30.6	29.7	28.8	27.9	27.0	26.2
98	34.2	33.3	32.4	31.5	30.6	29.7	28.8	27.9	27.0	26.2
99	34.2	33.3	32.4	31.5	30.6	29.7	28.8	27.9	27.0	26.2
100	34.2	33.3	32.4	31.5	30.6	29.7	28.8	27.9	27.0	26.1
101	34.2	33.3	32.4	31.5	30.6	29.7	28.8	27.9	27.0	26.1
102	34.2	33.3	32.4	31.4	30.5	29.7	28.8	27.9	27.0	26.1
103	34.2	33.3	32.4	31.4	30.5	29.7	28.8	27.9	27.0	26.1
104	34.2	33.3	32.4	31.4	30.5	29.6	28.8	27.9	27.0	26.1
105	34.2	33.3	32.3	31.4	30.5	29.6	28.8	27.9	27.0	26.1
106	34.2	33.3	32.3	31.4	30.5	29.6	28.8	27.9	27.0	26.1
107	34.2	33.3	32.3	31.4	30.5	29.6	28.8	27.9	27.0	26.1
108	34.2	33.3	32.3	31.4	30.5	29.6	28.8	27.9	27.0	26.1
109	34.2	33.3	32.3	31.4	30.5	29.6	28.7	27.9	27.0	26.1
110	34.2	33.3	32.3	31.4	30.5	29.6	28.7	27.9	27.0	26.1
111	34.2	33.3	32.3	31.4	30.5	29.6	28.7	27.9	27.0	26.1
112	34.2	33.3	32.3	31.4	30.5	29.6	28.7	27.9	27.0	26.1
113	34.2	33.3	32.3	31.4	30.5	29.6	28.7	27.9	27.0	26.1
114	34.2	33.3	32.3	31.4	30.5	29.6	28.7	27.9	27.0	26.1
115+	34.2	33.3	32.3	31.4	30.5	29.6	28.7	27.9	27.0	26.1

(Joint Life and Last Survivor Expectancy) (*continued*)

(Joint Life and Last Survivor Expectancy) (For Use by Owners Whose Spouses Are More Than 10 Years Younger)

Ages	60	61	62	63	64	65	66	67	68	69
60	30.9	30.4	30.0	29.6	29.2	28.8	28.5	28.2	27.9	27.6
61	30.4	29.9	29.5	29.0	28.6	28.3	27.9	27.6	27.3	27.0
62	30.0	29.5	29.0	28.5	28.1	27.7	27.3	27.0	26.7	26.4
63	29.6	29.0	28.5	28.1	27.6	27.2	26.8	26.4	26.1	25.7
64	29.2	28.6	28.1	27.6	27.1	26.7	26.3	25.9	25.5	25.2
65	28.8	28.3	27.7	27.2	26.7	26.2	25.8	25.4	25.0	24.6
66	28.5	27.9	27.3	26.8	26.3	25.8	25.3	24.9	24.5	24.1
67	28.2	27.6	27.0	26.4	25.9	25.4	24.9	24.4	24.0	23.6
68	27.9	27.3	26.7	26.1	25.5	25.0	24.5	24.0	23.5	23.1
69	27.6	27.0	26.4	25.7	25.2	24.6	24.1	23.6	23.1	22.6
70	27.4	26.7	26.1	25.4	24.8	24.3	23.7	23.2	22.7	22.2
71	27.2	26.5	25.8	25.2	24.5	23.9	23.4	22.8	22.3	21.8
72	27.0	26.3	25.6	24.9	24.3	23.7	23.1	22.5	22.0	21.4
73	26.8	26.1	25.4	24.7	24.0	23.4	22.8	22.2	21.6	21.1
74	26.6	25.9	25.2	24.5	23.8	23.1	22.5	21.9	21.3	20.8
75	26.5	25.7	25.0	24.3	23.6	22.9	22.3	21.6	21.0	20.5
76	26.3	25.6	24.8	24.1	23.4	22.7	22.0	21.4	20.8	20.2
77	26.2	25.4	24.7	23.9	23.2	22.5	21.8	21.2	20.6	19.9
78	26.1	25.3	24.6	23.8	23.1	22.4	21.7	21.0	20.3	19.7
79	26.0	25.2	24.4	23.7	22.9	22.2	21.5	20.8	20.1	19.5
80	25.9	25.1	24.3	23.6	22.8	22.1	21.3	20.6	20.0	19.3
81	25.8	25.0	24.2	23.4	22.7	21.9	21.2	20.5	19.8	19.1
82	25.8	24.9	24.1	23.4	22.6	21.8	21.1	20.4	19.7	19.0
83	25.7	24.9	24.1	23.3	22.5	21.7	21.0	20.2	19.5	18.8
84	25.6	24.8	24.0	23.2	22.4	21.6	20.9	20.1	19.4	18.7
85	25.6	24.8	23.9	23.1	22.3	21.6	20.8	20.1	19.3	18.6
86	25.5	24.7	23.9	23.1	22.3	21.5	20.7	20.0	19.2	18.5
87	25.5	24.7	23.8	23.0	22.2	21.4	20.7	19.9	19.2	18.4

(Joint Life and Last Survivor Expectancy) (*continued*)

Ages	60	61	62	63	64	65	66	67	68	69
88	25.5	24.6	23.8	23.0	22.2	21.4	20.6	19.8	19.1	18.3
89	25.4	24.6	23.8	22.9	22.1	21.3	20.5	19.8	19.0	18.3
90	25.4	24.6	23.7	22.9	22.1	21.3	20.5	19.7	19.0	18.2
91	25.4	24.5	23.7	22.9	22.1	21.3	20.5	19.7	18.9	18.2
92	25.4	24.5	23.7	22.9	22.0	21.2	20.4	19.6	18.9	18.1
93	25.4	24.5	23.7	22.8	22.0	21.2	20.4	19.6	18.8	18.1
94	25.3	24.5	23.6	22.8	22.0	21.2	20.4	19.6	18.8	18.0
95	25.3	24.5	23.6	22.8	22.0	21.1	20.3	19.6	18.8	18.0
96	25.3	24.5	23.6	22.8	21.9	21.1	20.3	19.5	18.8	18.0
97	25.3	24.5	23.6	22.8	21.9	21.1	20.3	19.5	18.7	18.0
98	25.3	24.4	23.6	22.8	21.9	21.1	20.3	19.5	18.7	17.9
99	25.3	24.4	23.6	22.7	21.9	21.1	20.3	19.5	18.7	17.9
100	25.3	24.4	23.6	22.7	21.9	21.1	20.3	19.5	18.7	17.9
101	25.3	24.4	23.6	22.7	21.9	21.1	20.2	19.4	18.7	17.9
102	25.3	24.4	23.6	22.7	21.9	21.1	20.2	19.4	18.6	17.9
103	25.3	24.4	23.6	22.7	21.9	21.0	20.2	19.4	18.6	17.9
104	25.3	24.4	23.5	22.7	21.9	21.0	20.2	19.4	18.6	17.8
105	25.3	24.4	23.5	22.7	21.9	21.0	20.2	19.4	18.6	17.8
106	25.3	24.4	23.5	22.7	21.9	21.0	20.2	19.4	18.6	17.8
107	25.2	24.4	23.5	22.7	21.8	21.0	20.2	19.4	18.6	17.8
108	25.2	24.4	23.5	22.7	21.8	21.0	20.2	19.4	18.6	17.8
109	25.2	24.4	23.5	22.7	21.8	21.0	20.2	19.4	18.6	17.8
110	25.2	24.4	23.5	22.7	21.8	21.0	20.2	19.4	18.6	17.8
111	25.2	24.4	23.5	22.7	21.8	21.0	20.2	19.4	18.6	17.8
112	25.2	24.4	23.5	22.7	21.8	21.0	20.2	19.4	18.6	17.8
113	25.2	24.4	23.5	22.7	21.8	21.0	20.2	19.4	18.6	17.8
114	25.2	24.4	23.5	22.7	21.8	21.0	20.2	19.4	18.6	17.8
115+	25.2	24.4	23.5	22.7	21.8	21.0	20.2	19.4	18.6	17.8

(Joint Life and Last Survivor Expectancy) (*continued*)

(Joint Life and Last Survivor Expectancy)
(For Use by Owners Whose Spouses Are
More Than 10 Years Younger)

Ages	70	71	72	73	74	75	76	77	78	79
70	21.8	21.3	20.9	20.6	20.2	19.9	19.6	19.4	19.1	18.9
71	21.3	20.9	20.5	20.1	19.7	19.4	19.1	18.8	18.5	18.3
72	20.9	20.5	20.0	19.6	19.3	18.9	18.6	18.3	18.0	17.7
73	20.6	20.1	19.6	19.2	18.8	18.4	18.1	17.8	17.5	17.2
74	20.2	19.7	19.3	18.8	18.4	18.0	17.6	17.3	17.0	16.7
75	19.9	19.4	18.9	18.4	18.0	17.6	17.2	16.8	16.5	16.2
76	19.6	19.1	18.6	18.1	17.6	17.2	16.8	16.4	16.0	15.7
77	19.4	18.8	18.3	17.8	17.3	16.8	16.4	16.0	15.6	15.3
78	19.1	18.5	18.0	17.5	17.0	16.5	16.0	15.6	15.2	14.9
79	18.9	18.3	17.7	17.2	16.7	16.2	15.7	15.3	14.9	14.5
80	18.7	18.1	17.5	16.9	16.4	15.9	15.4	15.0	14.5	14.1
81	18.5	17.9	17.3	16.7	16.2	15.6	15.1	14.7	14.2	13.8
82	18.3	17.7	17.1	16.5	15.9	15.4	14.9	14.4	13.9	13.5
83	18.2	17.5	16.9	16.3	15.7	15.2	14.7	14.2	13.7	13.2
84	18.0	17.4	16.7	16.1	15.5	15.0	14.4	13.9	13.4	13.0
85	17.9	17.3	16.6	16.0	15.4	14.8	14.3	13.7	13.2	12.8
86	17.8	17.1	16.5	15.8	15.2	14.6	14.1	13.5	13.0	12.5
87	17.7	17.0	16.4	15.7	15.1	14.5	13.9	13.4	12.9	12.4
88	17.6	16.9	16.3	15.6	15.0	14.4	13.8	13.2	12.7	12.2
89	17.6	16.9	16.2	15.5	14.9	14.3	13.7	13.1	12.6	12.0
90	17.5	16.8	16.1	15.4	14.8	14.2	13.6	13.0	12.4	11.9
91	17.4	16.7	16.0	15.4	14.7	14.1	13.5	12.9	12.3	11.8
92	17.4	16.7	16.0	15.3	14.6	14.0	13.4	12.8	12.2	11.7
93	17.3	16.6	15.9	15.2	14.6	13.9	13.3	12.7	12.1	11.6
94	17.3	16.6	15.9	15.2	14.5	13.9	13.2	12.6	12.0	11.5
95	17.3	16.5	15.8	15.1	14.5	13.8	13.2	12.6	12.0	11.4
96	17.2	16.5	15.8	15.1	14.4	13.8	13.1	12.5	11.9	11.3
97	17.2	16.5	15.8	15.1	14.4	13.7	13.1	12.5	11.9	11.3

(Joint Life and Last Survivor Expectancy) (*continued*)

Ages	70	71	72	73	74	75	76	77	78	79
98	17.2	16.4	15.7	15.0	14.3	13.7	13.0	12.4	11.8	11.2
99	17.2	16.4	15.7	15.0	14.3	13.6	13.0	12.4	11.8	11.2
100	17.1	16.4	15.7	15.0	14.3	13.6	12.9	12.3	11.7	11.1
101	17.1	16.4	15.6	14.9	14.2	13.6	12.9	12.3	11.7	11.1
102	17.1	16.4	15.6	14.9	14.2	13.5	12.9	12.2	11.6	11.0
103	17.1	16.3	15.6	14.9	14.2	13.5	12.9	12.2	11.6	11.0
104	17.1	16.3	15.6	14.9	14.2	13.5	12.8	12.2	11.6	11.0
105	17.1	16.3	15.6	14.9	14.2	13.5	12.8	12.2	11.5	10.9
106	17.1	16.3	15.6	14.8	14.1	13.5	12.8	12.2	11.5	10.9
107	17.0	16.3	15.6	14.8	14.1	13.4	12.8	12.1	11.5	10.9
108	17.0	16.3	15.5	14.8	14.1	13.4	12.8	12.1	11.5	10.9
109	17.0	16.3	15.5	14.8	14.1	13.4	12.8	12.1	11.5	10.9
110	17.0	16.3	15.5	14.8	14.1	13.4	12.7	12.1	11.5	10.9
111	17.0	16.3	15.5	14.8	14.1	13.4	12.7	12.1	11.5	10.8
112	17.0	16.3	15.5	14.8	14.1	13.4	12.7	12.1	11.5	10.8
113	17.0	16.3	15.5	14.8	14.1	13.4	12.7	12.1	11.4	10.8
114	17.0	16.3	15.5	14.8	14.1	13.4	12.7	12.1	11.4	10.8
115+	17.0	16.3	15.5	14.8	14.1	13.4	12.7	12.1	11.4	10.8

(Joint Life and Last Survivor Expectancy)
(For Use by Owners Whose Spouses Are
More Than 10 Years Younger)

Ages	80	81	82	83	84	85	86	87	88	89
80	13.8	13.4	13.1	12.8	12.6	12.3	12.1	11.9	11.7	11.5
81	13.4	13.1	12.7	12.4	12.2	11.9	11.7	11.4	11.3	11.1
82	13.1	12.7	12.4	12.1	11.8	11.5	11.3	11.0	10.8	10.6
83	12.8	12.4	12.1	11.7	11.4	11.1	10.9	10.6	10.4	10.2
84	12.6	12.2	11.8	11.4	11.1	10.8	10.5	10.3	10.1	9.9
85	12.3	11.9	11.5	11.1	10.8	10.5	10.2	9.9	9.7	9.5
86	12.1	11.7	11.3	10.9	10.5	10.2	9.9	9.6	9.4	9.2
87	11.9	11.4	11.0	10.6	10.3	9.9	9.6	9.4	9.1	8.9
88	11.7	11.3	10.8	10.4	10.1	9.7	9.4	9.1	8.8	8.6

APPENDIX I ▪ 333

(Joint Life and Last Survivor Expectancy) (*continued*)

Ages	80	81	82	83	84	85	86	87	88	89
89	11.5	11.1	10.6	10.2	9.9	9.5	9.2	8.9	8.6	8.3
90	11.4	10.9	10.5	10.1	9.7	9.3	9.0	8.6	8.3	8.1
91	11.3	10.8	10.3	9.9	9.5	9.1	8.8	8.4	8.1	7.9
92	11.2	10.7	10.2	9.8	9.3	9.0	8.6	8.3	8.0	7.7
93	11.1	10.6	10.1	9.6	9.2	8.8	8.5	8.1	7.8	7.5
94	11.0	10.5	10.0	9.5	9.1	8.7	8.3	8.0	7.6	7.3
95	10.9	10.4	9.9	9.4	9.0	8.6	8.2	7.8	7.5	7.2
96	10.8	10.3	9.8	9.3	8.9	8.5	8.1	7.7	7.4	7.1
97	10.7	10.2	9.7	9.2	8.8	8.4	8.0	7.6	7.3	6.9
98	10.7	10.1	9.6	9.2	8.7	8.3	7.9	7.5	7.1	6.8
99	10.6	10.1	9.6	9.1	8.6	8.2	7.8	7.4	7.0	6.7
100	10.6	10.0	9.5	9.0	8.5	8.1	7.7	7.3	6.9	6.6
101	10.5	10.0	9.4	9.0	8.5	8.0	7.6	7.2	6.9	6.5
102	10.5	9.9	9.4	8.9	8.4	8.0	7.5	7.1	6.8	6.4
103	10.4	9.9	9.4	8.8	8.4	7.9	7.5	7.1	6.7	6.3
104	10.4	9.8	9.3	8.8	8.3	7.9	7.4	7.0	6.6	6.3
105	10.4	9.8	9.3	8.8	8.3	7.8	7.4	7.0	6.6	6.2
106	10.3	9.8	9.2	8.7	8.2	7.8	7.3	6.9	6.5	6.2
107	10.3	9.8	9.2	8.7	8.2	7.7	7.3	6.9	6.5	6.1
108	10.3	9.7	9.2	8.7	8.2	7.7	7.3	6.8	6.4	6.1
109	10.3	9.7	9.2	8.7	8.2	7.7	7.2	6.8	6.4	6.0
110	10.3	9.7	9.2	8.6	8.1	7.7	7.2	6.8	6.4	6.0
111	10.3	9.7	9.1	8.6	8.1	7.6	7.2	6.8	6.3	6.0
112	10.2	9.7	9.1	8.6	8.1	7.6	7.2	6.7	6.3	5.9
113	10.2	9.7	9.1	8.6	8.1	7.6	7.2	6.7	6.3	5.9
114	10.2	9.7	9.1	8.6	8.1	7.6	7.1	6.7	6.3	5.9
115+	10.2	9.7	9.1	8.6	8.1	7.6	7.1	6.7	6.3	5.9

(Joint Life and Last Survivor Expectancy) (*continued*)

(Joint Life and Last Survivor Expectancy)
(For Use by Owners Whose Spouses Are
More Than 10 Years Younger)

Ages	90	91	92	93	94	95	96	97	98	99
90	7.8	7.6	7.4	7.2	7.1	6.9	6.8	6.6	6.5	6.4
91	7.6	7.4	7.2	7.0	6.8	6.7	6.5	6.4	6.3	6.1
92	7.4	7.2	7.0	6.8	6.6	6.4	6.3	6.1	6.0	5.9
93	7.2	7.0	6.8	6.6	6.4	6.2	6.1	5.9	5.8	5.6
94	7.1	6.8	6.6	6.4	6.2	6.0	5.9	5.7	5.6	5.4
95	6.9	6.7	6.4	6.2	6.0	5.8	5.7	5.5	5.4	5.2
96	6.8	6.5	6.3	6.1	5.9	5.7	5.5	5.3	5.2	5.0
97	6.6	6.4	6.1	5.9	5.7	5.5	5.3	5.2	5.0	4.9
98	6.5	6.3	6.0	5.8	5.6	5.4	5.2	5.0	4.8	4.7
99	6.4	6.1	5.9	5.6	5.4	5.2	5.0	4.9	4.7	4.5
100	6.3	6.0	5.8	5.5	5.3	5.1	4.9	4.7	4.5	4.4
101	6.2	5.9	5.6	5.4	5.2	5.0	4.8	4.6	4.4	4.2
102	6.1	5.8	5.5	5.3	5.1	4.8	4.6	4.4	4.3	4.1
103	6.0	5.7	5.4	5.2	5.0	4.7	4.5	4.3	4.1	4.0
104	5.9	5.6	5.4	5.1	4.9	4.6	4.4	4.2	4.0	3.8
105	5.9	5.6	5.3	5.0	4.8	4.5	4.3	4.1	3.9	3.7
106	5.8	5.5	5.2	4.9	4.7	4.5	4.2	4.0	3.8	3.6
107	5.8	5.4	5.1	4.9	4.6	4.4	4.2	3.9	3.7	3.5
108	5.7	5.4	5.1	4.8	4.6	4.3	4.1	3.9	3.7	3.5
109	5.7	5.3	5.0	4.8	4.5	4.3	4.0	3.8	3.6	3.4
110	5.6	5.3	5.0	4.7	4.5	4.2	4.0	3.8	3.5	3.3
111	5.6	5.3	5.0	4.7	4.4	4.2	3.9	3.7	3.5	3.3
112	5.6	5.3	4.9	4.7	4.4	4.1	3.9	3.7	3.5	3.2
113	5.6	5.2	4.9	4.6	4.4	4.1	3.9	3.6	3.4	3.2
114	5.6	5.2	4.9	4.6	4.3	4.1	3.9	3.6	3.4	3.2
115+	5.5	5.2	4.9	4.6	4.3	4.1	3.8	3.6	3.4	3.1

(Joint Life and Last Survivor Expectancy) (*continued*)

(Joint Life and Last Survivor Expectancy)
(For Use by Owners Whose Spouses Are
More Than 10 Years Younger)

Ages	100	101	102	103	104	105	106	107	108	109
100	4.2	4.1	3.9	3.8	3.7	3.5	3.4	3.3	3.3	3.2
101	4.1	3.9	3.7	3.6	3.5	3.4	3.2	3.1	3.1	3.0
102	3.9	3.7	3.6	3.4	3.3	3.2	3.1	3.0	2.9	2.8
103	3.8	3.6	3.4	3.3	3.2	3.0	2.9	2.8	2.7	2.6
104	3.7	3.5	3.3	3.2	3.0	2.9	2.7	2.6	2.5	2.4
105	3.5	3.4	3.2	3.0	2.9	2.7	2.6	2.5	2.4	2.3
106	3.4	3.2	3.1	2.9	2.7	2.6	2.4	2.3	2.2	2.1
107	3.3	3.1	3.0	2.8	2.6	2.5	2.3	2.2	2.1	2.0
108	3.3	3.1	2.9	2.7	2.5	2.4	2.2	2.1	1.9	1.8
109	3.2	3.0	2.8	2.6	2.4	2.3	2.1	2.0	1.8	1.7
110	3.1	2.9	2.7	2.5	2.3	2.2	2.0	1.9	1.7	1.6
111	3.1	2.9	2.7	2.5	2.3	2.1	1.9	1.8	1.6	1.5
112	3.0	2.8	2.6	2.4	2.2	2.0	1.9	1.7	1.5	1.4
113	3.0	2.8	2.6	2.4	2.2	2.0	1.8	1.6	1.5	1.3
114	3.0	2.7	2.5	2.3	2.1	1.9	1.8	1.6	1.4	1.3
115+	2.9	2.7	2.5	2.3	2.1	1.9	1.7	1.5	1.4	1.2

(Joint Life and Last Survivor Expectancy)
(For Use by Owners Whose Spouses Are
More Than 10 Years Younger)

Ages	110	111	112	113	114	115+
110	1.5	1.4	1.3	1.2	1.1	1.1
111	1.4	1.2	1.1	1.1	1.0	1.0
112	1.3	1.1	1.0	1.0	1.0	1.0
113	1.2	1.1	1.0	1.0	1.0	1.0
114	1.1	1.0	1.0	1.0	1.0	1.0
115+	1.1	1.0	1.0	1.0	1.0	1.0

IRS TAX FORMS AND PUBLICATIONS YOU SHOULD HAVE (AND WHERE TO GET 'EM)

Everything here can be accessed *free* (since it's already yours as a taxpayer) from the IRS website, *www.irs.gov*.

IRS Tax Forms

When ordering or downloading these tax forms, always request the instructions for them as well. Often the instructions contain key information not always found in the forms themselves. (The form writers probably felt, "What the hey; close enough for government work!")

- **Form 706, United States Estate (and Generation-Skipping Transfer) Tax Return.** Obviously you don't need this for yourself since it deals with your estate and that means you're dead, but you should order it anyway so you can see how the estate tax system really works. It will help with your estate planning. After your death, your beneficiaries will have to fill this out and calculate any estate tax owed. Your beneficiaries should keep your completed estate tax return as a permanent record of property values on your date of death. They will also use it to see if they are entitled to an IRD (income in respect of a decedent) deduction (Chapter 8). That's a big tax deduction they should not miss.

■ **Form 1099-R, Distributions from Pensions, Annuities, Retirement or Profit-Sharing Plans, IRAs, Insurance Contracts, Etc.** The 1099-R is the key information form that will clue you in as to what type of distribution you have received from your retirement plan (or as a beneficiary of one), the applicable tax treatment, and the tax forms you will be required to file with your tax return. Anytime you receive a distribution from a retirement plan, a 1099-R is triggered and a copy is sent by your plan or IRA financial institution to you and to the IRS. Before even attempting to file your taxes, you should scrutinize the amounts and codes listed on the 1099-R form to see how the amounts will be reported.

■ **Form 4972, Tax on Lump-Sum Distributions.** This form is used to report lump-sum distributions and capital gain treatment, and to figure the income tax on 10-year averaging and net unrealized appreciation in employer securities.

■ **Form 5329, Additional Taxes on Qualified Plans (Including IRAs) and Other Tax-Favored Accounts.** This form is usually attached to your personal tax return (Form 1040), but it can be filed by itself if you do not have to file an income tax return for the year. Form 5329 is used to report and figure the tax on early (before age 59½) distributions from retirement plans. It is also used to notify the IRS of any exception that may apply to the 10 percent early-withdrawal penalty. Form 5329 is the place to report and compute the 6 percent tax on excess contributions and the 50 percent tax on any amount of your required distribution not withdrawn. These 6 and 50 percent penalty taxes apply to all IRA owners and beneficiaries even if they are age 59½ or older.

■ **Form 5498, IRA Contribution Information.** Your IRA financial institution sends this to you and the IRS to report your annual IRA activity and the value of your IRA and Roth IRA accounts each year. The IRA activity reported here is not needed to prepare your tax return, but it does provide official documentation that can support items on your return. It shows your annual IRA and Roth IRA contributions, rollovers, Roth conversions, Roth recharacterizations, and the fair market value of your IRA account as of the end of the tax year.

▪ **Form 8606, Nondeductible IRAs.** This form also is usually attached to your personal tax return, but it too can be filed by itself if you do not have to file an income tax return for the year. Form 8606 is used to report an array of IRA transactions including nondeductible IRA contributions, distributions from IRAs that include nondeductible contributions, distributions from Roth IRAs, and distributions from Education IRAs. Roth conversions and IRA or Roth IRA recharacterizations are also reported here. This is the form where the pro rata rule is computed for distributions from IRAs that contain nondeductible contributions or after-tax funds rolled into the IRA from a company plan.

IRS Publications

IRS Publication Number	Title
559	Survivors, Executors, and Administrators
560	Retirement Plans for Small Business (SEP, SIMPLE, and Qualified Plans)
571	Tax Sheltered Annuity Plans (403[b] Plans) for Employees of Public Schools and Certain Tax-Exempt Organizations
575	Pension and Annuity Income
590	Individual Retirement Arrangements (IRAs)
721	Tax Guide to U.S. Civil Service Retirement Benefits
915	Social Security and Equivalent Railroad Retirement Benefits
939	General Rule for Pensions and Annuities

APPENDIX III

SAMPLE BENEFICIARY DESIGNATION FORMS AND "STRETCH IRA" BENEFICIARY INFORMATION SHEET

The following sample IRA beneficiary designation forms were developed by Seymour Goldberg, Esq., CPA, and are reproduced from *Consumer's Guide to the Retirement Distribution Rules* (copyright © 2002, Seymour Goldberg and Ed Slott) (www.guidetorules.com).

SAMPLE IRA DESIGNATION OF BENEFICIARY FORM #1
(Primary wife, children contingent)

JASON S. GOLDBERG
80 Kings Road
Southampton, New York 11530
Social Security No.: 785-11-2204
Date of Birth: 02/08/40

IRA Account Number: 10987654321

PRIMARY BENEFICIARY(S)

NAME	RELATIONSHIP	DATE OF BIRTH	SOCIAL SECURITY	PERCENT
Jennifer L. Goldberg	wife	12/11/45	123-45-6789	100%

CONTINGENT BENEFICIARY(S)

NAME	RELATIONSHIP	DATE OF BIRTH	SOCIAL SECURITY	PERCENT
*Mark Goldberg	son	02/22/64	234-56-7891	33⅓%
*Eric Goldberg	son	11/05/66	345-67-8910	33⅓%
*Jill Goldberg	daughter	04/17/68	456-78-9101	33⅓%

*In the event that any of my children shall predecease me, then in that event said deceased child's share shall be paid to the issue of such deceased child, per stirpes. In the event that a child shall predecease me leaving no issue, then in that event said deceased child's share shall be paid to my issue, per stirpes. In the event that any beneficiary entitled to receive benefits is a minor, then in that event said minor beneficiary's share shall be paid to a custodian under the Uniform Transfers to Minors Act or similar act for the benefit of such minor beneficiary until the maximum age permitted by law and thereafter directly to such beneficiary. The custodian shall be designated by the executor or administrator of my estate, as the case may be, to the extent permitted by law.

Dated: December 1, 2001   /s/

                                        Jason S. Goldberg

SAMPLE IRA DESIGNATION OF BENEFICIARY FORM #2
(Primary children, wife contingent)

JASON S. GOLDBERG
80 Kings Road
Southampton, New York 11530
Social Security No.: 785-11-2204
Date of Birth: 02/08/40

IRA Account Number: 10987654321

PRIMARY BENEFICIARY(S)

NAME	RELATIONSHIP	DATE OF BIRTH	SOCIAL SECURITY	PERCENT
*Mark Goldberg	son	02/22/64	234-56-7891	33⅓%
*Eric Goldberg	son	11/05/66	345-67-8910	33⅓%
*Jill Goldberg	daughter	04/17/68	456-78-9101	33⅓%

*In the event that any of my children shall predecease me, then in that event said deceased child's share shall be paid to the issue of such deceased child, per stirpes. In the event that a child shall predecease me leaving no issue, then in that event said deceased child's share shall be paid to my issue, per stirpes. In the event that any beneficiary entitled to receive benefits is a minor, then in that event said minor beneficiary's share shall be paid to a custodian under the Uniform Transfers to Minors Act or similar act for the benefit of such minor beneficiary until the maximum age permitted by law and thereafter directly to such beneficiary. The custodian shall be designated by the executor or administrator of my estate, as the case may be, to the extent permitted by law. In the event that none of the above classes survive me, then 100% shall be paid to the contingent beneficiary.

CONTINGENT BENEFICIARY(S)

			SOCIAL	
NAME	RELATIONSHIP	DATE OF BIRTH	SECURITY	PERCENT
Jennifer L.				
Goldberg	wife	12/11/45	123-45-6789	100%

Dated: December 1, 2001 /s/

Jason S. Goldberg

SAMPLE IRA DESIGNATION OF BENEFICIARY FORM #3
(Primary: trust for one child; contingent: remaining children, per stirpes)

PAUL TAYLOR
100 Main Street
Centerport, New York 11721
Social Security No.: 098-23-1234
Date of Birth: 02/04/31
IRA Account Number: 1234567

PRIMARY BENEFICIARY

NAME: In the event that I am survived by my son, CHARLES TAY-
LOR, then in that event the primary beneficiary of this Individual Retirement Account shall be:

"PAUL TAYLOR REVOCABLE TRUST FOR THE BENEFIT OF
CHARLES TAYLOR dated October 15, 1998 between PAUL
TAYLOR as Grantor and MARK TAYLOR as Trustee"

CHARLES TAYLOR'S Date of Birth: 01/01/61

Percentage of Benefits: 100%

CONTINGENT BENEFICIARIES

> In the event that my son, CHARLES TAYLOR, fails to survive me, then in that event the beneficiary of this account shall be:

NAME	RELATIONSHIP	DATE OF BIRTH	SOCIAL SECURITY	PERCENT
*1. JANE TAYLOR	daughter	04/06/63	987-65-4321	50%
*2. MARK TAYLOR	son	02/08/65	334-56-7890	50%

*In the event that any of my children shall predecease me, then in that event said deceased child's share shall be paid to the issue of such deceased child, per stirpes. In the event that a child shall predecease me leaving no issue, then in that event said deceased child's share shall be paid to my issue, per stirpes. In the event that any beneficiary entitled to receive benefits is a minor, then in that event said minor beneficiary's share shall be paid to a custodian under the Uniform Transfers to Minors Act or similar act for the benefit of such minor beneficiary until the maximum age permitted by law and thereafter directly to such beneficiary. The custodian shall be designated by the executor or administrator of my estate, as the case may be, to the extent permitted by law.

Dated: December 1, 2001   /s/

                                            Paul Taylor

SAMPLE STRETCH IRA BENEFICIARY INFORMATION SHEET

IMPORTANT—DO NOT LEAVE THIS BLANK

Location of beneficiary designation and distribution election forms:

_____

*Dated:*_____

Type of Retirement Account (use a separate form for each account)

IRA (traditional) ❑		401(k)	❑
Roth IRA ❑		403(b), TSA, or TDA	❑
SEP-IRA ❑		Keogh	❑
SIMPLE IRA ❑		Other Company Plan	❑

Name of Financial institution (bank, broker, mutual fund co., etc.)

Name _____

Address _____

Telephone number _____

Contact person _____

Account number _____

Primary Beneficiary(s)

Name	Relation	Share (% or Fraction)

Secondary (contingent) Beneficiary(s)

Name	Relation	Share (% or Fraction)

If you make any changes, be sure to update this form.

WARNING: This is NOT an IRA designated beneficiary form and should not be confused with one. It is an IRA beneficiary *information* sheet. Use it to provide your beneficiaries with key information about your retirement accounts, your beneficiary selection on each account, and, most important, where your designated beneficiary forms are and when they were last updated.

ACKNOWLEDGMENTS

J effrey M. Levine, JD, CFP, a financial planner with Linsco/Private Ledger (LPL) in Albany, New York, is a guy who makes things happen. But to me, he is much more than that. He is a motivator, one of those generous people devoted to helping others get what they want out of life.

Jeff attended a conference where I was speaking, after which I told him that I wanted to write a book on how people can protect their retirement accounts from extreme taxation. In the next breath Jeff said, "Let's call John McCarty [a gifted writer and editor, who had written numerous books] *right now.*" The *right now* part was the key; otherwise who knows when I would have called. John McCarty immediately picked up on my idea and called Laureen Rowland, a literary agent with the David Black Agency in New York City. Suddenly, we were a team focused on the importance and need for this book, with John as my collaborator and Laureen as my agent. Thank you, Jeff, for making this happen for me.

John McCarty is an experienced writer and agreed to help me write this book, but I don't think he really knew what he was getting himself into. His most recent book was *The Films of Mel Gibson.* Talk about switching gears. There I was, forcing him to learn all these IRA and tax rules that most professional advisors are scared to death of and then relying upon him to turn my writing and ideas into a digestible, useful, educational book that people would actually enjoy reading. But he did it, and he did it in record time. He is now a financial advisor (only kidding, he's still a great writer). Thanks, John, for being an amazing communicator and for being a really fast writer.

Laureen Rowland is no slouch either. What a bundle of energy. I'm glad she's on my side. I wouldn't want to be her opponent in anything, and that includes a game of "Go Fish." She is not only a terrific agent but also a former book editor and has graciously contributed those skills to this book. All readers will benefit from her input. Laureen put us together with Viking, who shared my vision, and that's why you're reading this right now. Thanks, Laureen, for getting this book published.

I'd like also to thank Jane von Mehren, associate publisher of Viking/Penguin and my editor, for spotting the vast potential of this book before she'd ever read a word of it, and for rallying the support of her publisher, Clare Ferraro, and president, Susan Petersen Kennedy. Jane also set the record for the fastest edit known to man. Thanks, Jane. To her tireless assistant editor, Brett Kelly, I offer my gratitude for ensuring everything went smoothly, and for delivering the dough. And to Nancy Sheppard, vice president and director of marketing, Carolyn Coleburn and Judi Kloos, publicity directors extraordinaire, and Joanne Kenny, manager of special sales, I extend my thanks for turning this book's launch into "the main event."

This book would not have been possible without Seymour "Sy" Goldberg, Esq., CPA. Sy is a longtime colleague and friend who started it all for me, and many others who ended up specializing in this unforgiving area. He jumped on IRA distribution planning before most professional advisors knew anything about it, and he has generously shared his expertise with me ever since. He has also contributed his IRA beneficiary designation forms to this book, which are included in the appendix for your use.

Thank you, Sy, for getting me started in the wonderfully confusing world of IRAs. You are a genius!

Thank you to Marvin R. Rotenberg, the national director of retirement services at Fleet Private Clients Group; thanks also to Beverly DeVeny, Mark LaVangie, and Richard B. James, who are part of Fleet's super IRA team. They help me tremendously throughout the year, every year, with the publication of my IRA newsletter, *Ed Slott's IRA Advisor.* Mark LaVangie is constantly finding those little nuances that make everything you read in it more accurate. Beverly DeVeny reminds me of every English teacher I have ever had rolled into one. She specializes in catching me repeating myself and edits out my redundancies, over and over again, all the time, over and over again, always. Together they are quite a team, and I am lucky to know them.

Rarely a day goes by without speaking with my friend and fellow New York Mets fan, Barry Picker, CPA/PFS, CFP, about IRAs and taxes. Besides being an IRA maven, Barry is the technical editor of my IRA newsletter. Thanks, Barry, for all your help over the years.

You thought O.J. had a dream team? I'd take this group over Johnny Cochran et al. anytime!

As you know from reading any single chapter in this book, these are some tough tax rules. No one person can know it all, yet all you need to know is here, thanks to the brilliant minds I have had access to over the years. (The key is not knowing it all, but knowing enough people who know some of it.) I could probably write another whole book about how helpful and generous these people have been with their time and talent, but for now I'll just list them and call them the IRA Guru Club, a collection of highly intelligent folks who know all about IRAs and how to send e-mail. I thank every one of them for helping me at one time or another grapple with the implications of technical tax rules. Most of these IRA experts have written extensively on the topic and I have included information on how to order their publications in "Resources."

Thank you all very much:

Seymour Goldberg, Esq., CPA
Natalie Choate, Esq.
Barry C. Picker, CPA/PFS, CFP
Michael J. Jones, CPA
Victor M. Finmann, Esq.
Bruce D. Steiner, Esq.
David A. Foster, CPA, CFP
Robert S. Keebler, CPA, MST
Marvin R. Rotenberg, national director of retirement services,
    Fleet Private Clients Group
Mark LaVangie, Fleet Private Clients Group
Beverly DeVeny, Fleet Private Clients Group
Richard B. James, Fleet Private Clients Group
Stephan Leimberg, Esq.
Gregory Kolojeski, president, Brentmark Software, Inc.
Gordon F. Weis, CLU, CPC, ChFC
Stephen J. Krass, Esq.
Shannon Evans, JD, LLM
Steven G. Lockwood, JD, LLM
Martin M. Shenkman, CPA, MBA, JD
Guerdon T. Ely, MBA, CFP
Jeremiah W. Doyle IV, Mellon Private Asset Management
Steven J. Trytten, Esq.
Gary S. Lesser, JD
John D. Bledsoe, CFP, CLU, ChFC, AEP
James Lange, Esq.
Thomas B. Gau, CPA, CFP
Mary Kay Foss, CPA
Peggy Cabaniss, CFP
Sally H. Mulhern, Esq.
Joel P. Bruckenstein, CFP, CFS, CMFC

Any accountant or lawyer that has ever read a tax book knows
Sidney Kess, CPA, Esq. He is the tax expert's tax expert. I have

been fortunate enough not only to know him personally, but to have had the honor of sharing a lectern with him. Sid has been a mentor to me, as he is with everyone he knows, and I thank him for all the opportunities and doors he has opened for me. A more kind and caring professional would be hard to find. Thank you, Sid.

The Estate Planning Committee of the New York State Society of CPAs is one of the most productive and elite professional groups I have ever been associated with. This is a group of skilled CPA colleagues that help each other help their clients. Being involved as both a member and a former chair of the committee has helped me to achieve many professional and personal goals, not to mention the relationships that began there. Most of my professional writing and speaking began with this group and I am thankful for the opportunities it has provided me over the years.

Remember in Chapter 5 where I advised you to get a professional insurance agent? Well, I don't only give advice. I take it. I have a terrific life insurance agent and financial planner who has become almost a part of our family over the years. His name is Alan Kahn, CPA, MBA, CLU, ChFC, and his company is the AJK Financial Group in Syosset, New York. His phone number is 516-677-0270. You can call him and tell him I told you to. Alan's service is second to none and I feel good knowing that when my family has to collect, they know exactly whom to call and what to do. Thanks, Alan. You are a credit to the insurance industry.

I also advised you to use a top-notch attorney. I did that myself as well. Mark I. Rozell is my attorney and I'm glad he is. Mark has helped my wife Linda and me to put together the kind of estate plan that I recommended to you in Chapter 8. No one likes to talk of or plan for their own death, but you need to. For my family and me, it is a great feeling to know that these things have been well taken care of with Mark's help.

Nothing would ever get done without the help of the home team, the wonderful people I work with every day. Anyone who knows me knows Laurin Levine. She not only manages our office, but also takes care of virtually every aspect of our business. She is a booking agent, a travel agent, an event planner; she makes appointments, cancels appointments, reschedules appointments, tracks me down while I'm on the road, makes calls, returns calls, proofreads, orders supplies, handles newsletter orders, and takes care of clients and subscribers, and when she's done with all that, she goes home and worries about it some more. She truly is all that, but most of all she is a real friend and fun to work with. Before you come in to the office, give her your lunch order—she also orders lunch. Thank you, Laurin, for being so much a part of our success. I share it with you.

Margot Reilly and Mike Lichter are our office tax pros. I have been working with them for years and they actually make taxes fun. It's hard to believe, but you should see them in action. They have made things so much easier for me over the years. Margot is always running around taking care of everything while I'm out of the office (which is almost always) and our clients love working with her. Mike and Margot are now partners running our tax practice. Thank you both and good luck!

There is one more person from our office whom I want to mention even though she no longer works with us. Kathy McCosker was a big help when she worked here and we miss her. She's busy raising a family now, but I put this acknowledgment in here so that maybe one day she'll read this and remember us . . . and maybe even come back to work. I hope so. Thanks, Kathy. See you soon?

And to my parents, Bob and Beverly Slott, what can I say other than "Thanks, Mom and Dad." Every success I have ever enjoyed had something to do with your encouragement. I hope I can do the same for my children. I am so lucky. Thank you, and I love you both.

ABOUT THE AUTHOR

A nationally known speaker who is much in demand as a teacher and consultant, Ed Slott, CPA, has been helping people for almost 20 years to avoid the costly mistakes that can drain retirement income and sabotage legacy goals. Called "America's IRA expert" by *Mutual Funds* magazine, he is quoted regularly in *The New York Times, The Wall Street Journal, Newsday, The Washington Post, The Los Angeles Times, The Boston Globe, Chicago Sun-Times, Time, Newsweek, US News & World Report, Financial Times, Fortune, Forbes, Money, USA Today, Business Week, Modern Maturity, Smart Money, Investor's Business Daily, Nation's Business, Trusts & Estates, Medical Economics, Physician's Financial News, Lawyer's Weekly,* plus a host of other national magazines and financial newsletters. He's also shared his expertise via appearances on virtually every major network and cable TV outlet in the country, including CBS, ABC, NBC, CNBC, CNN, FOX, National Public Radio, and Bloomberg TV.

The author of *Your Tax Questions Answered* (Plymouth Press, Ltd., 1997–98), which CNBC called "a great book," and the publisher of the aforementioned *Ed Slott's IRA Advisor*, his popular monthly newsletter of tax tips and strategies which is entering its sixth successful year of publication and is considered the bible on the subject among its 5,000-plus subscribers and media contacts, Mr. Slott is also a personal finance columnist for *Tax Hotline, Mutual Funds Magazine, Tax Savings Report, Personal Finance, Investment News,* and *Financial Planning Magazine,* as well as a frequent contributor to *The CPA Journal, The Practical Accountant, The Tax Advisor, Trusts & Estates,* and many other national and trade publications.

Mr. Slott's diverse client list includes such leading corporations as Fidelity Investments, American Express, Merrill Lynch, Nationwide Insurance, and Oppenheimer Funds as well as a host of other major mutual fund and insurance companies, brokerages, financial and estate planning professionals, accountants, and attorneys. His approximately 150 speaking engagements and workshops coast-to-coast each year put him before a combined audience of more than 50,000 people (financial advisors and the general public alike) annually.

Many of the largest financial institutions (banks, brokerage firms, mutual funds, insurance companies, and trust companies) use and swear by his training methods.

A former faculty member of the American Institute of CPAs and board member of the Estate Planning Council of New York City, Mr. Slott is a past chairman of the New York Society of CPAs Estate Planning Committee and has chaired the Annual Estate Planning Conference sponsored by the Foundation for Accounting Education (FAE).

Technical advisor to Money Magazine Online and a consultant to numerous other financial information web sites, including SmartMoney.com, CNNfn.com, and TheStreet.com, Mr. Slott also hosts his own site addressing complex IRA, retirement, and estate planning issues: www.irahelp.com.

He lives in Oceanside, New York, where he also grew up and was married.

ED SLOTT IS ...

"a 10+ on a 1-5 scale ..."[1]
"amazing ..."[2]
"tremendous, informative, funny and insightful ..."[3]

Discover the five simple steps to protecting your hard-earned retirement money from Uncle Sam *and* enjoy an hour, an afternoon, or a day with Ed Slott, America's IRA expert and one of the nation's top-rated speakers.

For more information on Ed Slott and *Ed Slott's IRA Advisor* newsletter, or to learn more about booking Ed Slott as a keynote speaker for your next conference or meeting, please contact:

Laurin Levine
E. Slott & Company
100 Merrick Road
Suite 200 East
Rockville Centre, NY 11570

Toll-Free Telephone: 1-800-663-1340
E-mail: slottcpa@aol.com

Or visit our website at **www.irahelp.com** (Go to Speaker Inquiry section)

---

[1] Amy Beattie, COO, CUSO Financial Services, L.P., San Diego, CA
[2] James D. Beatty, Beatty & Hines, P.C., West Des Moines, IA
[3] Steven Ford, Partner, Langdon Ford Financial, East Hanover, NJ

INDEX

FOR THE BEST IN PAPERBACKS, LOOK FOR THE

In every corner of the world, on every subject under the sun, Penguin represents quality and variety—the very best in publishing today.

For complete information about books available from Penguin—including Penguin Classics, Penguin Compass, and Puffins—and how to order them, write to us at the appropriate address below. Please note that for copyright reasons the selection of books varies from country to country.

In the United States: Please write to *Penguin Group (USA), P.O. Box 12289 Dept. B, Newark, New Jersey 07101-5289* or call 1-800-788-6262.

In the United Kingdom: Please write to *Dept. EP, Penguin Books Ltd, Bath Road, Harmondsworth, West Drayton, Middlesex UB7 0DA.*

In Canada: Please write to *Penguin Books Canada Ltd, 90 Eglinton Avenue East, Suite 700, Toronto, Ontario M4P 2Y3.*

In Australia: Please write to *Penguin Books Australia Ltd, P.O. Box 257, Ringwood, Victoria 3134.*

In New Zealand: Please write to *Penguin Books (NZ) Ltd, Private Bag 102902, North Shore Mail Centre, Auckland 10.*

In India: Please write to *Penguin Books India Pvt Ltd, 11 Panchsheel Shopping Centre, Panchsheel Park, New Delhi 110 017.*

In the Netherlands: Please write to *Penguin Books Netherlands bv, Postbus 3507, NL-1001 AH Amsterdam.*

In Germany: Please write to *Penguin Books Deutschland GmbH, Metzlerstrasse 26, 60594 Frankfurt am Main.*

In Spain: Please write to *Penguin Books S. A., Bravo Murillo 19, 1° B, 28015 Madrid.*

In Italy: Please write to *Penguin Italia s.r.l., Via Benedetto Croce 2, 20094 Corsico, Milano.*

In France: Please write to *Penguin France, Le Carré Wilson, 62 rue Benjamin Baillaud, 31500 Toulouse.*

In Japan: Please write to *Penguin Books Japan Ltd, Kaneko Building, 2-3-25 Koraku, Bunkyo-Ku, Tokyo 112.*

In South Africa: Please write to *Penguin Books South Africa (Pty) Ltd, Private Bag X14, Parkview, 2122 Johannesburg.*